THE REFERENCE SHELF *(Continued)*

Volume 25

No.

3. Representative American Speeches: 1952-1953. A. C. Baird. $1.75.

Volume 24

No.

1. Political Ethics and the Voter. T. A. Rousse. $1.75.

3. Representative American Speeches: 1951-1952. A. C. Baird. $1.75.

6. Latin America in the Cold War. W. M. Daniels. $1.75.

Volume 23

No.

2. Representative American Speeches: 1950-1951. A. C. Baird. $1.75

Volume 22

No.

3. Representative American Speeches: 1949-1950. A. C. Baird. $1.75.

Volume 20

No.

5. Federal World Government. J. E. Johnsen. $1.50.

Volume 18

No.

3. Representative American Speeches: 1944-1945. A. C. Baird. $1.25

THE REFERENCE SHELF

Vol. 30 No. 5

AMERICA'S EDUCATIONAL NEEDS

Edited by
GRANT S. McCLELLAN
Staff Member, Foreign Policy Association

THE H. W. WILSON COMPANY
NEW YORK 1958

Printed in the United States of America
Library of Congress Catalog Card No. 58-12646

PREFACE

This volume was prepared to provide material on the "problem area" designated by the National University Extension Association for high school debate and discussion in the academic year 1958-1959.

The topic of American education is fast becoming one of the "great debates" of our national history, comparable to the historic debates about foreign policy after each of the last two world wars and the debate on President Roosevelt's New Deal in the 1930's.

It is not a debate which started this year or last when Americans were suddenly startled to find a man-made moon circling the globe, thrust there by the technological and scientific prowess of our Cold War adversary, the Soviet Union. Three chief factors may be singled out as causes of the current controversy. First, it became apparent following World War II that the recent increase in births would soon confront our elementary and secondary schools with the formidable problem of providing more space for seating pupils and more teachers to man the classrooms. The later problem of need for enlarged facilities for colleges and universities also loomed on the horizon. Second, the dramatic achievements of the Russians in successfully competing with us in what too many have assumed was our special advantage—scientific and technological progress—rudely awakened the nation to the fact that not only was our educational plant in need of expansion, but that there might be other serious lacks in our school system. Third, however, as the education debate has matured, we are coming to realize that there is another, perhaps even more important, factor at work which urges on all of us the task of reappraising our educational system. And that is that the world is in one of its most revolutionary phases of change—a fast-paced change involving technological developments undreamed of even a few decades ago by all but the most highly trained scientists; change in the economic, social and political realms which is world-wide in scope; and change, too, which is affecting every aspect of our own national life.

Because education is so inextricably bound up with the whole life of any nation—its ideals as well as its means of livelihood—it is not surprising, when these are challenged by change, that attention should be directed toward its schools and what they teach. Thus as the great debate on education continues, it tends to concentrate on educational objectives, why and in what respects education has fallen short, and what remedies lie at hand both for the immediate and the long-range future.

To turn to the problems of education today, then, is to find oneself examining a host of topics concerning America, its history, its way of life and current changes in ideals, its fears in a world facing possible mutual destruction with other atomic nations caught in a nuclear arms race and its hopes in a world poised on the threshold of man's greatest adventure—the conquest of space.

The debate mounts and is inherently exciting because the stakes are so high. The articles in this compilation attempt to place the discussion in this context. Many other facets of our educational system also receive attention. Those dealt with here are among the most thorny and fateful issues involved. Foreign educational experience is also briefly examined, chiefly that of Western Europe and the U.S.S.R. The school systems of those countries may or may not be relevant to our own needs, but they figure as a lively part of the present debate.

The editor wishes to thank the authors and publishers who have courteously granted permission to reprint copyright materials included in this book.

GRANT S. MCCLELLAN

July 1958

A NOTE TO THE READER

For earlier compilations on aspects of American education in the Reference Shelf series the reader should consult *New Challenges to Our Schools* by Sturges F. Cary (Volume 25, No. 1); *Freedom and Loyalty in Our Colleges* by Robert E. Summers (Volume 26, No. 2); and *Educational Opportunities for Youth* by Walter M. Daniels (Volume 27, No. 5).

CONTENTS

I. DIAGNOSES AND CHALLENGES

EDITOR'S INTRODUCTION

If something goes wrong with one's health, as most people agree something is wrong with our education today, a proper diagnosis is the first step to a cure. Good diagnosticians in the medical profession are thus quite rightly highly esteemed both by their colleagues and their patients. It should be remembered, however, that the best diagnostician is at a disadvantage if his colleagues in medical research have not yet identified a particular malady, its cause and cure. So, too, with the topics dealt with in the articles of this compilation. Diagnosis is needed and doubtless more research. For it is apparent that some of the following inquiries into the shortcomings of American education are superficial and attempt to find scapegoats or easy cures. This seems especially true of many critics of American education when they single out educators and their philosophies as the chief, if not the sole, culprits. However much these are at fault, it should be borne in mind that education reflects, as well as molds, the culture of a nation. Cures which are prescribed in either-or terms, glorify the past or urge the aping of foreign examples, are also probably suspect.

The articles in this section are not put in such simple terms, nor are their authors unaware of the broader context in which the present debate is taking place. Often, however, the larger context is not specifically spelled out as each antagonist develops his position. This should be remembered in reading the following pieces and comparisons should be made between them so that the validity of the points made can be tested more accurately.

Most of the articles in this first section strike to the heart of the problem of educational philosophy. To appreciate them more fully, further reading, suggested in the bibliography, should be undertaken. Thus the first article, written by George S. Counts, professor emeritus of education, Teachers College, Columbia

University, is a case in point. Dr. Counts underscores in this article the fact that our educational system and its philosophy have reflected our total historical and cultural tradition. Many critics of our schools today, however, would counter with the charge that Dr. Counts, the late John Dewey, eminent pragmatist philosopher and educational leader, and others greatly influenced educational philosophy toward what these critics term the "life adjustment" schooling as against disciplined emphasis on the older "three R's"—reading, writing and arithmetic.

The second article is a more summary review of the present criticism of American education. Focusing on the problems of high schools, it serves to highlight the positions taken by various authors throughout the book. Next follow several indictments of our education, with rejoinders. First Dr. Arthur Bestor, professor of history at the University of Illinois, gives his forthright criticism of the "life adjustment" school of thought. Two short rebuttal statements are also given. Rear Admiral H. G. Rickover, USN, follows with further severe criticisms; other portions of his article appear in Section III where he pleads for adoption of European ideas on education. Marc Raeff, also a professor of history, carries the criticism further and pleads for a new respect for intellectual ability. His diagnosis indicates that we have "watered down" the educational fare so much that students carry away from school neither a well-rounded body of information nor the ability to think.

Last, the president of Teachers College, Columbia University, states the challenges of education as he sees them in the world today. In this case, whether the problem is to develop education for "adjustment" to the world-wide revolutionary changes he discusses or education for "coping" with those changes intelligently within a democratic society, it seems obvious that he has pin-pointed the striking problems with which future citizens, now students in schools and colleges, must deal.

It may be noted, in passing, that it has not been possible to deal adequately in this compilation with the problem of adult education, either by presenting diagnoses of its ills or suggestions on what needs to be done. The vast network of privately sponsored adult education work in the United States has not yet been squarely included in the current great debate. True, some increased private and public support for this work is now under way. The adult citizen, however, is in many ways the "forgotten man" of the educational debate. Yet it is he above all who needs up-dating and increased understanding to cope with the world-wide problems of today. Unless his needs are met, the students now in schools, whatever improvements can be made for their education, may not have to cope with a complex civilization but rather with preserving life in the aftermath of an all-out nuclear war.

THE SPIRIT OF AMERICAN EDUCATION[1]

Education, unless it is imposed from without, always constitutes a response to the traditions, the value commitments, the life conditions, and the genius of a people, influenced of course by the prevailing factors of power in a society.

The American educational scene is marked by great diversity and even by many contradictions. It has been said that the United States has no educational system, that within the borders of the country can be found almost any practice the inquirer may seek. It is a land of vast expanse, characterized by great differences in climate, resources, economy, and cultural tradition. . . .

How Education Is Controlled

In the sphere of control authority in the last analysis rests with the people. . . . Education in the United States has never been imposed from above. First as colonists along the Atlantic coast and later as pioneers in the wilderness of the interior, the people carried their institutions with them wherever they cast their lot. It was in this way that they established their schools, each community or settlement doing as it saw fit. No great statesman, no priesthood, no intellectual class, no committee of wise men, no centralized government devised the American system of education. With whatever merits or defects it may

[1] From article by George S. Counts, professor emeritus of education, Teachers College, Columbia University. *Teachers College Record.* 59:450-9. May 1958. Reprinted by permission.

possess, it is the authentic work of the people, with of course the assistance of inspired leaders. Almost universally the conduct of elementary and secondary schools is in the hands of local boards of education chosen in some fashion by the citizens of the community. The boards which control higher schools and universities are ordinarily somewhat further removed from the citizens, but even with them, at least in the case of public education, the contact is fairly close. . . .

A word should perhaps be said here about the origin of our people. What is now the United States was populated by the greatest migration of history. From the first colonial settlements, at the beginning of the seventeenth century, down to the present time something like forty million men, women, and children crossed the great ocean to make their homes in this land. Moreover, from beginning to end this great migration was essentially a migration of common people—common in the sense that they were without wealth or social rank. In fact the records show that they came overwhelmingly from the poor, the oppressed, and the persecuted of the Old World. . . . To this broad generalization regarding the source of the American people, there are of course many individual exceptions, but the exceptions were generally unsuccessful in the attempt to transport their conceptions of social relations to the New World. As a consequence, feudal institutions and traditions never took root in the colonies. Here, without doubt, is one of the most important and decisive factors shaping the history of the American people. The idea prevails to this day that America is a land without social classes; and anyone who seeks to arouse class antagonisms or even to speak of classes is generally regarded as un-American. . . . In educational matters the people exercise control, for the most part, through state and local boards of education. . . .

Although the Federal Government has played a role in the development of certain aspects of American education and although, ever since the Civil War, organized efforts have been made to secure substantial Federal funds for the support of public education, the school remains to this day essentially a function and a responsibility of the individual state. Opposition to Federal control is deep-rooted and is shared even by those who seek federal support. According to the American point of view, education is too powerful an instrument over the mind to be placed in the hands of any single authority. . . .

Basic to the American system, therefore, is the fact that the individual state is the primary legal authority in the field of education. Yet this statement conveys only a part of the picture. Within the state the local community rather than the central authority has always played the major role in the support, control, and general conduct of the public school. While enforcing minimum standards, promoting diverse limited objectives, and providing a measure of leadership, the state commonly delegates its authority under the Federal constitution to the local community. It is in the locality, therefore, that the process of shaping public education is concentrated. And here the people, operating within a framework of traditions, laws, and judicial pronouncements, make decisions governing the establishment and the conduct of their schools. The people do not discharge these functions directly, however. By one means or another, but commonly through popular elections, they create small lay boards of education to which their authority is delegated. It is asumed that at the time of election the broad issues confronting the schools will be thoroughly discussed by the electorate, and that the board members will be chosen on the basis of both their personal qualifications and their announced positions on the issues. It might be assumed further that during their term of office the board members will meet at stated intervals and, free from the pressure of special interests, make decisions respecting the conduct of public education in accord with the expressed mandates of the people.

In actual practice, however, the situation is quite different. In the first place, a large proportion of the people seem to have no interest in education and fail to participate in elections. At the same time, the board of education is rarely permitted to deliberate in solitude, insulated between elections from the play of social forces. And here we encounter a major political reality in the United States. In his study of the American democracy published in 1835, in the period of pre-industrial society, Alexis de Tocqueville observed with astonishment the tendency of Americans to form voluntary organizations.

> Americans of all ages, all conditions [he wrote] constantly form associations. They have not only commercial and manufacturing companies, in which all take part, but associations of a thousand other kinds—religious, moral, serious, futile, general or restricted, enormous or diminutive. . . . If it be proposed to inculcate some truth, or to foster some feeling, by the encouragement of a great example, they form a society. Wherever, at the head of some new undertaking, you see the government in France, or a man of rank in England, in the United States you will be sure to find an association.

And so it is today. The battles over the launching and the development of the system of public education in all of its aspects and departments have been conducted by these voluntary and private associations. . . . All of this is in the spirit of American democracy.

Ideas Which Affect Our Education

The controlling ideas and motivations in American education are many and contradictory. The following five, however, will be briefly developed in this lecture: the doctrine of equality, the drive for individual success, the devotion to practical utility, the spirit of pragmatism, and faith in the perfectibility of man. Although each of these ideas or motivations is often observed in the breach, they are all authentic elements in the total spirit of American education. They all have their roots in the long experience of the American people.

At the very base of the theory of education in the United States is a profound faith in the potentialities of the individual human being. Although this faith has been shaken in the twentieth century by the advance of industrialism, the appearance of a highly complex social order, and the results of biological and psychological investigation, the Americans continue to believe in the essential equality of men. . . .

The idea of equality, which is perhaps the most basic idea in democracy, has had a profound impact on the American system of education. It was responsible for the establishment of the *free* school without tuition charges and the *common* school attended by children from all elements of the population. It was also responsible for the development of the *single* educational system—one of the most magnificent achievements of American democracy. Except for the private schools which are permitted under the conception of liberty, the dual system developed in Europe, with its abbreviated program for the masses and its rich offering for the upper classes, has never taken root in the United States, except in the case of the Negro in the southern states, which constitutes our most severe violation of the democratic principle. The sequential organization of institutions, consisting of primary, secondary, and higher schools, is theoretically open to all elements of society and is commonly regarded by the Americans themselves as *their* system of education. The exceptions which exist are usually brushed aside as unimportant or irrelevant.

Another expression of the idea of equality is found in the organization of the public high school. During the early part of the present century, when the program of secondary education was expanding, the introduction of the more practical subjects pointing directly to the vocations precipitated a vigorous controversy regarding the form that the high school should take. Some argued in the name of efficiency that the different interests should be housed in different buildings and be provided with different managements; others argued in the name of equality that all of these interests should be brought together in one institution. According to the first proposal, the secondary school system of a large town or city would include a series of specialized schools, while, according to the second, it would consist of a single type of comprehensive school organized in sufficient numbers to meet the demand for adolescent education. Although both plans have found expression in America, the second is the more popular and seems to have triumphed. The typical secondary school in the United States is consequently an institution which embraces within its program the entire range of subjects from auto mechanics to Latin and from painting to trigonometry. It also enrolls among its pupils children from the most diverse cultural backgrounds and the most varied vocational and academic interests. The decisive consideration seems to be that the comprehensive high school serves the principle of equality by prolonging into the period of adolescence the common associations provided by the public elementary school. It thus constitutes an extension of the idea of the common school.

Idea of Success

A second controlling conception in American education is that of individual success. Indeed there is probably no principle that is more characteristic of the American mode of life and that has played a larger role in shaping the educational system. It is closely associated with the idea of equality. Even democracy tends to be identified with a species of individualism and the good society is regarded as one in which the individual is given an opportunity to succeed according to his industry and talents. Eminent statesmen and university presidents, as well as more humble citizens, vie with each other in praising the social order which permits the individual to rise above the station into which he was born. . . .

The establishment of the "free school" and the construction of the "educational ladder" were undoubtedly motivated by the desire to give the individual a chance to succeed in the American pattern. A glance at educational statistics in this connection will be of interest. The number of pupils in the upper four years of the secondary school has grown from approximately 300,000 in 1890 to over 8,000,000 in 1957. The corresponding figures for the higher schools are 110,000 and 3,400,000. I would like to believe that this phenomenal growth in about two generations expressed a desire on the part of the younger generation to become better citizens and to advance the arts and sciences. The explanation, however, undoubtedly lies in another direction. In 1890 the Bureau of the Census announced the closing of the geographic frontier—the very symbol of economic opportunity in the early America. At the same time the country was moving swiftly along the road of urbanization and industrialization toward a new civilization requiring formal schooling for many occupations. This upward surge of the masses into the higher levels of the educational structure, which can only be viewed in the nature of a profound social movement, seems to have been motivated by a desire for individual material success. At great sacrifice parents have struggled to "give their children an education" so that they might improve their social position and be freed from the necessity of hard physical labor. And now hard physical labor is being eliminated by the intervention of electronics and automation. And one of our foremost students of the developing American economy said not long ago that the economy of the future will place a premium on "brains."

Another striking instance of the triumph of the individual is found in the administration of the high school program of studies. An observer, noting the numerous curricula carrying vocational titles, would naturally conclude this implied a high degree of specialization. On closer examination, however, he would find himself in error. The subjects offered do indeed cover a very wide range. Also they are organized in specialized sequences, but many pupils do not follow them. They tend to experiment with this field and that, shifting from one specialization to another. And they do this without sacrificing their standing in relation to graduation. The rationale of this strange practice is found in the conviction that the future should always be left open. If a pupil, after having begun the pursuit of one of the more practical courses, should change his mind and decide to go to college, he and his parents would resent bitterly any effort on the part of the educational authorities to require him to begin a new series of sequences in the first year of the high school.

Idea of Utility

Devotion to practical utility constitutes a third and closely related ingredient of the spirit of American education. The American people from the beginning have been a practical people; they have been primarily concerned with the task of making a living and raising ever higher the standard of living. Coming originally for the most part from the "uneducated" classes of Europe they have had no great love of "book learning" as such or for the pursuit of knowledge for its own sake. In the earlier epoch they were engaged in felling forests, breaking virgin lands, erecting dwellings, and the physical conquest of a continent. More recently they have been engrossed in the building of railroads, the exploitation of mines, the construction of factories, the manufacture of goods, and the sale of merchandise. This preoccupation with practical affairs has left its mark on the system of education.

Perhaps the most striking expression of the principle of practical utility is the placing of control of education in the hands of practical men. With the exception of the colonial period, when the voice of the clergy generally ruled the educational councils, it has always been so. During the agrarian era educational policy, at least as it affected the lower schools, was determined almost altogether by small boards composed of untutored farmers and rural artisans. But with the rise of industrialism and the development of cities, control of the public school at practically all levels gradually came under the influence of the powerful commercial, financial, and industrial classes. The successful businessman therefore is the arbiter of educational enterprise in the United States today and is chiefly responsible for the practical turn given to the program. . . .

The result has been a revolution in secondary and higher education during the present century. One expression of the revolution is the vast expansion of enrollments already noted. Another is the transformation of the program of studies. The classical tradition which flourished through the centuries is but a pale shadow of its former self. Greek has all but disappeared from the high school, and Latin has had to retreat before the advance of modern studies. Even the humanities as a whole have encountered and do encounter great difficulty in maintaining themselves. It is the sciences and technologies which practical men have fostered. Along with all of this has gone a general downgrading of disinterested intellectual achievement in America. . . .

Pragmatism's Influence

A fourth influence which permeates American education from top to bottom, as well as American life and institutions in general, is the pragmatic or experimental temper. It is not by chance that John Dewey significantly developed the philosophy of pragmatism. Born in 1859 on the frontier in the state of Vermont, he later gave expression in his thought to the spirit of his people. Indeed he could have appeared nowhere else in the world. While he always had his critics in the United States and while his ideas are being attacked vigorously today in certain quarters, he remains a most authentic expression of American genius.

The pragmatic or experimental temper was bred in the American people from generation to generation by experience and circumstance. The great migration across the Atlantic and on to the Pacific practically compelled the development of this temper. All immigrants to a new and strange land invariably leave many of their possesions, both material and spiritual, behind them. This is particularly true if they migrate, not as complete social and cultural groups, but as individuals and families, as the migrants to America came. They had to break with the past again and again, moreover, as they moved westward. The fact that they came from diverse lands and cultures was another important factor in compelling them to adjust, adapt, and invent. . . .

Faith in Man

A fifth and final ingredient of the spirit of American education is faith in the perfectibility of man and his institutions. In fact this is the basic presupposition in our faith in education. Though this faith has often been naïve and superficial, . . . it is nevertheless one of the great faiths of the human race. It was a faith of the foremost founders of our Republic in 1776, 1787, and the succeeding years.

The powerful movements for intellectual and political liberation which swept over the Old World during the sixteenth, seventeenth, and eighteenth centuries were given a friendly reception in America. A distinguished French historian has said that the ideas of the Enlightenment took deeper root here than in France. Of these ideas, perhaps the most revolutionary was that of human progress and the indefinite perfectibility of man and his institutions. This idea found its natural home in America. The proposition that the future can be better than the past is an essential and distinctive part of our heritage. Although it may foster an irrational optimism and may be narrowly interpreted as material or mechanical advance, it is one of the great liberating ideas of history. Even our most conservative interests always claim to be battling in the name of progress. It was said long ago that "the Americans *love* their country, not, indeed, *as it is,* but *as it will be*. . . .

The American people believe today, with Jefferson, that education, appropriately conceived and administered, is an indispensable instrument for improving the nature and condition of man.

THE REAL TROUBLE WITH U.S. EDUCATION [2]

The U.S. educational system is not so bad as you might think if you listened only to the critics who have rushed to their typewriters since Russia's first Sputnik went up. It can, after all, claim credit for producing enough scientists and statesmen and artists and authors to give the United States a stable government and a standard of living that is the envy of the world.

But without any doubt it is bad enough—so bad, in fact, that the problem of doing something about it emerges as one of the great challenges to the United States of the mid-twentieth century; so bad that our efforts to do somehing about it inevitably will reshape our ways of living, patterns of spending, and scales of social values for the next fifty years.

Since World War II, the most obvious and most urgent problem of U.S. education has been sheer numbers. From the moment the baby boom of the 1940's surged into kindergarten, school boards all over the country have been scrambling to build new classrooms and hire new teachers—at last count, they were still something like 140,000 classrooms short. In the scramble, most of them have let go by default an older problem: the question of what to teach and how to teach it.

It is this rather than the numbers problem that really lies at the heart of the discontent with U.S. schooling. For one way or

[2] From "Education—Special Report." *Business Week.* p 155-61. April 19, 1958. Reprinted by permission.

another, the numbers problem is being handled. Where school programs were well planned and standards high to begin with, the deluge of new students has brought little serious deterioration. It is where the programs were already fuzzy and the standards low that education has caved in entirely.

Criticism of U.S. schools didn't start with the Sputniks. It has been going on for years. But Russia's sudden demonstration of scientific equality, if not superiority, has forced the whole country to look some of the facts in the face. Naturally, this has proved painful. In a very real sense, the educational institutions are the reproductive system of a society: To entertain serious doubts about them is a traumatic experience.

It is a healthy experience nevertheless. For the United States if it looks carefully and honestly, can identify its basic school problems and decide what it wants to do about them.

For various reasons, these problems come into clearest focus in the public high schools. The elementary schools have their troubles too. In fact, many of the most serious criticisms of U.S. education apply mainly to them. But about 9 out of 10 elementary school children go on to high school. If the elementary schools have done their job badly, it is the secondary school that has to pick up the pieces. And this applies not only to such things as reading ability and skill with figures but also to basic attitudes, values, and work habits.

The high school is the institution that takes in boys and turns out men. It is the place where somebody has to decide just how much these men shall differ one from another, how much the slow learner and the fast learner can take, how much the noncollege group, which is still the great majority, is to have in common with the smaller group that is going on to college. It is the point where the least common denominator of each succeeding generation is determined.

Within a few years, this point of decision may shift to the colleges. And certainly within three or four years the colleges are going to be beset with a numbers problem similar to the one that now swamps the lower schools. But that time has not yet arrived. For the present, the problem of U.S. education emerges as a high school problem.

It is a tough problem. But there are answers for it. And already you can find a surprising amount of agreement on what those answers are.

How Bad Are the Schools?

U.S. public education, says I. L. Kandel in his book *American Education in the Twentieth Century,* "is based on the principles that it must be classless, coeducational, nonpartisan in politics, and secular."

It is also based on the principle that it must be universal. Almost all states require school attendance at least through the age of 16. Some set the minimum age for leaving school at 18. This means that the high school has to deal with everybody, a complete cross section of the population. It is the only secular institution that shares with Christianity the conviction that all souls are worth saving.

The assignment of this responsibility to the public high schools is relatively recent. It was not until 1874 that the legality of spending public money for secondary schools was established. As late as the 1920's the high schools still considered themselves selective institutions, responsible only for dealing with the bright students or at least the moderately bright. Slow learners—an earlier and less compassionate age called them "dullards"—were expected to drop out and go to work or switch to a purely trade school when they found the going too tough.

But after 1920, the idea that high school education should be available to everyone began to make headway. And in the Depression of the 1930's, it became established policy. The main motive at the time was to keep young people out of the labor force. But the schools generally welcomed the new responsibility. They saw it as a chance to make education a mighty force in the future of the country.

U.S. educators were feeling their oats in the 1930's. The ideas of the "child-centered" approach, education of the "whole child," and "learning by doing" were spreading from the primary grades into the high schools. Teachers colleges were hammering away at the notion that it wasn't the subject matter but the method of teaching that counted. Success was to be measured not so much by mastery of a subject as by the "growth" that a student demonstrated; and "growth" was a hazy concept, often equated in the teacher's mind with docility.

With comparatively few qualms, the high schools seized on their new responsibilities not only as a chance to teach more students but as a chance to take a new approach to the education of all students.

In the excitement of the change, in the scramble to make the new arrivals feel at home, the schools worried less and less about the academically talented, the group that previously had been their sole concern. In theory, the new approach should have given the able students the same attention and held them to the same standards as before. In practice, they found it both easy and agreeable to lose themselves in the crowd. There wasn't enough premium on academic achievement to make them sweat.

Here and there a school—usually in a high-income neighborhood—stuck to its old standards. But for the country as a whole, the final result of making secondary education universal was to take most of the meaning out of the high school diploma. Just as bad money, according to Gresham's Law, drives out good, so the soft courses drove out the hard ones and low standards encouraged low performance.

If you take an inventory of U.S. education today—some 25 years after the high schools went through their great change—you find some imposing assets. In terms of number of children in school, literacy rates in the population, average educational level, college degrees, number of schools per capita, the United States has nothing to worry about. But any honest inventory also will show three frightening liabilities:

1. A shaky financial base. There are too many individual school districts, and they are entirely too dependent on real estate as a source of revenue. At the latest count, there were 53,000 independent school districts in the United States. Fiscal authorities guess there should be only half that many to get any sort of financial stability and to provide schools of economical size.

2. Low pay—and correspondingly low standards—for teachers. The average income of the U.S. school teacher is $4,520—

about on a level with the average factory worker, and something like half the pay of a locomotive engineer. In 1956, about 33 per cent of all elementary teachers had no college degree, 21 per cent of all public school teachers had done less than four years of college, 40 per cent of the secondary school teachers had not done as much as five years of college level work.

3. Basic confusion in philosophy. The paradox of dealing with the whole range of student abilities and yet remaining classless, coeducational, nonpartisan, and secular is still unresolved. There's good reason to think that the more able students are getting short-changed or are being allowed to short-change themselves. At the same time there's evidence that the less able are not getting the things they really need most.

It's hard to measure educational values. And so it is hard to say just how much of the torrent of criticism now flowing over the public schools is justified.

Where the attacks center on the elementary schools, the educators have their answers for critics, such as Rudolph Flesch, who have sprung forward with their own one-shot cures for what they conceive to be the trouble. Flesch's enormously popular *Why Johnny Can't Read* was a slashing attack on the methods used to teach reading—and a hard sell for Flesch's own version of the phonetic approach. To answer Flesch and similar critics, the schools have dug up tests given a generation or so ago. Almost without exception, todays' students can knock them over.

In Lincoln, Nebraska, some 5,000 children in grades 3 to 8 were given a reading test in 1921. The same test was given to a similar group in 1947. The 1947 group scored higher at every grade level, with the fifth grade group of 1947 topping the eighth grade group of 1921. In Evanston, Illinois, tests administered in 1933 showed substantially higher reading comprehension and vocabulary when they were given again in 1954.

In short, say the educators, teaching methods today are every bit as effective as those of a generation ago. If Johnny can't learn to read in 1958, he would have done no better in 1908. The difference is that today the schools will keep him and sweat it out with him. In 1908, they would have let him sit in second or third grade until he got tired and quit. The more enlightened schools, in fact, would have had a row of outsize desks at the back of the room for the likes of him.

When the critics train their fire on the high schools, the answers come with less assurance.

The educators can and do produce statistics to show that public school graduates generally score better in college entrance examinations than private school products. In the March, 1953, college boards, for instance, candidates from the public schools racked up a higher mean score than candidates from the independent (including parochial) schools in every test except advanced mathematics and French.

But all this proves is that a relatively limited number of crack students still are being well trained to stand a specific type of exam. It doesn't tell us anything about the students who don't take the college boards. And it doesn't answer the charges of such critics as Arthur Bestor (*Educational Wastelands*) and Albert Lynd (*Quackery in the Public Schools*) who insist that the schools are wasting time teaching "life adjustment" when they should be driving for intellectual achievement.

This is a criticism that goes to the heart of the trouble. For the weakness in U.S. education is not just a matter of classroom shortages or inadequate finances. It also involves the basic question of what the schools are trying to do.

It is not a criticism, however, that you can apply without some important qualifications. The strong medicine of academic challenge that Lynd and Bestor and Robert M. Hutchins and Stringfellow Barr prescribe may be just the thing that the bright student needs. But for the slow learner it would be a lethal dose.

As Paul Woodring points out in his book, *A Fourth of a Nation,* college professors are likely to take it for granted that even the dull boy can profit from the classics because professors "have never met a *really* dull boy of the kind that can be found in almost any public high school." It is true, Woodring goes on to say, that you can teach *Don Quixote* or *Hamlet* at the level of the lower third of high school sophomores, but in the process everything that makes them great books has to be dropped out.

The real task of the schools is to design a program that is flexible enough to accommodate both the boy who is going to college and the boy who is going to work in a filling station. There must be some sort of "life adjustment" and vocational courses in any comprehensive high school. But the schools will also have to see to it that these courses have standards of their own and that they don't crowd out the old academic curriculum.

The trouble is that the nonacademic subjects inevitably tend to become soft courses—pleasant, undemanding ways to pass the time and pick up credit toward a diploma—and as such they appeal to bright students as much as to anyone else. And in the ponderous machinery of the state education departments there usually are built-in devices to put pressure on the schools to make this line of least resistance even more tempting.

Here, for instance, is an excerpt from a letter written recently by a state industrial arts supervisor to a high school superintendent:

> I discussed with Dr.——— [the high school principal] the low enrollments in senior high school industrial arts courses. He pointed out that a large percentage of the pupils are college bound. I suggested that he study . . . the possibility of developing a course for these pupils within the framework of the state syllabus. I also recommended that metal, printing, and textiles be organized on one side of the shop and wood, electricity, and ceramics be included on the other side. This will provide for representation of all six major industrial sections.

In this popularity contest among courses, the losers have been the tough academic subjects—what the educators refer to as the "solids." Most states require a high school student to take four years of English and three or four years of history (often called social studies), but requirements in languages, science, and mathematics vary from nothing at all to only one year or two. It is possible to get a high school diploma without any algebra, without any languages, ancient or modern, other than English, and without any science other than what Glenn O. Blough, president of the National Science Teachers Association bitterly refers to as "cocoons, rocks, and hickory nuts dragged in by the children and deposited on the science table."

The result of this approach was summed up by Marion B. Folsom, Secretary of Health, Education and Welfare, in his memorandum to President Eisenhower outlining the Federal program of assistance to education that is now before Congress:

> Only one out of three high school graduates has had a year of chemistry, only one out of four has taken a year of physics, and only one out of three has had more than one year of algebra. There is a current shortage of more than 8,000 high-school science teachers and yet—of the 5,000 [college] graduates prepared to teach science last year—2,000 went into industrial jobs rather than the classroom.

Elsewhere in the same memorandum, Folsom commented tartly:

> All the forty-eight states now have special units and programs to promote the teaching of home economics, agriculture, and distributive trades. Only eight states, however, had special directors or units last year to foster and improve the teaching of science and mathematics. . . .

What Are the Answers?

The problems of U.S. education are a complex package. The answers, to the extent that there are answers, will also be a package. There isn't, and there can't be, a one-shot remedy.

Among educators at all levels and outsiders who are interested in education, there is fairly wide agreement developing on what some of the components of the package should be. The common ground includes the following changes:

Reorganization and broadening of the financial base. This means consolidation of the tiny school districts into economical units. It also means more state aid for hard-pressed districts, and, in one way or another, more Federal aid.

Upgrading of faculties. In part, this means higher pay and higher social status for teachers. But getting better teachers is not just a matter of hauling out the checkbook. It is a process that has to start far back in the colleges with teacher training—and even back of that with the able young men and women who now look at teaching as a possible career and decide they wouldn't touch it.

The widest possible use of movies, television, and other teaching aids—not as substitutes for the good classroom teacher, but to save his time and make the most of his abilities.

Special courses and special guidance for the academically talented students. This means grouping together the brightest boys and girls in every high school and providing them with courses that take them beyond the average of the others in their age group.

A thorough overhaul of courses to eliminate repetition and outdated material—and to add more advanced material.

A reassignment of subjects to the various grades so that the high schools will take on more of what's now considered college work, and the elementary schools take on some of the high schools' work.

The development and expansion of relatively new types of educational institutions—the community college and the two-year technical school.

All this applies primarily to the schools outside the biggest cities and schools in the better neighborhoods of the big cities. The city schools that draw their students primarily from the slum areas face a different situation. Theirs is a problem in sociology, not to say penology. They must work with a group that doesn't want to be in school anyhow and that bears a smoldering grudge against the society the school represents. The first thing these schools need is a program of social work. After that, they can start thinking about education.

Outside of these schools, the most encouraging thing you can say about U.S. education today is that it is making progress. The most disheartening thing you can say is that the progress isn't fast enough. Nothing is so irretrievable as time lost in education. Each year a new class shows up at the school gate, whether the school is ready or not. And each year a senior class marches out with a stack of diplomas that say it has been educated. If those diplomas are a lie, the schools never get another chance to make it good. And society has to live with the results for forty or fifty years.

In many ways, the financial problem of the schools comes ahead of everything else. In education, as in much of life, money can't fix everything, but you can't fix much without it.

The trouble with public school finances is that they lean far too heavily on local real estate for their revenue. All states supplement this by some form of payment to the school districts out of general revenues. But in the poorer parts of the country, even the taxing power of the states doesn't put enough financial muscle behind the schools. The variation in personal income available for taxation per child of school age is enormous—all the way from $12,256 in Delaware to $3,364 in Mississippi. This is why many serious students of education think that a program of Federal aid to the public schools is the only answer. But there is bitter resistance to Federal help, and it doesn't all come from the people who don't want to see any more money spent.

Education in the United States traditionally is a local affair. The separate school districts are fiercely independent and violently resentful of interference even from the state, let alone from Washington.

To some extent, this feeling undoubtedly arises because the school is the main branch of government that the parents have to deal with in bringing up their children. It is the point where collisions between the family and society are most likely to occur.

In any event, suspicion of Federal activity in education is deep-rooted. And opposition to Federal aid—with its implication of Federal standards and Federal supervision—is powerful enough to rule out any broad program of direct grants.

President's Program

This is one reason the program that President Eisenhower sent to Congress last January skirted so cautiously around the problem. Essentially, the Eisenhower recommendations are not a Federal education program but a first-aid kit. The main features provide for:

Matching grants to the states to encourage systematic testing of the aptitudes and abilities of students.

Matching grants for counseling and guidance.

Federal college scholarships, to be given on a basis of need, with preference for students in science and mathematics.

Matching funds for a four-year program to encourage local school systems to upgrade their science and math instruction.

A four-year program of graduate fellowships to train new teachers, and a system of direct grants of up to $125,000 to graduate schools.

Financial aid for the establishment and operation of training centers in foreign languages.

Limited as this is, it is tailored to what the Administration sees as the most urgent need of the moment—the training of more scientists and engineers for the great technological race with Russia.

The most important part of it is the testing and guidance program. This is supposed to spot, far back in the lower grades, the able students—estimated to be as many as 200,000—who now leave high school each year without going to college. The idea is that once they are identified the local schools can train them for college (and get them scholarships if necessary) instead of letting them drift through high school any way they may like.

This, for the present, is as far as the Federal Government is willing to go. It has even decided that this is not the year to push the plan for aid to school construction that it offered a year ago.

But with or without Federal aid, spending for education will go up. The school age population is growing faster than the tax base; just to maintain present quality, such as it is, the United States will have to spend more. The real question is whether it will spend enough more to get the improvement in quality that it needs.

Salary of Teachers

In a sense, teacher standards and teacher pay are simply part of the problem of school finance. Something like 60 per cent of the typical school district budget falls under the item "instructional services." The main reason for the low pay scales is that school boards all over the country have dragged their feet in a desperate effort to hold down taxes.

Low pay in turn has made it hard to keep good teachers or to be very fussy about the qualifications of new ones. More and more for the past fifteen years, the liberal arts or science graduates with anything on the ball have gone to work for industry, leaving teaching to the graduates of the schools of education. And while the schools of education have been trying to upgrade, they have found it harder and harder to sell teaching as a career for a man who thinks he has some real abilities.

Historically, the United States has been accustomed to get its teachers at bargain rates. The reasons for this curious bit of economics ceased to apply some years ago. But it is only now that the public is beginning to realize it.

A generation or so ago, teaching was one of the few occupations with a flavor of intellectuality that was readily open to the child of a poor family. (Law and medicine required long and expensive preparation, but a bright young man or woman could do a hitch in teachers college or normal school and go to work at once.) It was, moreover, one of the few respectable occupations open to women. As a result, teaching got more than its share of smart, earnest people, to whom it represented a step up the social ladder.

Today's salary scales in education still show the effects of that old situation. In spite of the social and economic changes that war and inflation have produced, the schools are still paying as though they could take their pick of thousands of eager young applicants.

In a study sponsored by the Ford Foundation's Fund for the Advancement of Education (*Teaching Salaries Then and Now*) Beardsley Ruml and Sidney G. Tickton found that if you allow for the effects of inflation, teachers now are getting just about what they were in 1904. The high school teacher in a big city (over 500,000) averaged $1,597 a year then. In 1953, his money income was up to $5,526, but deflated for rising costs that's worth only $1,577 in 1904 dollars. Meanwhile, other wage groups have been improving their status steadily. Ruml and Tickton calculate that in 1953 it would have taken $9,400 a year to give the big city high school teacher the same position with relation to other groups that he had in 1904.

The surprising thing is that good teachers have continued to come out of each June's graduating classes and that many of them—though not enough—have stayed in teaching. In that fact lies an important truth about teachers and teacher pay.

The best teachers teach because they like to. Some will talk naïvely but sincerely of "dedication" and "fulfillment." Others will simply say that they like to be doing something useful. In either case, what they mean is that teaching is a satisfying experience for them.

Such people will go into teaching as long as the pay and working conditions are not so bad as actively to discourage them. They are the people who should go into teaching, and the only people who should.

At present salary levels, even these people are getting discouraged. The United States will have to raise its scale of teaching salaries to keep them coming—and to keep them from drifting out of teaching once they have started. But you can't expect higher salaries to end the teacher shortage overnight by attracting droves of smart young people. There aren't that many potential good teachers coming out of the universities or working their way through the undergraduate pipeline. Even with adequate salaries, it will take a generation or so to recruit the faculty that we need.

There is no greater illusion than the idea that just by raising salaries high enough you could fill all the teaching jobs with smart young men who would make things hum. The eager young beavers you would recruit wouldn't be able to stand the kids. And the kids wouldn't be able to stand them.

All this is not an argument against higher salaries. It is a warning that you can't think about teachers in the same terms that you think about a factory labor force.

Many school boards have approached their teachers lately to talk about installing a system of merit pay, to replace or supplement the usual fixed schedules based on seniority and educational qualifications. They often have been astonished to find that the greatest opposition came from the best teachers, the ones who would qualify for merit pay under anybody's definition. The reasoning: Teachers shouldn't have to compete with one another; it hurts their teaching.

As one elementary teacher explains his stand, "Suppose I look at the class they want me to take next year and I see three slow learners in it. The way things are now, I'll take it and do all I can for them. But if I'm bucking for a merit increase, I'll think, 'Uh-uh, let somebody else take them. They'll louse up my record.' "

This is what a businessman would call a "civil service mentality." And that is a fair description: Teachers are civil servants, in law and in attitude. They think and act a little differently from the ordinary salaried worker. Pay is important to them, of course, but security, status, and protection from public harassment often count for more.

In all those areas—in teacher pay and teacher training, in the schools' finances and in the schools' basic concept of what they should be doing—there is wide agreement that things are not working as they should. It's clear that the U.S. education system has substantial shortcomings. But at least there is an equally substantial awareness of those shortcomings.

AGAINST THE "LIFE ADJUSTMENT" SCHOOL [3]

Q. Dr. Bestor, why is it that we suddenly find ourselves with an inadequate educational system? What went wrong in our schools?

A. The basic trouble is that the persons running our public-school system lost sight of the main purpose of education—namely, intellectual training.

In the last half century we have expanded our educational system enormously, and this has been all to the good. But educationists became so intoxicated with the idea of mere size that they were ready to lower standards in order to achieve it. Now we are paying the price of a "soft" educational policy. We have millions of college graduates and tens of millions of persons with high-school diplomas, but the Russian threat reveals us dangerously short of men and women with thorough and rigorous training in science and mathematics and other fundamental fields.

[3] From "What Went Wrong With U.S. Schools," interview with Arthur Bestor, professor of history, University of Illinois. *U.S. News & World Report.* 44:68-77. January 24, 1958. Reprinted from *U.S. News & World Report,* an independent weekly news magazine published at Washington. Copyright 1958 United States News Publishing Corporation.

Q. Why is it, for instance, that all of a sudden Russia has a lot of scientists and we're told that we didn't develop enough scientists? Was there something wrong with our system?

A. There was certainly something drastically wrong with our system. For a great many years, scientists and scholars in our universities and research establishments have been warning the country of the danger. Back in 1952, in an address to the American Historical Association, I referred to the danger as "anti-intellectualism in the schools." By this I meant the tendency of professional educationists to "pooh-pooh" the idea of mental discipline, and to say that the aim of public education ought to be "life adjustment" instead of thorough training in fundamental fields like science, mathematics, foreign languages, history and English.

In the light of Sputnik, "life-adjustment education" turns out to have been something perilously close to "death adjustment" for our nation and our children.

Q. What is the school of thought which believes in this "life adjustment" idea? Is it called "progressive education"?

A. Yes, but it is rather unfair to the originators of "progressive education" to blame them for the absurdities of what has passed for "progressive education" in the last 25 or 30 years. The original "progressive" educators, as I see it, believed in the importance of English, foreign languages, science, mathematics, history, and the rest, and they were looking for better ways of teaching these subjects—in particular, better ways of putting them across to larger numbers of young men and women. They were on the right track, certainly.

Q. But did "progressive education" go off the track?

A. Let me put it this way: Every teacher knows that he is most effective when he is able to show his students that the problems he is asking them to get to work on are connected with things they already know about and are interested in. A good teacher expects to go on from there, pushing his students into problems they have never thought of before, and calling upon them to master intellectual skills they will have to use later on. He is an adult, and he knows what these skills are. They are children, and they don't.

Now, if a teacher takes the child's experience not as a jumping-off place but as the end in itself, schooling can become utterly childish. You get a "child-centered school," to use a phrase that "progressive educators" began to use after they jumped the rails a quarter of a century or so ago.

You get the argument that the important things to teach in the schools are the things children are already excited about and choose for themselves. Because adolescents go out on dates, one pompous educational commission in my own state, Illinois, seriously recommended that, as part of their work in history, high-school students be asked to "make studies of how the last war affected the dating pattern in our culture."

Educationists blandly assert that spending class time on projects like these does not interfere with the teaching of basic subjects. This is simply not true. Time is limited. Whatever is done in school is done at the expense of something else that might be done.

We have wasted an appalling part of the time of our young people on trivialities. The Russians have had sense enough not to do so. That's why the first satellite bears the label "Made in Russia."

Q. There is a feeling among a lot of people that reading, writing and arithmetic are the fundamentals that all children should be taught, and there are lots of people who think that physics and chemistry and mathematics are essential to those students who have aptitudes in that direction. Now, what is your thought about that?

A. There is no contradiction whatever between these two propositions, with each of which I entirely agree. Reading, writing and arithmetic are absolutely fundamental for everyone. You must remember, however, that these are *elementary-school* subjects. We should insist on a mastery of these elements before a child gets to junior high school.

The study of science, of mathematics beyond arithmetic, of history, and of other basic subjects like these is the province of the high school. Work in these fields demands a foundation in reading, writing and arithmetic. It certainly should not be necessary to talk about the "three R's" beyond the elementary school.

What is "high" about a high school if it has to spend its time on these ground-floor skills?

Q. Why are not more students in this country taking mathematics? Is that because if a student just doesn't want to he doesn't, or is it because he lacks the proper counseling by the teachers?

A. It is both. In the first place, he may skip mathematics because no one forces him to take it. If he decides he isn't interested in it, he is allowed to make that decision for himself. Actually, he is in no position to make such a decision. He doesn't know how important the subject may be to him later on. Furthermore, he can't really know whether he likes a subject until he has actually sunk his teeth in it.

In the second place, there is a great deal of muddled thinking about "counseling" or "guidance" in the schools. Children have real problems—emotional, psychological and the rest—and they ought to be given whatever help is possible with these. This is one function of counseling.

But *academic* counseling is also needed, and it is a quite different thing. In essence it is straightforward, adult advice about what studies are necessary as a foundation for more advanced study. . . .

Q. The Secretary of Health, Education and Welfare, Marion Folsom, said, in a memorandum issued December 30 at the White House: "The best available studies indicate that, even in high school, one out of five students in the upper fourth of their class drops out of school before graduation. Further, among those who graduate in the upper fourth of their class, more than one out of three do not go on to college." It is also said: "Many intellectually able young people drop out of school chiefly because of lack of desire or incentive for education, or lack of money to pay for it." Of those who have the money to pay for it, why is there a lack of desire or incentive to go on to college?

A. American public schools give totally inadequate recognition to intellectual achievement. . . .

An educational system that refuses to single out for high and exceptional honors those who demonstrate in fair competition their brilliance and their willingness to work is not a democratic school system at all. It is simply an anti-intellectual school system. And it is no excuse to say that society as a whole has relatively little respect for intellectual achievement. In this matter the school has got to be the leader. If schools, whose business is intellectual training, do not really respect it, how can one expect society as a whole to do so?

There's another reason why such an alarming percentage of our ablest young men and women feel no desire to complete their education. Their intellectual interest and intellectual curiosity have been deadened because they have been held back to the level of the mediocre student so long that they have become completely bored. A "soft" educational system has put their brains to sleep.

Q. Is that due to a failure on the part of the teachers?

A. Yes, though I think the fault lies more in the system—including the system of training teachers—than in the teachers as individuals. The able student can tell the difference between a teacher who knows and loves his subject and one who doesn't.

The first passes on his fire, the second doesn't have any fire to pass on.

Our teacher-training programs are neither turning out nor selecting teachers of the first kind except by accident. Teacher training is controlled by the very people who have emphasized "life adjustment" at the expense of solid intellectual training in the schools. Their anti-intellectual point of view is carried over into teacher training. Their specialty is imparting the "know-how" of teaching, the tricks of the trade. The catalogs of departments of education in most universities offer an unbelievable array of courses in the techniques of teaching. The teacher-certification laws in every state require prospective teachers to take a minimum number of these. . . .

Q. Is the lack of incentive due to the fact that life outside of school is so attractive? Do you think jobs and good pay draw the youth?

A. That has something to do with it, but probably not a great deal. It is quite true that, so long as professional salaries of scientists and of scholars in the universities are very little higher than the wages of ordinary skilled workmen, there isn't much financial incentive to a student to spend an additional seven years after high school preparing himself for a career in research or advanced teaching. In the long run, however, intellectual curiosity counts far more than money in drawing able men and women into science and scholarship.

More dangerous than low salaries is the failure of the school, as a school, to awaken intellectual curiosity and to encourage the able student to go as far and as fast as he possibly can in basic subjects.

Q. The memorandum of the U.S. Department of Education further says: "The early identification of talent through the testing program would provide an opportunity for teachers, school counselors, parents and the community at large to encourage young students to remain in school, to work hard at basic academic subjects and to prepare for higher education."

Do we need to pay money to get that brought about? Isn't that the function of the school system?

A. These are certainly functions of the school system. The task is being inadequately performed at present, not, I think, so much because of lack of money as because of an unwillingness to push the able student ahead after he has been identified.

Q. Has there been a cult in this country which has been opposed to this type of thing?

A. Very definitely so.

Q. What is the belief of that particular school of thought?

A. It is the belief that democracy requires the leveling downward of the intellectually able. Take the recent report . . . by the Educational Policies Commission. [See article, "Changes Within the Democratic Pattern," Section IV, below.—Ed.] It pays lip service to the idea of "increased attention to the gifted young people," but it cancels most of this out by repeating a lot of antiquated nonsense about the danger of creating an "elite class." In particular, the report expresses nothing but hostility for "rigorous" programs of study for able students—exactly the kind that students of this caliber require—because in the past "such curricula were used to weed out the less able pupils and relegate them to inferior schools, thereby producing both an elite and a mass of followers."

Now I don't want inferior schools for anybody. But if you lower the standards of the schools for fear of giving too good an education to bright students, then you are deliberately *creating* inferior schools, and—most suicidal of all—forcing the best talent of the nation to go to waste in them.

Q. Then the "survival of the fittest" is not accepted as a doctrine?

A. Very far from it.

Q. Is it the theory, then, that we should have some kind of mass education that fits all varieties of ability, and concentrate on that rather than trying to develop an unusual class?

A. There is a very strong feeling in that direction. It has been a guiding one in too many of our school systems, to their very great detriment.

Q. Did this point of view prevail in the teachers colleges pretty largely?

A. It has certainly become very strong in departments of education—both in teachers colleges and in universities.

Q. Has it been resisted by citizens' groups of various kinds and parent-teacher associations?

A. I would say the parent-teacher associations have very rarely raised their voices. They don't often succeed in being anything but "yes men" on matters of educational policy. School administrators like it that way. Other organizations and individuals, however, have spoken out very freely. The Council for Basic Education, whose president is Dr. Howard Meyerhoff, executive director of the Scientific Manpower Commission, is rallying important scientific and scholarly groups in defense of the schools against anti-intellectualism. . . .

Q. What about the examinations you speak of? Does the Administration's new program meet the need? In his memorandum of December 30, Mr. Folsom proposed: "Grants to states, on a 50-50 matching basis, to encourage earlier, improved and more systematic testing of the abilities and aptitudes of students. Our concept is that the expanded and improved testing program would be placed in effect by the seventh, eighth, or at least the ninth grade, and would continue through high school. The states themselves would work out with their local school systems the best methods of accomplishing the desired objective." How do you feel about this proposal?

A. It doesn't fill the bill at all. In the first place, what we need is not more "aptitude" testing but much more testing of the *results* of our education. Of course we must locate potential talent, but we already have the machinery for doing so in existing testing programs in most places. Where the American system falls down, and falls down badly, is in finding out how much our students have actually learned at every stage.

European countries depend on thorough examinations of what students know and can do. These examinations come at each crucial stage in a student's advancement, and his promotion to a higher level of education depends on how well he does. [See article, "Changes in Europe's Secondary Schools," Section III, below.—Ed.]

This is the secret of how European countries have been able to maintain standards while moving toward mass education. We undertook mass education, but threw away the one essential safeguard of quality. Hence our present plight.

Q. We threw it away? When?

A. Thirty or forty years ago we had the rudiments of a good examination system in various places—the Regents' examinations in New York State, for example, and the College Entrance Examination Board exams. Hand in hand with expanding our school system we ought to have strengthened, intensified and expanded our examination system. Instead, educationists have attacked it, resisted it, and made it all but completely ineffective. If Federal funds are to go into educational testing, I believe emphatically that they should go for building up an independent, nation-wide system of examinations that would test, by a common standard, the results of the operations of our forty-eight state school systems.

Q. Secretary Folsom says: "The testing program would be a state, not a Federal, one." What do you think of that?

A. That is another fundamental defect of the proposal. I would compare a sound examination system with the report of an auditor. The nation needs to have a fair and impartial audit of the schools. Who ever heard of an auditor giving a 50-50 grant to the treasurer of a concern to enable the latter to audit his own books? This, in effect, is what Secretary Folsom's proposal would do.

The examination program should be a Federal program, kept in Federal hands. The Federal Government needs it in order to get a full picture of the nation's resources, to detect the weak spots, and thus to plan intelligently the kind of assistance it ought to give. And it ought to publish objective comparisons of the results of the educational programs of the various states, so that citizens in the weak states can put pressure on their own school authorities to improve standards.

Q. Isn't it the American tradition to leave responsibility for education in local hands?

A. Yes. And nothing I have said is in conflict with that principle. I do not suggest that the Federal Government tell the states how they are to educate their children. How the job is to be done is a question to be worked out by the states. All the Federal examination program would do would be to discover how well the job is being done and to publicize the results. . . .

Q. Now what about the shortage of teachers? What is that due to, do you think?

A. It's both a quantitative and a qualitative shortage. So far as the quantitative shortage is concerned, I think it has a great deal to do with salary levels. As far as the qualitative shortage—by which I mean the fact that students of real ability are simply not going into elementary and secondary-school teaching—the anti-intellectual character of so much public-school philosophy is in large part responsible. Students with first-rate minds are repelled by most courses in education. And once they have seen the anti-intellectual slant that has been imposed on the schools, many turn to another profession.

Q. Were there educational organizations that took those ideas as philosophy?

Yes, I think so. For the most part, I think the attitude of the National Education Association has been in favor of programs like "life adjustment" and has deprecated very strongly the fundamental intellectual discipline.

Q. Isn't this report by the Educational Policies Commission a report by the National Education Association?

A. Yes, in effect it is. The Educational Policies Commission is appointed by the National Education Association and by the American Association of School Administrators. It echoes the views of professional educationists. It has never taken an independent critical view of the prevailing philosophy in the schools. It has never issued a clear warning against the anti-intellectualism that has brought us to our present pass.

Recently there has been a good deal of retreating on the part of the educationists who have attacked foreign languages and attacked sciences and have advocated "life adjustment." The "life adjustment" educational program is certainly not talked about as much in educational circles as it was five years ago, and I think it probably is going to be decently buried soon. I believe this is all to the good. I am not by any means convinced that this represents a genuine change of heart. I've seen too many fads rise and fall in the field of education, and I'm suspicious that a lot of this is band-wagon-jumping at the last moment.

Q. How much can money do to overcome this thing? Is it a lack of money?

A. Primarily, it's a lack of clear purpose in education. The Educational Policies Commission spoke of "an infusion of public and private support on a massive scale," by which they meant financial support, of course. I myself think we need a massive infusion of ideas.

Q. Rather than more money?

A. Not "rather than" but "prior to." I think it will take a lot of money to do some of the things that need to be done, but my feeling is very strong indeed that we must decide precisely the things that need to be done, consider how much they will cost, and then put our money on these particular things and not on everything in general. It doesn't make sense to write a blank check payable to the order of the very educationists who have brought us to our present pass.

Q. Do you favor the Federal Government's taking over this whole job?

A. I think the Federal Government must exert its leadership in this matter in the national interest, yes. I don't think the Federal Government can run the school system. I think Federal money ought to be used to repair the standards of the schools we have, to reverse anti-intellectualism trends, and to back up the particular kinds of programs that we desperately need. . . .

Q. Is there danger that the present concern with science and mathematics will throw our educational system out of balance?

A. There is real danger of this. President Eisenhower has warned against it. We must, however, be careful to recognize the quarter from which the danger may come. Genuine scientists and mathematicians would never approve any such distortion of the school system.

I have had conferences with scores of scientists on educational questions. It usually turns out that I, an historian, am arguing strongly for more attention in the schools to science and mathematics, while they are arguing for more attention to English and history.

In other words, real scientists and scholars see eye to eye on the necessity of a school program that will develop intellectual competence in all the basic fields.

What I fear is that control over the new emergency programs will not be put in the hands of scientists and mathematicians, but will be seized by the very same educationists who have produced our present difficulties. Then we will really be in trouble.

The point is that we have neglected science and mathematics as part of a general neglect of intellectual training.

We neglected all the basic subjects because our educational-policy makers didn't think them important. They wanted the schools to deal only with so-called "practical" things, things in front of their noses—cooking, automobile driving, "better boy-girl relationships," "life adjustment" and the like. Now many of them are ready to concede that Sputnik has made science and mathematics "practical," and they are ready to plump for these two subjects. They have not really repudiated their anti-intellectual attitude toward education. They have simply taken up another fad.

If educationists of this stamp control the new programs that the present crisis may bring forth, then we won't get good teaching even of science and mathematics. They will be taught as a series of specialized tricks, not as a fundamental way of thinking. And there will be a hacking away at humanistic disciplines like history, English literature and foreign languages, because the educationists will still brand them "impractical."

Q. How can this be prevented?

A. I think we need—*at once*—a national advisory commission on public educational policy, composed of absolutely top-level physicists, chemists, mathematicians, historians, foreign-language specialists, professors of English literature, economists, and representatives of other disciplines fundamental to a sound school program. Rear Admiral H. G. Rickover proposed this. . . . I endorse everything he said on the matter. Indeed, I proposed such a commission back in 1952 in resolutions presented to the American Historical Association.

In view of the present emergency, I think Congress should take steps to create such a commission by statute, and should do so prior to proceeding with any of the other educational proposals before it. Such a commission should supervise the scholarship program, should fix the fields and the standards for any Federal examination program, and should indicate the precise way in which money for strengthening science teaching should be spent. More than this, it ought to sponsor studies of foreign school systems, and should in general work toward far-reaching reforms in the public-school curriculum and teacher training.

We desperately need guidance from the real scholarly world to offset the damage done to our school system by the advice that has come from commissions representing merely the narrow point of view of professional educationists.

Q. Is the trouble with the quality of teaching in the schools mainly a matter of educational philosophy or of lack of knowledge of subject matter?

A. The two go hand in hand, because a false educational philosophy is one that asserts that knowledge of the subject is not particularly important. It has been frequently said that a teacher does not have to know advanced, up-to-date science in order to teach science in the secondary school. The blind leading the blind. Educationists love to repeat as truth an absurd half-truth: "We don't teach the subject, we teach the child." . . .

Q. One of the assertions you frequently hear is that it is not the progressive educationists but the parents themselves who wanted and demanded vocational courses, "life adjustment" and so forth. What do you think of that charge?

A. I have two things to say. One is that the demand for these other kinds of programs is the demand of a very small minority of parents. The really overwhelming demand of parents today is for the three R's and for substantial advanced study. The educationists listen respectfully to the thoughtless few, and ignore or denounce the intelligent and thoughtful many. A citizen who stands up and says he wants more science, more history or more foreign languages in his child's school is likely to have his ears pinned back by the school authorities. I know from personal experience.

Educationists, in other words, sometimes make a very selective use of public opinion. Expressions in favor of vocationalism or "life adjustment" are taken to be the voice of the people. Expressions in favor of sound intellectual training are not regarded as public opinions at all—because educationists have decided in advance that such demands are "undemocratic."

There is a second thing to say. Even were it true—which it is not—that the overwhelming number of Americans want a watered-down school program, public-school authorities have no business bowing to the demand. They have a professional responsibility, like a doctor's. It's not the job of a doctor whose patient comes to him and says, "I would like a dose of opium," to give it to him. It's the doctor's job to refuse. He has responsibilities of a professional sort. He has been trained, or should have been trained, so that his guidance is what is needed, medically speaking, not what his patient wants to take.

It seems to me the professional responsibility of a teacher at any level to say to students, parents and the community: "These are the things that are fundamental in education. If you want them, I am prepared to offer them. But if you don't want them, that is the end of it. My job is to help you become educated. What you propose will not produce an educated man or woman. I will have no part in misleading and miseducating you."

AN ANSWER[4]

In his criticism of our public schools, Professor Bestor has conveniently ignored all evidence of the successes of our high schools and has emphasized only their alleged failures. . . .

For years, public-school seniors have consistently outranked seniors in private schools on the achievement examinations of the College Entrance Examination Board, although the private schools, being selective in character and emphasizing academic curricula, closely resemble the schools that Professor Bestor advocates. . . .

In the 1956 class at Yale, which admits public and private-school graduates in about equal numbers, 32 of the 40 men elected to Phi Beta Kappa were public-school graduates. Sixteen of the 17 top scientists who designed the successful Explorer rocket were graduates of public high schools.

The criticism of the schools for failing to teach enough students science ignores the fact that, in recent years, our public high schools have graduated more than 50 times as many students who have studied chemistry as have been graduated by all of our colleges with majors in chemistry and chemical engineering and more than 100 times as many students who have studied physics as were graduated from the colleges with majors in physics, engineering physics and aeronautical engineering combined. . . .

Our need today is not for a change to the European system of class schools which would close the door to higher education at the age of 10 or 11 to all but a favored few. We cannot afford to follow the Russian example and eliminate all but one third of our young people from our secondary schools by the end of the tenth grade.

[4] From "The Debate Over Quality of U.S. Schools—a Symposium," statement by Howard G. Spalding, high school principal, Mount Vernon, New York. *U.S. News & World Report.* 44:99-100. May 16, 1958. Reprinted from *U.S. News & World Report,* an independent weekly news magazine published at Washington. Copyright 1958 United States News Publishing Corporation.

In a nation with as many needs for educated people competent in many fields, the talents of all of our young people need to be fully developed. All need to be prepared for the difficult duties of democratic citizenship.

The most dangerous educational mistake that could be made in a democracy would be to assume that only the gifted are worth educating to their full potential. It is this assumption that has guided European schools for generations. The bitter social cleavages and the lack of political stability which today threaten the very existence of France, and which hamper the operation of democratic government in many other nations, are a direct result of the class education which the schools of these nations have provided.

Much less do we need to adopt a system of standardized examinations administered by a Federal bureaucracy. Such a system would provide a perfect instrument for dominating the schools, for stopping the local experimentation on which progress depends, and for manipulating the social, political and economic thought of our young people.

The localization of control of instruction is a strong safeguard against the evils of "thought control" and the use of governmental power to shape the opinions of our people.

What we do need urgently is, without change in our basic educational structure, an intensification of our efforts to make our best schools better, and to bring up to the same high level of efficiency all schools throughout the nation. The pattern for effecting the needed improvements can be found in hundreds of excellent public high schools which are already rendering a high quality of educational service.

FROM AN EDUCATIONAL RESEARCHER [5]

Mr. Bestor's contempt for professional educators reaches its depths in his countless references to "life adjustment" education.

[5] From "The Debate Over Quality of U.S. Schools—a Symposium," statement by Sam M. Lambert, Director of Research, National Education Association. *U.S. News & World Report.* 44:101. May 16, 1958. Reprinted from *U.S. News & World Report,* an independent weekly news magazine published at Washington. Copyright 1958 United States News Publishing Corporation.

If he knows anything at all about the subject, he knows that life adjustment has never been proposed as an alternative to a thorough training in science, mathematics and other academic fields.

Life adjustment as an idea in education began with concern for two groups of young people.

First were the dropouts, those who were unable to learn from the standard college-preparatory curriculum and who left school in discouragement, only to find in our industrial economy no regular employment open to untrained teen-agers.

The second group was the large number of in-between youth, not aspiring to college preparation, not suited for strictly vocational courses, who were in high school because they and their parents wanted their schooling continued.

The college-preparatory curriculum has always been offered. There is ample evidence that its graduates hold their own with graduates of private college-preparatory schools. The life-adjustment idea was aimed primarily at developing a genuine educational program for those who could not profit from the college-preparatory approach.

Two national conferences on life-adjustment education were held—in 1951 and in 1954—and a number of useful state programs were developed. Some of the enthusiasm spilled over to vitalize the whole secondary program. But, today, "life adjustment" as a separate movement has neither prophets nor followers. It has made its contribution to secondary education in calling attention to the needs of a neglected group of students and in proposing improvements that have been beneficial to secondary education for all American youth.

U.S. EDUCATION: AN INDICTMENT [6]

We are slowly thinking our way through a thicket of bitter disappointment and humiliating truth to the realization that a

[6] From "Education in the Nuclear Age," address delivered December 6, 1957, by Rear Admiral H. G. Rickover, USN, developer of the first atomic-powered submarine. Text from press release issued by United States Atomic Energy Commission. Washington 25, D.C. 1957. p 2-6. mimeo. Reprinted by permission. (For another excerpt from this address see "In Favor of Europe's System" in Section III, below.)

nineteenth century educational philosophy is as hopelessly outdated today as the horse and buggy. Nothing short of a complete reorganization of American education, preceded by a revolutionary reversal of educational aims, can equip us for winning the educational race with the Russians.

Let me digress a little to go into this matter, though it is seemingly remote from today's event. I should like to do this because I think it is a matter of vital importance. . . .

Ours is a democracy. We cannot move forward faster than the majority of the people will permit us to go. Today the people are aroused because they sense that something is fundamentally wrong with American education when a country—three fourths illiterate a generation ago—can in twenty years catch up with us in so important a field of knowledge as science and engineering. The mass of well-reasoned criticism which is currently filling the air and the news columns is, however, so large as to be almost indigestible. . . .

In my work in nuclear energy, the defects of our school system forced themselves upon my attention as long as ten years ago. Since then I have had occasion to interview more than a thousand young college men and officers. The design and development of nuclear power plants is a difficult scientific and engineering project encompassing the most advanced concepts in physics, mathematics, chemistry, metallurgy, electrical engineering, electronics, and mechanical engineering. Young men with sound fundamental scientific and engineering knowledge and proper motivation are needed to carry the project forward. Despite the numbers who apply, I have never found more than a very small percentage who had the necessary qualifications. I could not but come to the conclusion that something was radically wrong with the schools and colleges to whom the education of these young men had been entrusted.

I think we have come to the pass we are in today because our mass media wrap us in a cocoon of soothing "Coué-ism" along the lines of "every day, in every way, things are going to be better and better." Few of us read serious books. We are therefore singularly defenseless against the continuous flood of optimistic predictions of a future with delightful superabundance

—just around the corner—which American science will provide. We are equally defenseless against the clichés of our folklore which assure us that America is and always will be the most technically advanced nation. Or that ours is the most marvelous system of education in the world since more teen-agers are in school in the United States than anywhere else. This silky cocoon has kept us in isolation from the educational practices of even our closest allies in Europe. A few hours' check of their curricula, teaching standards, and of the end results of their educational system would disabuse us speedily of our illusions.

It seems to me that the first step in tackling the American educational problem is to collect all the pertinent data concerning education in other Western nations and to present it to our people clearly and with dispatch. I am thinking of the sort of thing done by the Department of Health, Education and Welfare when it published its recent useful *Report on Education in the USSR.* We need all the information and we need it now. At little cost much help for planning educational reforms could be made available.

Some may say that one cannot make valid comparisons between the educational systems of different countries since—to paraphrase a famous saying of Lord Haldane—it is in its education that the soul of a people mirrors itself. Even so there are other ways to measure education besides the soul.

Take spelling, for example: *elementary* schools in Europe seldom fail to teach their pupils how to spell, yet American *high* school graduates are notoriously bad spellers. Or take educational efficiency: The American student is two to three years older than youngsters of equivalent education abroad, at every age from nine to completion of his professional education. Or, to take a more elevated level:

Through 1955 the Nobel Prize Committee in awarding prizes for original work in physics and chemistry granted, in proportion to population, three times as many to Germany as to the United States; two and one half times as many to England; one and one half times as many to France. Most astonishing perhaps, Holland with a population one sixteenth of ours received four to our 22 prizes; Switzerland with one fiftieth received five prizes; Austria with one twenty-fifth got three. Or take the field of nuclear fission alone. Twelve basic discoveries in physics, chemistry and mathematics brought atomic power into being. Of these, three each were made by German, English and French; one each by Danish and Italian scientists; and only one by an American. Yet the population of France, Germany, England, Denmark and Italy combined is only one third greater than that of the United States; their total national wealth is far less than ours. But in this particular field of trained brain power they were 11 times as rich as we.

Or again, take the successful development of the atomic bomb. We provided excellent direction, extensive facilities, unlimited funds; but the major contribution in brain power came from such men as Italy's Fermi and Segrè, Denmark's Bohr, Hungary's Teller, Von Neumann, Wigner and Szilard, Germany's Hahn, Strassmann, Bethe and Einstein, England's Chadwick and Cockcroft—to mention but a few of the top men. In fact, it was of no small concern to the Joint Congressional Committee on Atomic Energy that, as the late Representative Hinshaw put it, the very topmost of our scientists is 60-70 per cent foreign born and educated. Even some of our own foremost scientific contributors received their university training abroad.

Of course, no educational system can guarantee that it will bring forth genius at any given rate; all it can do is to make it easy for genius to be discovered early, nurtured and encouraged, and allowed to flower according to its own inner motivations. Can we truly say that our education does this? I think not. Nor does it even seek out, nurture and develop mere talent—as contrasted with genius. It fails to develop in our most intelligent youngsters the desire to make the best use of their good minds. Hence we see 200,000 of the top quarter high school graduates lost each year to higher education while the nation suffers the most acute shortage of trained professionals in all fields, and a disastrous shortage of vitally needed scientists and engineers.

It is estimated that industry and the defense establishment urgently need at least twice as many scientists and engineers as we are currently graduating. Even more disastrous in the long run is the severe shortage of properly qualified teachers of science and mathematics in high schools and in colleges. It will take many years merely to bring the present corps of 60,000 junior and senior high school science teachers to the level of competence required to give our youngsters sufficient education so that they can enter engineering colleges properly prepared. As it is, only one third of our high school graduates are really qualified; the remainder must take remedial work which puts a heavy burden on the colleges' scant number of teachers. No wonder most engineering schools lose 50 per cent of those who enter. In 1955 we actually gained only 125 physics teachers. This works out to one for every 225 of the country's high schools.

One of the great defects of our educational system is that it does not respond to changing national needs for specific kinds of professional people. Because of the considerable latitude allowed to the student in selecting subjects, not only in college but even in high school, he may be so unprepared to study for a given profession as virtually to bar him from it unless he has begun deliberately to prepare himself for it in high school. For example, we need a great many physicists *now.* But a youngster who has taken no physics and little mathematics in high school, as is true of most of our high school graduates, and who then takes the usual two years of liberal arts in college is, in effect, precluded from becoming a physicist. And yet in today's rapidly changing technological civilization it is absolutely essential that the educational system be sufficiently elastic to permit students to shift quickly into study for those professions most needed at any given moment.

This inelasticity of our school system is the direct result of the sentimental attachment we hold for the concept of a comprehensive school in which all children—stupid, average, talented and bright—march sedately up to the eighteenth year, absorbing so little real education that it takes another four years at college before the preprofessional stage of education is completed. In order to make some small allowance for different mental capacities we allow junior and senior high school pupils considerable leeway in selection of subjects. Electives are a necessary consequence of forcing the educational strait jacket of the comprehensive school on *all* children in the name of educational democracy. We thus thrust upon our teen-agers decisions which may adversely affect not only their own professional careers but also the country's ability to obtain the professionals it needs. . . .

The greatest single obstacle to a renovation of our education comes from the fact that control, financing and direction of education is, in the United States, in the hands of many thousands of local school boards, whose members seldom qualify as educational experts. State control is slight and Federal assistance is rejected. We therefore are at an impasse. It is exceedingly difficult and time-consuming to convince thousands of school boards that they must change the curriculum of the local high school; to persuade forty-eight states that their colleges and universities ought to confine themselves to education and not to vocational training and service activities which have no place in institutions of higher learning; or for that matter to win over thousands of alumni on whose bounty our privately endowed colleges and universities so largely depend.

In no other Western country are educational institutions so precariously placed financially, so dependent on local politicians, on the whim of small communities where few have ever had a higher education. Half our colleges are continuously threatened with bankruptcy. The future looks bleak unless in some way Federal assistance can be made acceptable and some sort of national standard can be established to which diploma- and degree-giving institutions must conform.

England which was faced with a tradition of private education and of control by thousands of local school boards finally worked out a compromise by which government and local school authorities were able to cooperate. The local school boards had to go however, and were replaced by a small number of county councils. Government aid remains voluntary but is conditioned on acceptance of uniform standards of excellence in curriculum and in teacher qualification. Moving slowly step by step, England has been able to overcome her own political obstacles to good public education; but it took her over a hundred years and she has been that much behind continental Europe. Might this not be one reason why, despite her far-flung Empire, her enormous head start in industrialization, England was rapidly overtaken by Germany, both industrially and finally militarily? Education is too vital for a nation's welfare safely to be debated overlong.

In our own country, the schools have been primarily engines for Americanizing children of diverse backgrounds; for teaching all children to get along with others whose economic and cultural standards might be different; for developing the qualities which citizens in a democracy need in order to carry out their political responsibilities. These tasks our schools have accomplished excellently. As long as the country devoted all its energies single-mindedly to development of the highest standard of living for the greatest number of people, the kind of education received by American youngsters was entirely adequate. But in the pursuit of this aim, we have neglected two things:

First, we have not counted the cost to us of our high standard of living in terms of rapid exhaustion of irreplaceable mineral and fuel resources; and

Second, we have failed to recognize the damage done to our talented children by squeezing them into the strait jacket of the comprehensive school.

We must devise better ways to educate our talented youth. We cannot spare a single child who has the capacity to become a professional. In science and engineering we need many more trained people to help us develop substitutes for diminishing natural resources and to keep us ever advancing technologically.

Faced with the task of expanding the aims of American education we must yet not lose its great qualities of humaneness and its ability to lay the spiritual foundations for harmonious democratic life among people of varied capacities and cultural standards.

Change, of course, is always painful. Too often those whose way of life is dependent on the old and familiar routines resist fiercely, counting their own interests above those of the nation, though never conscious of this. Nothing is easier than to convince oneself that what is good for him is good for the country.

I can perhaps make more clear what I think of the health of our educational system by reminding you what is done in a hospital when a patient is seriously ill. He is placed on a critical list. Those who are concerned for him are notified. If he is an important man, bulletins are issued hourly. A continuous watch is maintained and extraordinary measures are taken to revive his health so that as soon as possible he may again become a useful member of society.

Once the American public realizes the desperate consequences of our great shortage of trained man power in terms both of national well-being in a resources-poor future, and of our very existence as an independent and strong nation; once the connection is made in everyone's mind between education and lack of vitally needed scientists and engineers—there will I hope be action to undo the educational harm of the past half century.

WE DO NOT TEACH THEM HOW TO THINK[7]

American education, in the grip of a crisis for over a decade, has been forced into self-examination by the launching of the Russian Sputniks. Stunned, perhaps, but also awakened to the harsh realities of the modern world, the American people sense the crucial roles played by systems of education in Russia's scientific success and in our own failure. In spite of its economic poverty, former technological backwardness and ideological rigidity, the Soviet system has proved capable of producing engineers and scientists whose achievements are equal (and perhaps at times superior) to those of the best brains in the West.

Among the many reasons is, of course, the fact that the Soviet dictatorship has relentlessly emphasized and unstintingly supported the technological and scientific training of Russian youth. Not only are *more* engineers and scientists (and scholars in other fields as well) "produced" in Soviet Russia, but their fundamental preparation is no worse than that of their average American counterparts. Moreover, scholars, scientists and engi-

[7] Article by Marc Raeff, associate professor of history at Clark University. New York *Times Magazine*. p7+. January 26, 1958. Reprinted by permission.

neers enjoy the respect and support of the people at large and of the educated in particular.

There are many serious drawbacks in the Soviet approach, the two most conspicuous being the dictation of professional specialization and constant ideological indoctrination. It would be suicidal for American culture to try to ape the Soviet system slavishly. Yet we cannot escape the fact that as long as it remains the political and ideological system we abhor, it presents a very serious challenge to American political and cultural security.

Recent comparisons between the Soviet and American educational systems have stressed the great amount of time and attention paid by Soviet schools to science. But the weakness of American education does not lie exclusively, or even primarily, in that it gives less attention to science; its failings are much more fundamental.

Before analyzing these failings, it would be well to remember that—ideology apart—Soviet education today is not the peculiar product of a totalitarian regime. As a matter of fact, Soviet Russia today essentially follows the traditional system of secondary (and primary) education prevalent in all continental Europe. Moreover, it is a system which still survives, in part, in the better private preparatory schools in the United States.

What is wrong, fundamentally, with American education? Two things: it does not train for mental work and teaches little.

It would seem that the first business of a school is to train the student to work with his head. This is a habit that takes time to develop and should be started early. The trouble with American schools, especially high schools, is that they seldom force the student to make serious efforts. They do not accustom him to systematic, constant, hard work. There seems to be a general reluctance in our civilization to "push" a child, to make him do the things we believe are right. What utter nonsense! The child, at least up to 13 or 14 years, wants guidance, needs direction and feels confused and insecure when all the decisions are left to him. After all, what are parents and teachers for if they cannot give the child the essential support and direction he needs?

There is no reason why this protection, direction and support which we lavish in terms of physical care should be denied to intellectual and emotional needs. Accustoming a child to consistent, systematic hard work early will give him confidence in his own mental powers and will help him to accumulate and digest knowledge easily. The time to start is when the child is impressionable and eager to acquire knowledge about the surrounding world. Teachers in Europe have repeatedly testified to the fact that, far from discouraging students, a stiff program and great demands on their time and effort stimulate and encourage them.

How many of our bright students get bored and discouraged because so little is required of them? Why do so many of us remember our "tough" teachers most fondly? It is because they taught us something, instead of merely amusing us. For example, at an age when children like to memorize, it is easy to assign them tasks of memory which would develop this faculty and at the same time build up a store of knowledge for later use.

While our children are frittering away their time at unrewarding, unchallenging and easy mechanical tasks, the European child learns that the acquisition of knowledge is a serious, time-consuming, absorbing business. At an early age he finds out that learning does not stop with the class bell. Each day he continues his education at home when he does his homework—a homework which often requires a great deal of effort, thought and exchange of ideas with others.

Unlike his American counterpart, the European high school student is not asked to decide for himself which of the many areas of modern learning he wants to acquire. After all, is a 12- or 13-year-old really mature enough to decide intelligently what is best to know and to take upon himself the emotional responsibility of selecting a course of studies with an eye to his future career? I am sure that this freedom of choice, so much vaunted by us, far from helping the child to maturity and responsibility, disorients him by putting too much stress on his self-reliance.

The European student has no choice (or very little), but he has a well thought out, comprehensive, stable curriculum. This curriculum takes up all the important subjects gradually, at the logical time, in their most fruitful and natural sequence. The basic "tool" subjects, such as the native language (spoken and written), mathematics, natural sciences, history (in a chronologically meaningful order) and geography are studied every year, and the student progresses in them gradually and logically.

Other subjects, such as foreign languages (two or three, at least), special fields in science (organic chemistry, physics, advanced mathematics, physiology, geology), fine arts, psychology and philosophy come at their proper time, after a solid groundwork has been laid for them. Thus, by the time the student graduates from the *lycée* or *Gymnasium,* at the age of 18, he has a firm grounding in the essential elements of his cultural and scientific heritage; he knows how to use his mind; he is ready for advanced, specialized studies at the university.

Instead of providing a well-integrated and logically complete curriculum, our high schools are like cafeterias, offering discrete fragments of modern knowledge, not related to each other, not grounded in any serious common foundation, and changing their "bill of fare" at every twist and turn of popular fad and fashion. From a disparate array ranging from accounting to zoology, the student is asked to make his selections. Often he takes those courses which are most amusing and easy, or which appear to have immediate practical value. He avoids those requiring much work and long preparation (which means basic subjects like mathematics or physics).

Furthermore, he can take most courses in any order he wants. So it may happen that he takes chemistry before physics, or physics without adequate grounding in mathematics, or makes a chronological jumble of history courses. Taking up an ill-assorted, disconnected set of subjects every year, the student's attention is never called to the common foundations and the essential problems of each; his mental energy is dispersed as he switches rapidly from one field to the other, without stopping long enough to master any thoroughly.

What is the result? The student comes to college woefully unprepared. To make up for his deficiency he takes the notorious survey courses (or, in some cases, General Education courses). In these courses the lost time is made up hurriedly and superficially and the information is seldom properly digested or assimilated.

In what way is the student unprepared? To begin with, some students come to college incapable of even reading their text-books intelligently—so we need college courses in remedial reading. Many students cannot follow the main argument or find the central point in their readings because they have been accustomed to look only for the trivial details (around which the so-called "objective" tests are built). The number of students who cannot even express themselves in correct and clear English is appalling. Often I have had to guess what the student was trying to say in his paper. Often, too, I have had to give a poor grade because the sentences were unintelligible. As for a clear essay, it is frequently a task beyond the student's capacity.

His ignorance of anything he did not study in a special course is dismal. Is it permissible for a person in the mid-twentieth century to finish higher education with distinction, obtain a Ph.D. from a reputable university in a social science field without *ever* having had any physics or chemistry, and no geography since grade school?

Or to take another example: In an advanced undergraduate course on the history of Western thought, I could not adequately discuss the development and nature of modern science because the students did not know what Kepler's laws of planetary motion were about or what contributions Galileo had made to the study of motion. And this in an age of space satellites and moving machines!

How can such students begin to understand that science is not magic or mere technology, but that it rests on principles and concepts which are closely related to Western religion, art and thought? No wonder that technical training remains narrow, superficial and, worse yet, isolated from the rest of our culture. And it is not surprising to find that the scientist or scholar is frequently misunderstood and unsupported by his own society.

Perhaps the most serious failure of the American educational system has been its tendency to produce intellectual passivity. It has not helped to develop active, critical, inquisitive minds. Our schools, especially high schools, pride themselves on the fact that they train for democratic citizenship, that is to say that they develop a critical spirit and an ability to discuss. But that is far from being the case. I am afraid our schools have taken the *technique* of question asking for the *substance* of the process by which inquiring minds are developed. They provide students with slogans, generalities and formulas by which to judge and criticize, but they don't give the knowledge which alone makes criticism meaningful.

I once had occasion to hear a high school discussion of the causes of the defeat of France in 1940. Rarely have I heard such a silly and useless exercise: the students were completely ignorant of the most elementary facts of recent French history and European politics. And yet they were asked to "discuss." The result was a meaningless juggling of slogans and clichés suggested by their teacher, who himself was not well informed.

A corollary of the school's failure to provide the foundation for intelligent opinion is the unquestioning respect so many people have for the "expert." Was not America's espionage hysteria and receptivity to McCarthyism a warning sign that indoctrination and uncritical acceptance of self-styled experts had gone far enough?

It is not opinions that a school should provide (as it does, incidentally, in Soviet Russia), or even a wishy-washy "on the one hand, on the other hand" objectivity. The school must give solid knowledge, so that students have something with which to develop intelligent opinions of their own. Recent student discontent in eastern Europe shows that knowledge is stronger than indoctrination.

And how is a student to develop an inquisitive spirit and creative intellect if, during most of his school years, he has never been asked to work with his own mind? Our schools are so afraid, it would seem, to tax the student's time and energy that they don't dare to give him much work for home. And what homework they give is of the most superficial sort, consisting mainly in repeating what has been done in class.

Here again we could learn a great deal from Europe. There the student is given a large amount of homework from the very start. In this homework he is asked to do some creative "relating" and imaginative thinking himself. In mathematics, for example, the American student is expected primarily to find the correct final answer. The French student's task, however, is to explain in writing—a good training in composition, incidentally—the steps and reasons involved in the solution of a problem.

We pride ourselves on developing the child's self-reliance and independence. True, in matters of behavior, in getting along with others, we do a fairly good job. But we don't make any such effort in developing the mind. The European child develops his intellectual independence and inquisitiveness, his critical spirit and sophistication by doing a lot of his studying and thinking by himself, in his homework. Our schools offer pre-cooked, processed foods. No wonder that the students cannot cook a meal themselves; they don't even want to shop for anything that is not neatly packaged and pre-cooked.

This is not the stuff creative scientists and scholars are made of. This produces the subordinate bureaucrat and the narrow, unimaginative technologist. In general, our students merely memorize disparate facts and ready-made generalizations which can be regurgitated at the examination. It is frustrating for a teacher to hear a student say: "Yours was a good course, I took so and so many pages of notes," when a little prodding shows quite clearly that nothing has ever percolated from the notes into his mind.

The students, however, are not so much to blame as are their schools and teachers. There are many wonderful and capable teachers in this country—men and women who have dedicated their lives to the poorly remunerated task of teaching the young. And many of them have done a splendid job, in spite of the system. Unfortunately, these dedicated teachers are a declining minority; they are the older generation that is vainly struggling against the cobweb of education administration.

It is the average younger teacher, the product of our education departments and teachers colleges (and the administrator who supports him) who is to blame. He mistakes the form, the technique of teaching for the content and process of teaching. Our teachers are trained *how* to teach, but are they provided with the knowledge and understanding of *what* to teach? I often wonder. Time is wasted on trivial details as the length and nature of tests, "group dynamics," the size of the paper to be used, the form of the report cards—with little attention being paid to the subject the teacher will have to teach.

We feel that a Ph.D. or even an M.A. in a given field qualifies a person to teach that subject in a college, without the "benefit" of any education courses. But if it is adequate for college teaching, it ought to be adequate for the high schools as well. It has not been unusual in my experience to have a prospective (or even active) public school teacher come to my history classes, eager to learn more of the subject-matter, only to be forced to withdraw at the insistence of the education department in order to take more courses in education.

Education has two main tasks: First, it should provide well-integrated, solidly grounded, general knowledge of *all* the essential fields. In the second place, education must help to *develop* the mind. As with everything that develops gradually, it is essential to give the proper habits early. Inasmuch as men are unequally endowed with intellect, the school system must be discriminating, too.

Democracy in this context should mean that all gifted individuals are given the opportunity to develop and apply their talents fully. To gear *all* education to the least common denominator only discriminates against the more intelligent and able, to the great detriment of society and with no corresponding benefit for the less gifted. Give everyone as much serious and solid education as he can take. But do not water down education for the sake of giving everybody some "higher" education.

What can be done about all this right away? We all agree that much more money has to be put into education. The apportioning of the funds, too, should be modified so as to raise the financial and social standing of the teaching profession. But this is only part of the story. It is unrealistic, as well as wasteful, to act as if every high school graduate were capable (or desirous) of continuing his studies. We don't expect every college graduate to become a Ph.D. Why then view *all* high school students as potential college material? This only drives the standards down to the lowest common level.

The standards of education must be raised rapidly and in this the colleges should take the lead. With an expected increase in college enrollment, the colleges are in a strong position to make their weight felt and again become more selective. Stressing quality and not quantity, they should admit only that fraction—perhaps quite a small one—which can be expected to make the things of the mind its main concern. Then let the "feed-back" mechanisms operate freely; let the higher standards of the colleges set the pace instead of forcing the colleges to bow to the high schools' performance and changing whims of a poorly informed public.

We have several kinds of high schools already; why not extend the system? Those unwilling or unable to go to college—provided it is not for economic reasons—may go to trade schools or similar institutions where their education will terminate. The regular academic high school should become the purveyor to the college, admitting its students selectively, and treating them as potential creative scholars, scientists, engineers or administrators.

The radical overhauling of American education has been long delayed. The impetus may be provided by America's reaction to the Sputniks. But, to be fully effective, the educational system needs the nation's constant interest and enlightened support.

Such support can come only from a population which from childhood on has been introduced to the essence of mental activity, a people that has developed a genuine understanding of the process of learning and has acquired respect for knowledge and intellectual accomplishment. In the development of such a population lies the greatest challenge and noblest task of American education.

GREAT CHALLENGES FOR EDUCATION [8]

Our people and our country face awesome tasks and responsibilities in the decades ahead. Let us take a quick look at some of the great challenges we must meet.

[8] From article by Hollis L. Caswell, president, Teachers College, Columbia University. *Teachers College Record*. 59:69-75. November 1957. Reprinted by permission.

1. We must learn to live with great uncertainty and with ever-present danger in our international relations, maintaining confidence and moving step by step toward achievement of a durable peace. This is a goal men have long sought unsuccessfully but a new urgency is now given this problem, for the alternative is a war of destruction, awful beyond imagination.

2. Somehow people of various cultures who hold different values and have markedly different customs must learn to live side by side in harmony and with mutual respect, dealing constructively with problems which inevitably intertwine their destinies. . . . In this great and complex task of achieving intercultural understanding and cooperation our people and our country must lead.

3. We must discover how to use atomic energy to foster the well-being of mankind. The extension of its use involves not only the most intricate technical problems but far-reaching questions of public policy and economic development.

4. Automation promises a second industrial revolution, or if you prefer, the extension of industrialization to its ultimate development. Machines replacing men to an extent we can hardly imagine present demands for technical competence far exceeding those we now must meet. To operate the increasingly vast and complicated system of economic production in the years ahead will require that a greatly increased proportion of our people achieve mastery of intricate, high-level skills.

5. As machines replace men, less and less work time will be required to produce the materials we need. . . . For millions of people the job no longer dominates their lives, and it will do so for fewer people in the years ahead. To what ends shall the substantial time that is freed be devoted? This is a question of great seriousness. . . . At the same time, demands on many professional workers have increased, so that once favored groups find themselves with the heaviest work loads and least opportunity for leisure.

6. Our world today is characterized by a pervasive sense of insecurity and purposelessness. Many persons question the basic goals of life and countless numbers are emotionally disturbed and mentally unstable. There is on every hand evidence of a

need for clearer understanding of and commitment to values which make life a great adventure eminently worth living.

7. The extension of mass organization in many aspects of our life threatens submergence of the individual. There is danger that American society, which in the past has been distinctively mobile, may become more rigid. There is reason to believe that more and more people are seeking security in conformity to groups. Should these tendencies become dominant, our national ideal of providing opportunity for individual initiative and development would be undermined.

These seven challenges indicate that we have a tremendous task ahead, probably the most difficult one our country has ever faced. But it is imperative that they be met if our people are to move forward into a hopeful and better future. Whether or not we succeed depends more on education than on anything else. Military and economic strength give us current dominance, but in the final analysis lasting solutions to these problems will be achieved only through an education that cultivates greater understanding of man in the modern world, fosters firmer devotion to our basic ideals, and evolves more effective means for their achievement under the new conditions of an atomic age.

Consequently, as we look to the future and ask what kind of education we should have we must direct our thinking and plans to meet challenges such as these. The import they have for education can only partially be comprehended, for their influence will be pervasive, powerful, and of long range. However, we must make projections of desirable lines of development, testing each step ahead by its actual results in experience. I shall indicate four broad requirements which I believe education for the future should meet, and point out what seem to me to be some dangers and limitations in certain current educational practices and trends.

Requirement I: All of our people must have an education which provides a balanced and interrelated emphasis on general or liberal objectives on the one hand and on vocational or professional objectives on the other. One of the strong features of American education has been the extent to which it has sought to meet this requirement. There have been marked differences of opinion regarding relative emphasis, but fairly wide agreement to the proposition that all students should receive an education which meets both general and vocational needs.

At present, however, there is increasing evidence of a desire to divide the two. In many suggestions there is the implication that the intellectually talented should have their work restricted to academic fields and that those destined for skilled and semi-skilled jobs should have programs largely of a vocational nature. The most extreme illustration of this is the proposal by Rear Admiral Rickover that children with IQ's above 115 should be separated from other students at ten or eleven years of age and be educated in different schools. The program for this group should be "purely academic" to use his words. The inference may be drawn that education of the remainder should be largely vocational, since he recommends patterning the program on the traditional European plan. . . .

The challenges I have mentioned suggest clearly the need for both more effective general education and increased technical competence. I would consider it most unfortunate if these needs were dealt with by restricting the education of an intellectual elite to academic fields and of those preparing for technical work to a vocational program. In our country, it seems clear to me, every person needs to have both a good general education and preparation for his lifework. The wisdom and special competencies of the mass of our people will in the long run determine our future. . . .

Requirement II: Education must become increasingly effective in influencing the behavior of students. Many years ago John Ruskin wrote: "Education is not teaching people what they do not know; it is teaching them to behave as they do not behave." Yet down through the years schooling has been overwhelmingly devoted to teaching students what they do not know. The faith of the rank and file of teachers in the value of memorizing facts and definitions is amazing. "Learn the causes of the American Revolution," "Define a noun," "Give the formula for sulphuric acid," "Take the next ten pages for tomorrow." So goes too much of our teaching.

The kinds of problems we have been facing as a people and a nation and those we will face in the future require an education that leads people to act differently than they otherwise would. For example, if the challenges in the international field are to be met successfully, our people generally must have guided experience in education which will cause the actions they take that influence people of other cultures actually to reflect greater understanding and appreciation of those cultures. . . .

There needs to be a systematic long-range effort to interpret educational objectives in behavioral terms. . . .

But the most difficult task remains to be achieved—the devising and introduction into teaching practices of procedures which will lead to the desired developments in behavior. It is all too easy to accept new objectives verbally and then insist that old methods and content which we have been using all the while will serve the new purposes. . . .

Many a teacher who faces the challenges of education for the decades ahead and asks honestly how he can teach so as to improve the behavior of pupils will find to his dismay that "his own learning touches not on these things." We must seek new knowledge and develop more effective means of making education a vital and guiding force in the lives of our students. In a world that moves as fast as ours we may never safely accept without question what we are doing in the present as adequate for the future.

Requirement III: Education in school should become increasingly concerned with developing attitudes and methods of work which lead the individual to continue his education throughout his life. Many educators over the past several years have been deeply concerned with the great diversity in the educational program. They have felt the need for some common core of knowledge that would mark the educated man, as was true in earlier times. Various means have been proposed to achieve this end. More and more colleges have reduced electives and have prescribed an increased number of common courses. There is a tendency to move toward a greater number and increased uniformity of requirements in high school.

The plain fact is that the diversity which has characterized education is a reflection of the culture in which we live. Knowledge is extended so greatly and increases so rapidly, conditions of life change so fast, and the problems we face are so varied that there is utterly no hope of achieving solely through formal agencies an education adequate to our needs. Our people will become able to deal with the unpredictable effects of powerful forces such as automation and atomic energy only as they continuously educate themselves to understand the influence these forces exert on their lives and on the future of our country. The most important outcome of formal education today, when we look to the great challenges of tomorrow, is the development of attitudes and methods of work which will cause the individual to continue his education so that he will at all times bring the tools of the educated man to bear on his present problems.

There are bound to be tremendous gaps in the education of every individual in the modern world. There is simply too much to be known, there are too many complexities to modern life for any individual to comprehend. Thus we must select those things which at a time and in a given setting hold greatest significance, and use them as a means of reaching toward the unknown of the future.

It is my opinion that at present there is a tendency to place too great emphasis on developing a common body of knowledge in comparison with cultivating attitudes and methods of work that cause the student to meet whatever situations he may face with thoroughness and competence and appreciation. It is far more essential that a student have real appreciation of a few selections of good literature, that he develop the habit of reading for enjoyment, and that he achieve a sense of confidence in his own taste than it is that he cover the works of a prescribed group of writers. It is far more important that he have the experience of analyzing and dealing thoroughly with a few of the most important social problems than that he have a smattering of information about a great many. At best he can only sample the vast accumulation which our culture represents. That sampling should be such as to make him forever a student. This will give greatest assurance that as our people and our country face the great challenges of the future we will bring the resources of education to bear on their solution.

Requirement IV: Education should be so conducted that the individual and his development are the constant focus of attention. The challenges I mentioned earlier in this discussion involved a threat to one of our basic national values: the threat of submergence of the individual person in mass organization. They also implied the great need for individual initiative and leadership and for improved person-to-person relationships. In fact, the basis of our concept of democracy is the independent, deliberate, informed, and altruistic judgments of individual citizens on matters of public policy and personal action. If this base should be undermined, our entire way of life would be threatened.

Education has been a chief means of fostering these desirable qualities. While we have had *education* for the masses in America, we have always striven to avoid in so far as possible *mass education.* Over the years in our schools various devices have been used to adjust to the individual student and to give the kind of personal attention that makes him feel he is valued and considered as a person. The guidance movement has been a major expression of this concern. . . .

Teaching is to a significant degree an art, and the better the teacher the more this is apparent. Many outcomes of teaching may be related quite directly to specific teaching procedures, but some of the most significant influences of fine teachers are very subtle in nature and rest largely on the direct personal relations of teacher and pupil. For example, the power to stimulate the pupil to high endeavor, to help him grow in his appreciation to develop a spirit of inquiry, to create the drive to continue his education, to develop a sense of beauty and an appreciation of the mysteries of the world in which he lives—these are qualities which must be cultivated pretty largely by the teacher through a multitude of small actions in day-by-day association with the pupil.

Consequently, as we look to the future, it seems to me we should bend every effort to see that the personal element holds a large place in the process of education. Many institutions today are weak in this respect and promise to be even weaker as enrollments increase. There are too many cases in which students do not have the sense of personal interest and direction from teachers. Especially is this true in large institutions. Many college students go through their freshman and sophomore years and some even further without receiving any indication whatever of personal interest and guidance from the faculty. All too often high school students have the same experience. Procedures that lead to this result will, in my opinion, greatly limit the over-all effectiveness of education and will tend to intensify the undesirable submergence of individuals in mass organization in our society generally.

The extension of mass techniques of teaching by the use of television and increase in class size, both of which limit the personal relations of teachers and pupils, in my opinion, should be appraised against this broader setting. Many people view teaching as a matter of getting across so much knowledge and certain skills and are willing to let the evaluation of education rest largely on testing of achievement in these areas. To me teaching is far more than this and its most important outcomes cannot possibly be realized when the personal element is minimized or eliminated. The challenges to be met in the future make this even more essential than it has been in the past.

Requirements for education other than the ones I have selected might well seem of greater importance to other educators. I would readily agree that there are many additional points that merit consideration. On this alone I would insist: As science and industry remake our world with incredible speed, education must also proceed with vigor and vision to new levels of effectiveness if civilization is to be preserved and advanced. We must not think small in relation to education. Just as the scientist and engineer project ever bigger and more revolutionary developments, so educational leaders must move forward with broad-scale plans and programs to meet the more complex, extensive, critical, and pressing need of the decades ahead for effective education.

II. MORE SPECIFIC PROBLEMS

EDITOR'S INTRODUCTION

The problems of classroom shortage, teacher shortage and pay, rising costs of higher education, and the desirability of using Federal funds in solving such problems are reviewed below. A myriad other specific problems relating to present or future educational needs also exist; but only a few of these can be glanced at here. It is significant, however, that in dealing with educational problems one touches immediately on vital areas of American national life. Thus any discussion of education today can hardly avoid a consideration of the problem of desegregation in public schools in both the South and the North or the continuing problem of juvenile delinquency and the schools. To call for Federal financial aid to education is to raise at once the question of Federal controls. The problem of the freedom of universities to teach and the freedom of students to know is likewise a critical national problem of recent years. And the plight of science within our educational system involves our national security. Further specific issues are covered in Section IV dealing with plans for the future and improvements now under way.

In the *Life* magazine editorial, which has been both much praised and much criticized, the controversy regarding "life adjustment" theories introduced in Section I is presented as *the* specific problem of American education today. The case for progressive education is summarized next by one of its famous proponents, William H. Kilpatrick. The problem of teacher shortage is dealt with by Irving Adler. And Beardsley Ruml, in the next article, takes a rather unusual tack on the problem of teacher salaries at the college level. In the following two articles brief notes are given on two problems of colleges and their students—the problems of too many students and too high costs.

Louis M. Hacker, educator and author, next deals with the problems of the free and the open university. The former problem, the need for free universities where scholarship and inquiry are unfettered by political authorities or social prejudices of the day, is an old one. Whether universities should be open to all who would attend is in certain ways a newer problem as some educators in face of mounting requests for admission would pick and choose among those to whom they offer their wares. In "The Law of the Land" the Supreme Court gives its official verdict striking down segregation in the public schools. Howard A. Meyerhoff's article is a revealing analysis of the place of science today in the educational world and also a plea that it be correctly balanced in the total spectrum of liberal education.

The section concludes with four articles dealing with Federal financial aid to education. First are statements for and against providing such funds for religious educational schools. They are followed by two statements on the possible effects of Federal aid on our educational system.

THE DEEPER PROBLEM IN EDUCATION[1]

It is still a shock to realize the penalties a good teacher must pay, just to do his country's most important job. We must do something quickly about improving teachers' salaries, training and status. But teachers and the public must also get together on a problem less tangible but more basic—how to straighten out the debris left by 40 years of the progressive educationists. It is a legacy of distended play facilities, substandard curricula and principals whose intellectual confusion can no longer be disguised by the compulsory smile on their faces.

American schools have done a tremendous job in educating people at a rate beyond the dreams of most nations. Such a quantitative achievement was bound to hit some snags on the quality side. And it serves no purpose to polarize the educational debate by shouting "un-American" at the late John Dewey's bones (a distinctive Americanism, in fact, was one of Dewey's intellectual boasts), or by making blanket denunciations of

[1] From editorial. *Life*. 44:32. March 31, 1958. © 1958, Time Inc. Reprinted by permission.

"frills" in education (if How to Run a Beauty Shop has no place in a general high school curriculum, a good challenging music appreciation course very definitely *has*). The problem underlying all our confusion is—to use words long out of favor in pedagogical circles—a matter of tradition and philosophy. Only by grasping this can we figure out where and how our education system went wrong.

Until the arrival of Dewey and his disciples, American schools had the stated objective of educating individuals in an inherited and enlarging body of learning. Confident of their own established values in ethics, law and culture, the old-fashioned teachers deliberately set out to pass down these values as part of a living tradition. They held that it was all one cultural heritage —everything from Boyle's Law to Cicero's First Oration against Catiline—and the more of it you learned the wiser and more mentally alert you would be.

Dewey and his disciples revolted against this certitude, which had indeed grown more than a little ossified in its teaching methods. But history records no more egregious case of throwing out the baby with the bath. Instead of modernizing the old-timers' teaching methods, the new educationists went deeper and denied tradition in anything.

"We agree," Dewey once said, "that we are uncertain as to where we are going and where we want to go, and why we are doing what we do." In a kind of country club existentialism, Dewey and his boys genially contended that the traditional ends of education—and indeed of human life—like God, virtue and the idea of "culture" were all debatable and hence not worth debating. In their place: enter life adjustment. The alternative to educating the individual thus became, as John Keats puts it in his excellent new book, *Schools without Scholars,* "to bring the individual by a process of conditioning, to a realization of his functional role in society."

The Deweyites thus transformed conditioning techniques into ends in themselves. As they tracked through U.S. education, teachers colleges assumed the dignity of lamaseries. They called their system science, but they worshiped its doctrines like a cult. In thousands of schools teachers were denied the chance of learning more about their subjects in favor of compulsory education courses in how to teach them.

Within the schools discipline gave way to increasingly dubious forms of group persuasion. "With teen-agers," one high school principal said proudly, "there is nothing more powerful than the approval or disapproval of the group. . . . When the majority conforms, the others will go along." It would not easily occur to the modern educationists that such blind fostering of group pressure is a travesty of free democracy. Such criticism honestly puzzles them, as do suggestions that they might concentrate more on dry "learning" subjects, like mathematics and languages, to the exclusion of teen-age problems, beauty care, fly-casting. . . .

By their own trusted empirical test, the poor performance of their students has proved the educationists wrong. U.S. high school students are plain ignorant of things grammar school students would have known a generation ago. Years of barren discussion courses in English have made a whole generation chronically incoherent in the English language (the mutterings of a U.S. teen-ager trying to discuss his beliefs generally sound like a sanitized version of Elvis Presley). By substituting "projects" for study, the educationists have soothed students' curiosity, but left them with little intellectual patience for solving problems. Cut off from any but the most obvious contact with his tradition, *e.g.*, an occasional project visit to the local courthouse, the student has lost his sense of history, at a time when his country needs this most. Surely the history of the Crusades can give a young American a better grasp of the problems implicit in the UN or NATO than dressing up as a Pakistani delegate in an imitation UN assembly at school.

With Dewey's world so demonstrably in tatters, one might think the educationists would run up the white flag. Far from it. Entrenched in public school administrations, they defend with the adhesiveness of a band of brothers every article of their gobbledygook canons. In Holland, Michigan, the Christian High School, a respected institution of impeccable academic standards, has recently been denied accreditation by the North Central

Association of Colleges and Secondary Schools because it refused to dilute its academic standards with shop and cooking courses. A sample of the canons by which such schools are judged: "Is the control and atmosphere of the individual's rooms and classes based upon teacher authority or group self-control and group defined standards . . .? To what extent are opportunities provided for children to develop moral and spiritual values through the process of direct experience in working with each other . . .?"

We cannot expect to cure such lopsided standards just by giving teachers the pay they deserve, building the schools we need, and ordering up more science courses. A few important steps *can* be taken by state and local authorities. For one thing, most of our state teachers colleges should be abolished as such and converted into liberal arts colleges, with subordinate education departments. There must also be some drastic upgrading of curriculum requirements.

But most of all we need to do some thinking about the true ends of education. The worthwhile innovations in method brought by Dewey's educationists should be kept. But their exclusive devotion to techniques and group adjustment should never again be allowed to hide the fact that American education exists first of all to educate the individual in a body of learning, with a tradition and purpose behind it. A man so educated is far better equipped as a democratic citizen than the merely "well adjusted." For he will have not only the social ease to make his civilization comfortable, but the intellectual discipline to help save it.

A DEFENSE OF PROGRESSIVE EDUCATION [2]

It should be stated first of all that progressive education is part and parcel of the general advance in modern thought. It is simply the proper and legitimate development and application in the field of education of what the best university thought offers in psychology, biology, sociology, mental hygiene and the social sciences.

[2] From "Progressive Education: A Debate." William H. Kilpatrick, professor emeritus at Teachers College, Columbia University. New York *Times Magazine*. p 25+. September 8, 1957. Reprinted by permission.

In many areas of life the modern world has seen great developments come from the creative application of science and scientific method. Pasteur, for example, around 1870 gave us the germ theory, and in consequence the treatment of surgery and methods of medicine have been entirely remade, to the great advantage of mankind. Similarly, around 1890 William James, taking his start from biology, gave the world a scientifically oriented psychology to displace the previously prevalent but relatively inert "mental philosophy."

Students of James and others, along with students of Freud, have given us new conceptions of thinking, of the learning process, and of child nature and development. Out of these and out of closer current study of democracy and civilization has come the modern study called Education.

No claim is made here that all scholars in the field of education think alike—in such a rapidly growing subject they could not. Nor is it denied that new insights may upset some present beliefs—in a changing civilization this, too, is to be expected. But the discussion given here is believed to represent the most generally accepted thought on the subject among those who uphold the progressive outlook in education.

It is frequently charged that the progressive type of school fails to teach the three R's. Widespread tests show the contrary. Better modern insights into the teaching-learning process have led the school to reject both the kind and degree of formal drill and memorizing which formerly prevailed. For the same reason the elementary school has given up the formal teaching of separate subjects. The child learns at home to talk, not by formal drill lessons but by using language in life situations; similarly the school now centers on actual child life experiences and situations, and helps the children to learn by facing these situations.

This is so different from the old type of school that many are troubled at the change. However, many carefully made scientific evaluations show—practically without exception—that the progressive school teaches the three R's and the other school subjects better than did the old methods. Some pupils, to be sure, do not do well in school—and in college—but the average teacher is now far better prepared than formerly; and the average pupil does definitely better. Critics who charge otherwise are ignoring what the standardized tests actually show.

As to the charge that the modern school allows children to do as they please, this again is not true. The charge comes, it appears, from those who see no middle ground between letting children do as they please and controlling them by threats and punishment. Between these two hurtful extremes there is ample middle ground for successful dealing with children and here the progressive school takes its stand.

To see how and why progressive education treats its pupils differently from the old way, it may help to consider the two main guiding aims of the school: (1) to support and improve society that people may live helpfully, and not hurtfully, together; and (2) to develop each individual to the fullest extent of his capabilities. Under our democratic outlook, which calls for the betterment of all individuals, these two aims are but two sides of one process, each supporting and correcting the other.

Three fundamental principles underlie and guide modern education.

The first is that education must aim primarily at character-building, not simply at acquiring subject-matter. To say this is not to belittle subject-matter, which is clearly and incontestably essential to any proper education. However, to say that subject-matter is necessary is not to say that it is sufficient. Proper character-building includes more than mere subject-matter can supply; it calls also for a properly adjusted personality and for certain necessary interests and guiding attitudes. A properly built character will be guided by intellect; but that kind of guiding intellect cannot be built from subject-matter alone. It is this all-round character at which education must primarily aim.

Second, in democratic America our aim must be the development of all, each to the extent of his native ability and the extent that he can be induced to put forth the necessary effort. And this development must be for all-round living, not simply for the ivory tower as some have thought, nor simply for vocational success as too many others have thought. Our democracy demands the fullest feasible development of all, not merely of those good at book learning.

Third, according to modern psychology, *only actual behaving can build real character.* The older outlook seemed to hold that memorizing a rule would build obedience to that rule into one's character. We now know that this is a vain hope; only actual personal acceptance of the rule and behavior in accordance with it can build anything into character.

For example, one learns responsibility in any effective character sense only by behaving responsibly in appropriate life situations, and this behaving cannot be merely on the outside, it must be even more important on the inside. The older education, by its emphasis on memorizing and on examinations of a kind that cramming could meet gave little if any school opportunity for character-building behavior.

The progressive school undertakes to direct its work along the lines of these guiding aims and these three underlying principles of teaching. On the one hand, the teacher remains in final control on all points; but, on the other hand, he tries as best he can to guide his pupils to constructive cooperative and responsible "acting on thinking."

He helps them to make proper choices (of a kind that he can approve) as to successive activities to undertake; he helps them plan these activities, see the need for background knowledge, acquire methods of attack, and evaluate the work as it proceeds. Specifically, in all the teacher's dealings with his pupils, he is studying each one in order to guide him according to individual needs and abilities, with the intent of stressing responsible constructive thinking.

From early years pupils study community life; as they get older they engage in community projects and thus build interest in community affairs and responsible citizenship. As the pupils get still older, the teacher must encourage a serious attack upon current controversial issues, which of course involves careful study of appropriate literature. But always the teacher must avoid taking sides on the controversial issues under discussion. The democratic school must avoid indoctrination.

Some have claimed that the progressive school is subversive, seeking to set aside American democracy for socialism or worse; others have claimed that it is anti-intellectual. Both charges are totally false. The democracy set forth above is exactly the American democracy of Thomas Jefferson and Abraham Lincoln brought educationally up to date.

As to being anti-intellectual, one can hardly resist feeling irritated at the charge. We of the progressive outlook deeply respect the minds of human beings and show this by striving to foster its development in the many aspects which psychology now recognizes, not merely the single aspect formerly stressed.

For mind is not merely intellectual, and intellect is not merely memory or even grasp of what someone else has said. Intellect runs through all content of life, not merely information. It concerns itself also with attitudes, with values, with all that one cares about. Primarily, intellect takes all these things into account when it carries thinking into overt action. This is what is meant by "acting on thinking."

How well the progressive type of secondary school can succeed intellectually we see from an eight-year study of 1,475 students first in high school and then in college. The more definitely their high school education differed from the conventional, the more the students succeeded in college: "consistently higher academic averages and non-academic honors . . . clear-cut superiority in . . . the willingness and ability to think logically and objectively, and active and vital interest in the world about them . . . more often cooperative, tolerant and self-directing."

That over $600,000 was spent on this study suggests that it was done with considerable care. In such a record there is certainly no anti-intellectualism.

TEACHER SHORTAGE: CAUSE AND CURE [3]

There are three distinct, though related, aspects to the problem of staffing the public schools: getting enough teachers, improving their quality and training them properly for their jobs. . . .

There has been a chronic shortage of teachers since World War II. Many factors have combined to create this shortage,

[3] From article by Irving Adler, author and teacher. *Nation*. 186:407-9. May 10, 1958. Reprinted by permission.

but the basic factor is the rising birth rate. The number of live births in the United States has risen from 2.3 million in 1933 to 4.2 million in 1956. Predictions that the birth rate would level off at about this time have turned out to be wrong. It is still rising, and the trend toward early marriage and larger families promises to keep it rising. More births naturally mean more children going to school. The total enrollment in elementary and secondary schools has increased 39 per cent in the last ten years, while the number of teachers has increased only 32 per cent in the same period. The result has been overcrowding of classes.

One of the reasons for the lag in the number of teachers lies in the birth-rate figures themselves. The birth-rate graph is a great wave sweeping through the population and affecting different age levels with the passage of time. The supply of children now entering school comes from the crest of the wave. But the supply of young adults from whom teachers must be recruited comes from the 1933-1938 trough. At the same time that we have more children to teach, we have fewer young adults to draw from for our teacher supply. This bare statistical fact is something that we cannot do anything about. But it doesn't mean that the teacher shortage is inevitable. A declining adult population by itself does not necessarily mean a shortage of personnel. It might have been offset by a rise in labor productivity which freed people from industry and agriculture to enter the teaching profession. This counter-trend did not develop because of the influence of other factors arising from national policies. But policies can be changed, so there is an area in which we can do something about the teacher shortage.

The national policy that, more than any other, has aggravated the teacher shortage has been the Cold War and the accompanying armaments race. It has had a triple effect on teacher supply: the growth of the armed forces to unprecedented peacetime levels has been a direct drain on manpower; the growth of industries that manufacture military equipment has been a further drain; the accompanying inflation, by keeping teachers' real wages low, has made the teaching profession seem uninviting to many young people. The third point has had particular effect on the supply of teachers for secondary schools.

However, the trends have not been all in the wrong direction. The number of teachers did increase by 32 per cent in ten years. Also, the fraction of the college population that prepares for teaching has steadily increased, from 24 per cent of all college students in 1947 to 32 per cent in 1957. However, this increase does not automatically assure a comparable increase in the number of teachers, because only four out of five who prepare to teach in elementary school, and three out of five who prepare to in secondary school, actually become teachers. Here we see the effects of higher salaries offered by industry. Moreover, the number of students preparing for different types of teaching positions does not match the actual need. Although the need for elementary- versus secondary-school teachers is in the ratio 2 to 1, the number of students preparing for these levels is in the ratio 3 to 2, and is declining. A special weak spot is the number of students preparing to teach mathematics and science. At the very moment when there is an increasing need for them, this number has been shrinking. While 9,000 science teachers were graduated in 1950, the class of 1956 produced only 4,300. The number of graduates who prepared to teach mathematics dropped in the same period from 4,600 to 2,500, and of the latter only two thirds actually became teachers.

This picture is brightened somewhat by a new factor that has come into play in the last few years—a campaign to enlist as teachers mature college graduates who have been out of school for five years or more. This campaign has been directed especially towards married women who become available for work as their children grow up. Because of their maturity, their experience with children and their educational background, these women are potentially good teachers. . . .

If we want to raise teachers' salaries to a level that can compete with salary scales in industry, we need substantial Federal aid to education. But this plea has been falling on deaf ears. . . .

There are no short cuts to solving the school crisis. Not opportunistic emphasis on "military necessity," but disarmament and the reduction of international tensions are the roads to overcoming the teacher shortage. Only when we take this way will money and men now tied up in military preparations be made available for serving the schools.

When there is a shortage of teachers, the schools are always under pressure to relax standards and to accept as teachers people with lower qualifications. One of the paradoxes of the present situation is that this pressure has been successfully resisted. Although here and there unqualified people have been granted emergency teaching certificates, on the whole professional standards have been maintained and have even been raised. The teachers in the schools today are better educated than those who taught ten years ago. A decade ago, only 46 per cent of teachers were college graduates; today, the figure is 70 per cent. Ten years ago, only twenty states required elementary-school teachers to have a B.A. degree; today, thirty-seven states have this requirement. Of course, the other 30 per cent and the other eleven states show that the problem of professional standards is still not completely solved. For example, in Iowa 21 per cent and in Nebraska 33 per cent of all elementary-school teachers have had less than two years of college training. In Nebraska, the situation is getting worse; 53 per cent of teachers appointed last year have had less than two years of college. But while Nebraska is moving backwards in this respect, the country as a whole is moving steadily forward.

The rise in standards of preparation is a direct result of a change in salary policy that has taken place in the last two decades. In the past, elementary-school teachers used to be paid less than those in secondary school; low standards were simply the reverse of the low-salary coin. After the war, however, the movement for a single salary schedule swept the country. In 1941, only one-third of the country's urban school districts had a single salary schedule; by 1949, nearly all of them had it. Higher salaries made it possible to require higher standards of preparation. It is interesting, too, that the states that have the highest standards have had the least difficulty in attracting young people to the teaching profession.

PAY AND THE PROFESSOR [4]

The forward-looking school, the progressive school, at whatever level or however deeply committed to professional and vocational training, is necessarily concerned with what happens to liberal education. The liberal studies are the foundation of the liberal community. They provide the dimension that gives meaning to all other understanding and know-how. They are the explicit liberalizing force, creative in all free men everywhere.

With us, the liberal studies have found a home in the liberal college. But this is by no means a necessary, nor has it been a unique, home. In other times, in other places, even with us, the liberal studies have flourished outside institutional ivy walls.

Even so, the liberal college is a central instrument in expounding the standards and substance of liberal education, and for that reason if for no other, the liberal college is worth attention for its own sake. In this spirit, my remarks here are limited to the situation in the four-year liberal college, independent of university affiliation or responsibility. Nor will I attempt to include the special circumstances of state, municipal, or parochial institutions of a collegiate character. Let us look simply at the traditional liberal college, since to me the liberal college is the mind, the heart, and the conscience of liberal thought in our country—as it has been and as it will continue to be.

My title, "Pay and the Professor," may be judged by many as being a bit vulgar to be used in association with so profound a subject matter as liberal education. But I have looked up the word "vulgar" in a very large dictionary, and I am convinced that my title, even if vulgar, is not inappropriate. All professors have income of some kind, and the common, vulgar form of income is pay. It is just one of those facts of life, common though it be, that for years and years has not been getting the fullness of attention it deserves.

The facts about what has happened to pay and the professor over the past fifty years are now known with sufficient accuracy

[4] From article by Beardsley Ruml, business man and educator. *Atlantic Monthly.* 199:47-50. April 1957. Reprinted by permission.

for those who formulate policy. A year or so ago the Fund for the Advancement of Education asked Sidney Tickton and me to put together such figures as might be readily available on this subject, and the report which we made to them was published as a bulletin of the Fund under the title "Teaching Salaries Then and Now."

Fifty years ago, a salary of $3000 a year was good, but not uncommon. Allowing for changes in the cost of living and Federal income taxes, and assuming that the professor has a wife and two dependents, in 1953 he would have had to have $11,200 in order to have equivalent economic status with that of his professorial colleague at the turn of the century. The figures for 1956 would be about the same.

Fifty years ago a salary of $4000 for a professor was uncommon but by no means nonexistent. Today's equivalent would be $15,580.

A salary of $5000 in those days generally went with some administrative responsibilities. Today we still have administrative responsibilities, and the salary would be $20,345.

In 1904, probably the top professor's salary was paid at the University of Chicago, and there to only a few men. The rate was $7000, and today's equivalent is $31,250. In those happy, not too distant days, a first-class professor was considered economically as worthy as a first-class anybody else who was working for pay and not risking his own capital.

I do not attempt to appraise the injustice that is revealed by these figures, although it must be large and wide. However, about one impression there can be no dispute: the economic position of the top personnel in the liberal college has been drastically downgraded in the past fifty years. Recruitment of new personnel, both in the quantity needed and of the quality which we would desire, is completely out of the question at present pay scales.

In my opinion, for the liberal college professor an average of $15,000 is required under prevailing cost-of-living and tax circumstances, and top salaries of $30,000 should be widely distributed among the liberal colleges of the United States. But these tops should be on a merit basis, with merit defined as talent and effort applied in the arts and skills of liberal reading, writing, and instruction.

After the Fund's bulletin on teaching salaries came out, there was naturally a considerable amount of discussion as to why what had happened had happened. There is an element of bitter comedy in the hard-won statistical series of the Twentieth Century Fund, the National Planning Association, the Committee for Economic Development, and the Council of Economic Advisors. They show how wonderfully we have done economically, with production per man-hour soaring, the hours of work shrinking from decade to decade, the death rate falling, health rising; and their projections of past trends to the future date of 1976, the two-hundredth anniversary of the Republic, all point to an increase in productivity and a decrease in working hours. But there are no projections for pay and the professor in these economic series. Can it be that at or about 1976 both pay and the professor will have substantially disappeared, along with other antiquities not easily mechanized?

The question of why what had happened had happened seemed interesting and important. Once again the Fund for the Advancement of Education made it possible to collect a few facts, not to do a research by any means, but merely to take a look at the old and new catalogs of a dozen or so of our most characteristic liberal colleges. This helped me to gain and clarify a number of impressions. Unfortunately the data and statistics are not really comparable, and I have no doubt that a truly systematic research might reveal a number of errors of substance and of emphasis as well as bring out much that I have overlooked. For this reason I shall not name specific institutions, much as that would add to the interest of this discussion.

What can be said in general with reference to the dangerous economic situation of the liberal college as clearly revealed in the shocking levels of professorial pay? Has the failure been on the income side? Endowments and gifts have risen greatly, perhaps not as much as the statistical indicators, but they have risen, particularly regular annual contributions from alumni.

During fifty years, tuition rates have gone way up, far beyond the statistical requirements, averaging increases of more than

600 per cent and going as high as 1000 per cent and 1700 per cent. The number of units required for graduation is virtually unchanged.

Enrollment is up, an average of perhaps 200 per cent, and of course it will go much higher. This increase in enrollment is sometimes given as a reason for a college's economic hardships, but a decrease in enrollment would have been much worse. It is surprising that with large increases in enrollment, very large increases in tuition rates and substantial increases in endowment income and gifts, there should be any problem about pay and the professor.

When we look inside the college itself, the causes become apparent. Administrative expenses are up, but dollarwise they are not too important, particularly when it is understood that they are largely devoted to money raising and publicity efforts that generally produce a net gain, or for various types of student supervision which an earlier generation probably needed but did not get. In many colleges, a large part of this supervision, particularly for health and guidance, is paid for in student fees. Athletic deficits are frequently large, but are more or less unpredictable.

And so we come to the heart of the matter, the teaching program. The teaching program is incredibly inefficient, and has not made the progress that might have been expected over the past fifty years. The pay that the professor gets today is the direct consequence of what he earns, now as compared with then.

The number of courses offered has doubled and trebled, even though the units required for graduation remain the same. The number of courses offered per member of the faculty has dropped by a third, although in some institutions it is still close to where it was. The ratio of students to teachers is also down a third—it now stands at about ten to one, sometimes less.

Where does the responsibility lie and what can be done about it? The question is more easily asked than answered.

It would appear that if we are to have academic freedom and professorial tenure, the responsibility is with the faculty. But when we examine the realities of the situation, the faculty as we imagine it simply does not exist. True, there is a group of men paid the same day out of the same bank and walking in the same procession at commencement time. But from an operational point of view, we have only a series of departments interested in the size, offerings, and prerequisites of their particular department, meeting together for departmental protection.

Since the faculty does not exist, so neither does the curriculum exist. It is nothing more than a listing of departmental offerings from which a selection is made by the student to add up to the requirements for a degree. The occasional required course and the course requirements for concentration are a consensus of departmental interests. Departments offer their own introductory courses and frequently these are prevocational rather than liberal. This device is useful in forcing selection upon students, increasing departmental enrollments, and justifying the numbers on the department's teaching staff.

Well, if the liberal college has neither a faculty nor a curriculum, the responsibility must be placed on the administration. Theoretically, this might be true, but practically it is completely theoretical. The big job of the administration is public relations. Its job is to put out fires, not to start them. The faculty, departmentalized though it be, will form a defensive circle and moan to high heaven at any aggressive initiative by an administrative wolf. The administration wants the support of the alumni, and perhaps of a foundation or two. Such support is not easily come by, especially if there is a question as to the public morals of the student body or the vocal loyalty of the paid teaching staff.

So we come to the trustees. The trustees have powerful legal rights and, I suppose, the duties that go with them. Will the trustees act? Of course they will—they will back up the administration.

The financial problem of the liberal college is therefore essentially one of internal disorganization. Bluntly, the liberal college is organizationally and financially bankrupt. It has been forced to raise its prices unconscionably, it cannot pay a going scale of wages, it looks to committees of friends to make up its deficits, it talks at times as if it could not supply its growing market.

What the liberal college seems to need is the functional equivalent of a committee in receivership that would be responsible for preserving the body corporate and its liberal purpose. It would necessarily have the power of decision, the authority to tell departments, administrative officers, and trustees where the road to solvency lies. Or else it should dispose of the real estate.

It is my opinion that an efficient receivership committee can be found in the personnel of every liberal college's board of trustees, administration, and faculty. But, if not, a couple of alumni could be brought in.

Frankly, because of the great demand coming along for admission, the basic situation of the private liberal college today is very strong indeed. But it requires administrative discipline—a discipline that is sensitive to the fundamental issues of academic freedom and professorial tenure, but which at the same time can re-create a faculty with a common purpose, dedicated to reestablishing a curriculum whose central purpose is the advancement and diffusion of knowledge and understanding in the liberal arts.

Of course we will not call it a receivership committee. We will call it a Joint Committee on Educational Policy and Administration. And we will get a few thousand dollars from some foundation whether we need it or not, just to sanctify its work. This is strictly ethical since it does the foundation as much good as it does the liberal college, and it provides at once a responsible outside audience to which the reports of the committee, neatly typed and bound, can be addressed.

The joint committee in each particular college will find particular conditions of their own that require attention. But I venture a guess that three situations will be discussed by all.

First, the number of hours spent by a student in class or otherwise under faculty supervision is too large. The common practice is fifteen hours a week, more if laboratory work is taken, sometimes less in junior and senior years. I suspect that this tradition springs from the Carnegie Unit which was established to equate educational institutions for professorial pension rights.

Whatever the history, the burden on the student is too great and the cost of instruction is wasteful. If an hour in class should require two hours of preparation, which seems to me not unreasonable, then a twelve-hour classroom schedule instead of a fifteen would require thirty-six hours a week devoted to the curriculum. This is about all that should be expected of the average adolescent boy or girl, who needs to eat, sleep, and make friends as well as spend many serious hours listening, talking, and writing on the formal subjects offered by the liberal college.

This reform, justified on purely educational grounds, would save some 20 per cent in faculty, which would help in a somewhat lesser amount in pay for the professor.

The second inefficiency that our joint committee will find is in the use of physical plant. A canvass should be made of just how many hours a year each instructional room is used, and a percentage figure should be computed against some definition of "full utilization." It will be found that afternoon, evening, and Saturday use is very light, and that in many if not most of our liberal colleges summer use is for all practical purposes nonexistent. Full summer use may mean a change from a two-semester to a four-term basis of curriculum organization. Full Saturday use might mean the end of intercollegiate athletics, but it need not interfere with intramural sports.

Here the increase in capacity would be substantial and the increase in dormitory rentals from increased use in many cases would finance the modern lecture hall facilities which so many colleges lack. The yearly professorial schedules of nine months' teaching should not be increased, but within administrative possibilities option should be given as to whether the professor's time off campus would be taken in fall, winter, spring, or summer.

Finally our joint committee will take a detailed look at the proliferation of course offerings, the frivolous causes for many of them, and the shrinking ratio of students to the teaching staff. It will also observe whether tenure and title are being given instead of pay.

It seems to me reasonable that the ratio of students to teachers should be twenty to one. It also seems reasonable that the tuition paid by the students should go into pay for the professor. Such a rule would provide incentive for efficient instruction and would put trustees, officers, and alumni in the tenable position of offering to the faculty and students freely the instruments of instruction. At the present time in some liberal colleges, not one penny of endowment income or alumni gifts, except where specifically designated, goes into faculty salaries. Perhaps this is as it should be, but I do feel that the tuition paid by the students should go to their teachers in full.

This twenty-to-one rule, and 100 per cent application of tuition to teaching staff, means that the tuition rate could be multiplied by twenty to give the average teaching salary for any particular college. In general, this would turn out to be about right as an average and would make possible maxima that would be reasonable as compared with other professions.

The twenty-to-one rule, a ratio of one teacher to twenty students, is not taken seriously at the present time and when discussed is bitterly attacked. Most of the opposition comes as a result of misunderstanding, of a naïve acceptance that a ratio of ten to one makes a better college than a ratio of twenty to one. It is thought that the suggestion depends on an increase in the size of every class. But the increase in ratio could come from restoring the formal lecture to its traditional place as a method of teaching. And very little lecturing will be required. A college with a faculty of two hundred will need only eight lecturers to bring the discussion and seminar groups to a maximum of fifteen students or fewer. The really wasteful teaching is done in the classes that have between twenty and sixty members.

I have heard it said that a twenty-to-one ratio does violence to the romantic ideal that the best liberal education would be Mark Hopkins on one end of a log and a student on the other. But if Mark Hopkins had lectured three times a week, which he certainly would have been able and probably willing to do, and if in addition he would have been willing to sit on that log a couple of times a day, he would not only have been grossing his own salary, but he also would have been contributing to the pay of his as yet not so talented juniors.

There is nothing arithmetically or educationally incorrect in an over-all ratio of students to teachers of twenty to one in the liberal college. But it cannot be done under prevailing conditions of departmental organization.

There is one important good development, and that is the inevitable rise in demand for admission. If the joint committee will see to it that this demand is met by curriculum reorganization and without increase in faculty numbers, the problem of pay and the professor will have been largely solved.

Does this mean that the contributions of alumni, friends corporations, and foundations will no longer be of help and a public good? Not at all. But these contributions will strengthen living institutions with their own intrinsic vitality and will no longer go to the support of the remains of an eroding educational tradition.

The community, national, state, or local, public or private—the community in a free society—has two kinds of interest in the education of its young people in the liberal studies. The first interest is to make sure that a large, a very large, proportion of each oncoming generation knows what freedom for the individual really is, that freedom is valued, that it will be respected, that it will be defended. The second interest is to give an opportunity for some thousands, or even hundreds, in each generation to be creative with respect to human freedom. We have not yet, nor shall we ever, come to the end of the road in our insights and in our institutions widening the frontiers of human freedom. The talent that can take us further along the way must have the education and the opportunity to give to the community the leadership in freedom for which a free society is in being.

THE NEW AVALANCHE OF COLLEGE-AGE AMERICANS [5]

Take all the colleges that have been built in America since the Puritans founded Harvard in 1636.

[5] From article in Education Section, by H. R. Allen. *Newsweek*. 51:82-4. March 3, 1958. Reprinted from *Newsweek*, March 3, 1958.

Take the vast University of California system, with its nearly 42,000 students; Vermont's rustic little Marlboro College, with its 29; bustling Chicago City Junior College, with its more than 13,000.

Put them all together—1,900-odd colleges, junior colleges, and universities that have been built in the United States in 322 years. They add up to a $3 billion-a-year enterprise in higher education, a combined faculty of more than 225,000, a grand total enrollment of almost 3.5 million students this semester.

Yet over the next twelve years, if the tidal wave of World War II "babies" is to enjoy the same educational advantages as their parents, America will have to duplicate all these facilities—or, since that obviously is not possible, the educators must devise new selection and admission methods so that every qualified high-school graduate has a fair chance to earn a college degree.

The rush on the colleges is already on, of course. Classrooms and dormitories are jammed. "Most colleges and universities are now operating at or near what they consider their maximum capacity," Dean Ronald Thompson of Ohio State University said last month. "Most of our better colleges are turning away more and more students each year."

Another authority, Francis H. Horn, professor of higher education at Southern Illinois University, estimates we will need 200 new colleges within the next fifteen years, many of them junior colleges.

Recently a Greater Philadelphia citizens' committee envisioned an "absolute shortage" of places in the 42 public and private colleges in that area by next year. Georgia Tech has announced it will not be able to increase its 1,200-freshmen enrollment by a single person until it gets more buildings.

By 1970, there will be some 14.5 million college-age Americans. Based on past percentages, that means at least 7 million will be enrolled in higher education. The proportion of the 18-21 college-age group actually attending college has been steadily rising—from 4 per cent in 1900 to 15.3 per cent in 1940. Today it is nearly 35 per cent, and some experts feel that the percentage could easily exceed 50 per cent by 1970.

What are the colleges doing?

To overcome the critical shortage of instructors, a few colleges are experimenting with television, more independent study (with students working on their own and conferring periodically with a teacher), and even "teaching machines" which flash correct answers after a student has written his answer. They are tightening their curricula and casting a fishy eye at the kind of courses president Carroll V. Newsom of New York University has denounced as yawn-provoking "trivia" and a waste of money.

Paced by Harvard, with its $82.5 million drive for buildings and faculty salaries, the schools are tapping alumni foundations, anybody at all with money.

The state of Florida, which expects its college enrollment to triple by 1970, has started a $16.5 million program. California has authorized two new state colleges. Last fall New York State voted a $250 million bond issue for a building program for its state university.

But it seems certain that the demand for an education will exceed the supply of colleges and teachers. The question pressing harder day by day is: "Who should go to college?"

The question might better be put as two: Of those who would normally expect to go, who should be allowed to go? Of those who probably will *not* go, who should be helped to go?

In assessing the first group, most educators probably would go along with 42-year-old President Louis T. Benezet of Colorado College.

"Given a certain minimum of ability," says Benezet, "which is often lower than we care to admit, [those who should go to college are] those who really want to go to college with a clear understanding of what college really is. This does not mean because it is the social thing to do, or because the old man expects it, or to make more money."

Where to set the floor?

"You can't," says President Samuel Gould of Antioch. "I could show you students in the lowest 40 per cent [of their high-school classes] who do well in some colleges."

One way to meet the "floor" problem—by doing away with it—is proposed by President James H. Case Jr. of Bard College.

Case would "admit virtually everyone to college who applies," then, at the end of the freshman year, "weed out absolutely mercilessly all those who do not respond fully."

Case's plan would find little favor with a sizable portion of American educators and scientists—chemist Harold C. Urey, a 1934 Nobel Prize winner, for one. Urey, lambasting college students' preparation in English, mathematics, science, and literature, declared last November: "Most should never have gone to college."

In the final analysis there is little doubt that college entrance, based on high-school grades and test scores, will become more and more competitive.

For the cream of the crop, says William Fels, president of Bennington College, "there must be institutions that take the responsibility for giving students a knowledge of what has been called 'the best that's been thought and said.' . . . There are only a limited number of people who are able to converse on this level. These are the people who should go to college."

Not even Fels, however, would rule out the idea of taking in the youth who may be a little short on grades but long on personality and potentiality.

"We should take a lot more risks than we do," he says. "Instead of the 'well-rounded' man, we should go in and take some of the odd specimens. Many a well-rounded man has a short radius."

But it is not the horde of youngsters who will be storming their gates that worries college educators so much. They feel that, by testing and stiff grading, they can cope with these. More heavily on their consciences are submerged thousands of able teen-agers—their talents needed as never before—who probably will never get beyond high school.

"We know," says former Harvard president James B. Conant, "that one-third of our school population now goes to college. But this third does not necessarily include the top 15 to 20 per cent."

Money and brains: Among college-caliber students who don't go on to college, lack of money is the reason most often given. "The Lord in His wisdom," says President Irvin Stewart of the University of West Virginia, "did not see fit to distribute brains and money in equal proportions." The cost of a year at college has doubled since 1940—to about $1,500 at an average public institution and about $2,000 at a private one.

The Educational Testing Service estimates 150,000 more bright youngsters would be in college today if they could afford it. More scholarships could take care of some of these. But many educators suspect that in a fair number of ostensibly financial cases, there is a more serious reason: Many bright kids aren't interested in college.

Junior colleges may help. Studies show that many youngsters who had not planned to go to college will attend a home-town junior college, perhaps finish at a four-year institution.

Two sources of untapped brains that especially concern educators these days are minority groups—especially Negroes—and women.

The National Scholarship Service and Fund for Negro Students estimates that only about 12 per cent of Negro youth enter college. Yet, in a two-year project the NSSFNS uncovered 1,732 young Southern Negroes who could qualify for college; it helped 523 enter non-segregated colleges. One, the son of a retired schoolteacher, now is working on his Ph.D. at Harvard.

As for women, the American Council on Education estimates that only two women attend college for every three men (except, oddly, at Negro institutions, where the ratio is reversed). The Educational Testing Service reported this winter that nearly 20 per cent of high-ability boys in high school—but only 9 per cent of girls—who said they did not plan to go to college eventually changed their plans.

What is the long-range prospect?

The President's Committee on Education Beyond the High School has said:

> By dint of strenuous effort by all concerned, the resources available to higher education can be greatly enlarged. . . . There will at best be much unfinished business in 1970—but meantime anything short of maximum efforts could place the long future of our democratic society in serious jeopardy. . . . If an unwelcome choice were required between preserving quality and expanding enrollments, then quality should be preferred.

RISING COLLEGE COSTS [6]

A continuing rise [in the cost of higher education] within the next ten years, to twice or even two and one-half times the present outlay, is considered not at all unreasonable by many experts. . . .

The living expenses that are an important part of the total cost of college [have hit all time highs this year]. . . .

But tuition and fees are likely to rise even more steeply than living costs. This will be due primarily to the long-delayed and widely advocated increase in salaries for college faculties.

The average 1958 salary for college and university faculty members is $6,120, according to an Office of Education study. Several college heads have declared that at such levels, professors are subsidizing their students as well as teaching them.

As Samuel B. Gould, president of Antioch College, told students January 28:

> Every one of you owes or will owe this college over $2,000 for your education if you are here the normal amount of time [a study-plus-work course of five years]. The fact is that the $2,000 you are not paying is coming directly out of the pockets of the faculty of this institution. It is their personal gift to you which they make at the sacrifice of what we normally consider necessities of life.

But the upward trend in over-all expense will also reflect a national enrollment increase of nearly 100 per cent—from 3,036,938 for fall, 1957, to a projected 5,796,000 for fall, 1969. Money will be needed for new campuses and buildings, new personnel, and for replacement and maintenance of physical facilities.

The high cost of going to college began to be apparent in the late 1930's. In a nation determined to educate more of its youth through the college level, it has become more and more noticeable with inflation. In some instances, of course, inflation has raised family incomes so as to keep pace with—or exceed—the money needed for a higher education. . . .

[6] From "Costs of College Soaring; Likely to Double by 1970," by Milton Bracker, New York *Times* reporter. New York *Times*. p 1+. April 20, 1958. Reprinted by permission.

As more and more persons of college age have gone to college, the cost of supporting them has had to be borne by families in relatively lower brackets. Putting it another way, the wealthy have always been able to send their children to college and, presumably, will always be able to.

But the enlarged middle income group, which "always thought it could take care of itself," as one educational economist observed, "is now finding that it can't."

Defining the middle income group is no easier in terms of higher education than in terms of housing. In that field, the question was posed recently whether it meant $4,000 a year or $20,000.

But as most frequently mentioned in terms of educational costs, it would appear to mean families with an annual income of from $7,500 to $20,000. And with the upper figure tending to rise steadily, it would appear that an increasing number of parents face a challenge to the long-established philosophy or custom of paying cash for a college education.

Although parents rarely complain to colleges on the announcement of tuition increases—and occasionally such an announcement has brought in letters expressing understanding and even approval—fathers and mothers are quick to speak of the problem as it affects their personal finances. . . .

Whether eagerly, indifferently or reluctantly—more and more parents are changing their attitude toward buying higher education on time.

Probably more of them are reluctant than eager. . . .

Many installment plans and loan facilities are already in operation. They are proliferating rapidly and seeking to make their terms more attractive. There is a running debate among experts on college financing as to whether the college itself, or a commercial agency, should provide the credit.

Tuition Plan, Inc.

Dating to 1938, the Tuition Plan, Inc., of 1 Park Avenue, is a private financing enterprise that works with 150 colleges in forty states.

Under the plan, a parent signs a contract for one, two, three or four years. The plan pays the college direct, at the outset of the academic year. The parent sends monthly payments to the plan. The cost is 4 per cent above cash for one year, 5 per cent for two years, 6 per cent for three or four years. If there is a collection problem, the college is out of it; it is a matter between the plan and the parents. On the two, three and four-year deals, automatic life insurance covers the education funds even if the parent dies.

Harvard is an example of a college that prefers, in the words of John U. Monro, director of the financial aid office, "not to send the people to the bank." Providing credit for students, Mr. Monro held, "is an appropriate thing for the college to do."

On April 11 Harvard announced four new steps relating to bill payments, loans and scholarships. All are intended to help students and their families meet higher costs of education. These steps were in addition to a general increase in the amount of scholarship and loan aid for needy students from $1,330,000 this year to $1,830,000 for next year.

Harvard's Four Steps

The steps were:

1. Relaxation of traditional grade standards for the renewal of scholarships and aid grants.

2. Setting up of a monthly payment plan (as opposed to Harvard's standard five-payments-a-year system) for a flat fee of $10 for new students or $5 for those already enrolled.

3. Raising of the limit on the present no-interest (until after the completion of professional school) loans from $400 to $600 a year in ordinary circumstances and from $600 to $1,000 in unusual circumstances; and the total that may be borrowed during four years of college from $2,000 to $3,000.

4. Initiation of a bursar's office loan program enabling any student's family to borrow up to $600 a year, at 6 per cent interest, the loan to be repaid at $50 a month after graduation. This is separate from the student loan system and is designed especially for families who do not wish to apply, or are ineligible, for a scholarship or other grant.

Loans to Students

Student loan funds have not been under pressure in all institutions. In some colleges, a recent flurry of applications is believed to be a sign of the recession. But in others, loan funds are actually "going begging." This may be the case where many students live at home; where tuition is relatively low; and where the competition for admission is not the same as in the Ivy League group. . . .

To ease the strain on college loan funds, a strain that in general is expected to mount, a student loan rediscount corporation has been discussed. It would be incorporated on a nonprofit basis with philanthropic capital. It would leave to the individual college the actual collection of debts. . . .

Besides the many banking, insurance and credit union plans, and the efforts of colleges themselves to ease the financial burden, there have been measures proposed and taken on Government levels.

Testimony before the House Ways and Means Committee in January [1958] incorporated the recommendation, by the President's Committee on Education Beyond the High School, that tax laws be revised to permit deductions or credits for higher education.

On behalf of four groups, John F. Meck, vice president and treasurer of Dartmouth, backed a plan that had already been set forth in several bills before the Eighty-fifth Congress.

Noting that the idea of tax relief on tuition payments dated back many years—and had languished before previous Congresses, Mr. Meck supported a proposal that would allow 30 per cent of tuition and fees actually paid by the taxpayer to the institution as a credit on the amount of tax otherwise payable. This would mean the same benefit in dollars to all involved, regardless of income tax bracket. . . .

FREE MINDS AND OPEN UNIVERSITIES [7]

The profession of learning and knowledge—within the corporation of the university and its ancillary bodies of learned

[7] From article by Louis M. Hacker, educator and author. *Nation*. 186:309-12. April 12, 1958. Reprinted by permission.

societies and journals—seeks to extend knowledge, to conserve it and diffuse it, constantly bringing the processes of nature, social organization and human conduct under better control. Such are the roles and obligations of scholarship and scientific research.

It is equally necessary to train youth, and those adults who were by-passed by formal learning when they were young, for more useful lives, giving them—at the same time that they are being trained for greater productivity—the tools of analysis by which they can differentiate between right and wrong, the honest and the spurious, beauty and corruption. Citizenship requires virtue, usefulness and boldness; to free the mind of both prejudice and fear are the demands we impose upon educators, at the same time that they exercise their functions of scholars and scitists. To this extent educators are teachers of morals dedicated to the perpetuation of a moral universe.

Educators are prepared for their dual functions by universities; standards of competence and performance are safeguarded by these universities, the faculties within them, and the professional associations or learned societies to which educators belong. In consequence, universities, faculties and academic societies must be permitted to choose and police their own company. . . .

Youth is a period of challenge and experimentation. Youth is suspicious of indoctrination. Youth wants to start out by assuming that there are alternative roads to freedom. Young men and women seek to explore, debate, question every verity, every assumption, every custom and institution—not to reject them, necessarily, but to test their validity with a powerful new resource they have discovered, their minds.

It is the function of educators, as teachers or moralists, to let such minds range freely. For this reason, no body of doctrine or belief or, indeed, error can be kept shut to them like a kind of Bluebeard's chamber. They must be permitted to read and ponder over, see and hear and be exposed to the writings of Marx, Freud and Keynes, the pictures, sculpture and music of Picasso, Moore and Stravinsky, at the same time that they are reading, seeing and hearing the great conservators of our tradition and taste.

By the same token, the open university means that youth has the same rights we seek for ourselves as citizens to form its own clubs, maintain its own discussion groups and platforms, run its own newspapers—without let or interference on the part of university administrators or faculties. To protect them in their later lives from investigation—for more often than not these adventures are only youthful peccadillos—university administrators have no right to ask for membership lists or demand faculty surveillance.

Revolt is not taught in the classroom. The youthful Alexander Hamilton was not made a rebel by his teachers at King's College or the young Shelley by his tutors at University College. Youth becomes rebellious when injustice and inequalities are abroad in the land, leaders are corrupt and society has no confidence in itself.

It is, in consequence, the status of learning in our contemporary world that is alarming. Educators, as scholars and teachers, have been and continue under a cloud of suspicion. Because of an undue concern with security, particularly in the sciences, learning is being regarded as a sensitive area. What Professor Edward Shills so aptly calls "publicity"—free access to scientific knowledge, the rights of publication, open discussion in conferences, and travel by scholars and scientists to other lands and from other lands to ours—is being restricted. Dubious witnesses are being given credence; youthful associations are being exposed to demonstrate unreliability; legislators and self-appointed groups continue to voice their want of confidence in teachers.

Teachers have been asked to sign special loyalty oaths; to purge themselves before investigating committees by giving names of associates; and to surrender an important protection against self-incrimination—the safeguards afforded by the Fifth Amendment. They spend their time and substance defending themselves against calumniators, some of whom are engaged in their traffic professionally. Only too frequently, the administrators of universities have not defended their colleagues under attack; worse still, they have not had the courage to restore to academic life men who have been discharged from teaching posts simply because they refused to answer questions about their private lives by legislative committees. There is a virtual blacklist existing in the American university world that is as mean and cruel as any inquisition.

Why do I raise these uncomfortable questions? It is because I believe that neither universities, nor in fact our free society, can survive and knowledge advance unless we can guarantee to scholars and scientists both publicity and privacy. And unless we are to accept beyond question that universities, their faculties and professional associations, should protect themselves against incompetence and the second-rate, the very heart of the principle of free inquiry is surrendered.

We must assume, as a result, the defense of integrity from within through self-policing, and by that I mean by faculties and not by administrators or governing boards. Therefore, the teacher who abuses the privileges of the classroom to indoctrinate can be simply adjudged incompetent by his peers. . . .

All other questions raised affecting the private beliefs and associations of educators are irrelevant. They are citizens and as such have the rights of freedom of speech and association all of us properly claim under the First Amendment. And the rights to due process—at the hands of their peers—when their conduct is being called into question, must be equally assured. Due process in this context means a hearing before an academic body, the right to counsel and a full record of proceedings, the opportunity to confront and cross-examine witnesses and to appeal adverse findings.

Questions of political belief have no bearing on such an inquiry unless they are relevant to a man's responsibilities as a teacher and scholar. That is to say, unless there is substantial evidence of the perversion of the academic process, neither retention of a teacher nor his employment should be affected by beliefs or associations, whether they be political or religious.

In the light of such considerations, the position taken by too many university administrators is not only puzzling but a surrender of their own trust. Thus . . . [one] university president, . . .

after having defended the university's right to examine all sorts of heterodox opinion, goes on to say:

> But the freedom the universities claim is not a negative concept. It is not freedom from all restraints, from all commitment, but the positive freedom to perform the traditional functions of research and teaching in the spirit of truth. . . .
>
> University faculties have only one true valid defense against such attacks; namely, that they demonstrate, on demand, that their educational methods and their traditional findings have been arrived at by trained personnel through the use of thoroughly rational procedures.

Why "on demand"? Universities and their members, their methods and preoccupations, are constantly under scrutiny, in fact, twenty-four hours a day and 365 days a year. Accrediting associations visit classrooms, test curriculums, evaluate results; university admissions offices admit students to higher studies on the basis of examinations or a knowledge of the competence of college teaching staffs; learned societies and their journals are organs of debate where ideas are tested and new contributions to knowledge closely examined. Within the university itself, no matter how large, the achievements and weaknesses of every department and faculty are known to all the rest, and are equally known in other universities.

The profession of learning watches over its own integrity. We must reject the assumption that its integrity can be preserved only if, "on demand," legislators or self-appointed bodies can periodically call upon the universities to justify themselves.

The Association of American Universities is even willing to surrender the right to privacy altogether. For it has said:

> Legislative bodies from time to time may scrutinize [the universities'] benefits and privileges. It is clearly the duty of universities and their members to cooperate in official inquiries directed to these ends. When the powers of legislative inquiry are abused, the remedy does not lie in noncooperation or defiance; it is to be sought through the normal channels of informed public opinion.

Of course. An "informed public opinion" can be created if university administrators themselves, regarding this as their first obligation, will ceaselessly exercise themselves in the education of the public, their alumni and their own governing bodies, in the fact that learning has always accepted its responsibilities toward truth. They are likely to get a better hearing if they will demonstrate, by their own works, that an open university exists to satisfy all the legitimate needs of the community for its services and for continuing education. But we must not forget that "noncooperation and defiance," too, have their place; for such conduct, on the part of persons who refuse to be cowed, leads to an orderly examination of their claims to privacy by the judicial process and frequently adjudication in their favor. The invocation of the law's protections, in the recent Watkins, Jencks and Sweezy cases, proves that "noncooperation and defiance" can stop unlawful persecutions.

What of society's claims on learning? There is no quarrel with the position of public authority that it can require that curriculums be devised to meet professional standards and even, more broadly, to examine the means by which the stability of the world in which we live is to be maintained. But curriculums are one thing; the content of the courses themselves entirely another. . . .

Granting, in this troubled world of ours, that security is a proper public concern, it must be recognized that any security program is restrictive of the free communication which, as I have pointed out, scholarship and science must have to advance. We must recognize, particularly in regard to science, that we have pushed over-compartmentalization and over-classification, both internally and externally, much too far. . . .

The price of freedom, obviously, is responsibility and today, particularly, the obligations of the world of learning are heavy. Universities cannot command the respect they must have unless they eschew all those demands on them—whether to furnish entertainment for the outside world and their alumni, needlessly attenuate their curriculums, provide unneeded services for their students—which have nothing to do with the advancement and diffusion of knowledge and speculative research. They must live austerely, managing their resources with the economy and efficiency which we demand of government and business enterprise. There is an enormous amount of waste today in university management in part because university administrators are unfamiliar with financial procedures, in part because they too easily take on commitments under the pressures of would-be benefactors. University administrators should have the courage to say "no" to proffers of financial support for undesirable and unnecessary purposes just as they should seek help for legitimate ones. There must be more cooperation among universities in forming library collections, setting up specialized institutes, and starting and maintaining scholarly journals. They must pay their faculties well to prevent them from seeking unduly additional sources of employment and by better salaries to obtain for them that regard from the outside world which they rightfully should have.

At the same time, universities must keep an open mind and an open door to experimentation in new disciplines and skills. They must constantly expand the educated class, for in the final analysis the protection of learning will come here. If more and more men will become convinced—and they can be, because they are educable—that speculative effort, or free inquiry, leads to truth, then the university is safe and privacy is safeguarded. By the same token, the stability and progress of society demand more and more training at middle as well as at advanced levels. Universities have a responsibility toward selecting and educating men and women who ultimately will enter into the field of higher learning itself. With this objective there obviously can be no compromise, although in the selection process there is no certainty that youthful promise inevitably leads to adult maturity and creativity. I say, flatly, that the only purpose of the university is *not* the education of Ph.D.'s and therefore only future university professors.

Different kinds of training for what we are beginning to call a mass democracy, in consequence, are required; as well as all kinds of terminal degrees, and programs and courses that do not need degrees at all.

If universities are going to be restrictive, selective and *élitist* —as too many privately-supported institutions have announced they plan to be, constantly raising the requirements for admission and refusing to make adequate plans to expand with our suddenly growing population—they will perforce shut their doors to the great majority of young people and adults who are not only educable but whose trained services we so desperately need.

There is no magic in smallness. The great success of the University of California and the New York municipal colleges, as distinguished institutions of learning, proves that quality and size are not necessarily contradictory. . . .

Freedom of knowledge means freedom for scholars and scientists; but it also means free access to them for every legitimate community need and by every qualified student regardless of age, previous conditions of education, and whether or not he has a degree intention. Whether a student's purpose is formal training (on a full or part-time basis, during the day or during the night, in regular term or during the summer) or the advancement of his self-interest and tastes, or for occupational improvement, the university should receive him. In order to meet all the complex needs of our world and make possible the education of men and women with all sorts of adult responsibilities, universities should be available day and night and 365 days in the year, at the same time that they continue to explore—through every form of communication, including television and correspondence courses—the means for the extension of educational services.

Learning will be free and will flourish the more persons it exposes, by the educational process and in formal courses, to the rigorous methods of analysis, experimentation and speculation. Our world requires more educated persons at all sorts of levels; and knowledge, as well as our society, will remain free as we continue to encourage the development of an increasing number of educated men and women. This is where the true defense of learning really is to be found. This is the nature of an open university.

THE LAW OF THE LAND [8]

These cases come to us from the states of Kansas, South Carolina, Virginia, and Delaware. They are premised on different facts and different local conditions, but a common legal question justifies their consideration together in this consolidated opinion.

[8] From *Brown v. Board of Education of Topeka* [decision in desegregation case], May 17, 1954, by Chief Justice Earl Warren, speaking for a unanimous court. In *United States Supreme Court Reports.* Superintendent of Documents. Washington 25, D.C. 1954. v347. p483-96.

In each of the cases, minors of the Negro race, through their legal representatives, seek the aid of the courts in obtaining admission to the public schools of their community on a nonsegregated basis. In each instance, they had been denied admission to schools attended by white children under laws requiring or permitting segregation according to race. This segregation was alleged to deprive the plaintiffs of the equal protection of the laws under the Fourteenth Amendment. In each of the cases other than the Delaware case, a three-judge Federal district court denied relief to the plaintiffs on the so-called "separate but equal" doctrine announced by this Court in *Plessy v. Ferguson*. . . . Under that doctrine, equality of treatment is accorded when the races are provided substantially equal facilities, even though these facilities be separate. In the Delaware case, the Supreme Court of Delaware adhered to that doctrine, but ordered that the plaintiffs be admitted to the white schools because of their superiority to the Negro schools.

The plaintiffs contend that segregated public schools are not "equal" and cannot be made "equal," and that hence they are deprived of the equal protection of the laws. Because of the obvious importance of the question presented, the Court took jurisdiction. Argument was heard in the 1952 Term, and reargument was heard this Term on certain questions propounded by the Court.

Reargument was largely devoted to the circumstances surrounding the adoption of the Fourteenth Amendment in 1868. It covered exhaustively consideration of the Amendment in Congress, ratification by the states, then existing practices in racial segregation, and the views of proponents and opponents of the Amendment. This discussion and our own investigation convince us that, although these sources cast some light, it is not enough to resolve the problem with which we are faced. At best, they are inconclusive. The most avid proponents of the postwar Amendments undoubtedly intended them to remove all legal distinctions among "all persons born or naturalized in the United States." Their opponents, just as certainly, were antagonistic to both the letter and the spirit of the Amendments and wished them to have the most limited effect. What others in Congress and the state legislatures had in mind cannot be determined with any degree of certainty.

An additional reason for the inconclusive nature of the Amendment's history, with respect to segregated schools, is the status of public education at that time. In the South, the movement toward free common schools, supported by general taxation, had not yet taken hold. Education of white children was largely in the hands of private groups. Education of Negroes was almost nonexistent, and practically all of the race were illiterate. In fact, any education of Negroes was forbidden by law in some states. Today, in contrast, many Negroes have achieved outstanding success in the arts and sciences as well as in the business and professional world. It is true that public-school education at the time of the Amendment had advanced further in the North, but the effect of the Amendment on northern states was generally ignored in the congressional debates. Even in the North, the conditions of public education did not approximate those existing today. The curriculum was usually rudimentary; ungraded schools were common in rural areas; the school term was but three months a year in many states; and compulsory school attendance was virtually unknown. As a consequence, it is not surprising that there should be so little in the history of the Fourteenth Amendment relating to its intended effect on public education.

In the first cases in this Court construing the Fourteenth Amendment, decided shortly after its adoption, the Court interpreted it as proscribing all state-imposed discriminations against the Negro race:

> It ordains that no State shall deprive any person of life, liberty, or property, without due process of law, or deny to any person within its jurisdiction the equal protection of the laws. What is this but declaring that the law in the States shall be the same for the black as for the white; that all persons, whether colored or white, shall stand equal before the laws of the States, and, in regard to the colored race, for whose protection the amendment was primarily designed, that no discrimination shall be made against them by law because of their color? The words of the amendment, it is true, are prohibitory, but they contain a necessary implication of a positive immunity, or right, most valuable to the colored race

—the right to exemption from unfriendly legislation against them distinctively as colored—exemption from legal discriminations, implying inferiority in civil society, lessening the security of their enjoyment of the rights which others enjoy, and discriminations which are steps towards reducing them to the condition of a subject race. [Slaughter-House Cases (1873) and *Strauder v. West Virginia* (1880)]

The doctrine of "separate but equal" did not make its appearance in this Court until 1896 in the case of *Plessy v. Ferguson,* . . . involving not education but transportation. American courts have since labored with the doctrine for over half a century. In this Court there have been six cases involving the "separate but equal" doctrine in the field of public education. In *Cumming v. County Board of Education* . . ., and *Gong Lum v. Rice* . . ., the validity of the doctrine itself was not challenged. In more recent cases, all on the graduate-school level, inequality was found in that specific benefits enjoyed by white students were denied to Negro students of the same educational qualifications. *Missouri ex rel. Gaines v. Canada* . . .; *Sipuel v. Oklahoma* . . .; *Sweatt v. Painter* . . .; *McLaurin v. Oklahoma State Regents.* . . . In none of these cases was it necessary to reexamine the doctrine to grant relief to the Negro plaintiff. And in *Sweatt v. Painter* . . . the Court expressly reserved decision on the question whether *Plessy v. Ferguson* should be held inapplicable to public education.

In the instant cases, that question is directly presented. Here, unlike *Sweatt v. Painter,* there are findings below that the Negro and white schools involved have been equalized, or are being equalized, with respect to buildings, curricula, qualifications and salaries of teachers, and other "tangible" factors. Our decision, therefore, cannot turn on merely a comparison of these tangible factors in the Negro and white schools involved in each of the cases. We must look instead to the effect of segregation itself on public education.

In approaching this problem, we cannot turn the clock back to 1868 when the Amendment was adopted, or even to 1896 when *Plessy v. Ferguson* was written. We must consider public education in the light of its full development and its present place in American life throughout the nation. Only in this way can it be determined if segregation in public schools deprives these plaintiffs of the equal protection of the laws.

Today, education is perhaps the most important function of state and local governments. Compulsory school attendance laws and the great expenditures for education both demonstrate our recognition of the importance of education to our democratic society. It is required in the performance of our most basic public responsibilities, even service in the armed forces. It is the very foundation of good citizenship. Today it is a principal instrument in awakening the child to cultural values, in preparing him for later professional training, and in helping him to adjust normally to his environment. In these days, it is doubtful that any child may reasonably be expected to succeed in life if he is denied the opportunity of an education. Such an opportunity, where the state has undertaken to provide it, is a right which must be made available to all on equal terms.

We come then to the question presented: Does segregation of children in public schools solely on the basis of race, even though the physical facilities and other "tangible" factors may be equal, deprive the children of the minority group of equal educational opportunities? We believe that it does.

In *Sweatt v. Painter, supra,* in finding that a segregated law school for Negroes could not provide them equal educational opportunities, this Court relied in large part on "those qualities which are incapable of objective measurement but which make for greatness in a law school." In *McLaurin v. Oklahoma State Regents, supra,* the Court, in requiring that a Negro admitted to a white graduate school be treated like all other students, again resorted to intangible considerations: ". . . his ability to study, to engage in discussions and exchange views with other students, and, in general, to learn his profession." Such considerations apply with added force to children in grade and high schools. To separate them from others of similar age and qualifications solely because of their race generates a feeling of inferiority as to their status in the community that may affect their hearts and minds in a way unlikely ever to be undone. The effect of this separation on their educational opportunities was well stated by a finding in the Kansas case by a court which nevertheless felt compelled to rule against the Negro plaintiffs:

> Segregation of white and coloerd children in public schools has a detrimental effect upon the colored children. The impact is greater when it has the sanction of the law; for the policy of separating the races is usually interpreted as denoting the inferiority of the Negro group. A sense of inferiority affects the motivation of a child to learn. Segregation with the sanction of law, therefore, has a tendency to retard the educational and mental development of Negro children and to deprive them of some of the benefits they would receive in a racially integrated school system.

Whatever may have been the extent of psychological knowledge at the time of *Plessy v. Ferguson,* this finding is amply supported by modern authority. Any language in *Plessy v. Ferguson* contrary to this finding is rejected.

We conclude that in the field of public education the doctrine of "separate but equal" has no place. Separate educational facilities are inherently unequal. Therefore, we hold that the plaintiffs and others similarly situated for whom the actions have been brought are, by reason of the segregation complained of, deprived of the equal protection of the laws guaranteed by the Fourteenth Amendment. This disposition makes unnecessary any discussion whether such segregation also violates the Due Process Clause of the Fourteenth Amendment.

THE PLIGHT OF SCIENCE EDUCATION [9]

The expansion and fragmentation of knowledge have . . . reached the point of diminishing returns in science. . . .

No one can deny that science has lost much of its alleged "purity" and has become increasingly vocational. Thirty years ago scarcely one scientist in ten entered industry. Science was a cultural, ivory-tower subject and profession, plied in the classroom, the university laboratory, or the museum. The curriculum

[9] From article by Howard A. Meyerhoff, executive director of the Scientific Manpower Commission. *Bulletin of the Atomic Scientists.* 12:333-7. November 1956. Reprinted by permission.

in each field was designed accordingly, and it had a strong natural philosophic and scholastic flavor. The scientist vigorously differentiated himself from the engineer, whose vocational training prepared him for industrial employment rather than scholarship.

In the year 1956—one generation later—nearly 50 per cent of the practicing scientists, whether bachelors, masters, or doctors, are employed in industry. In many schools the curriculum has been shaded or modified, the better to prepare the science major or the graduate student for an industrial career. The graduate thesis, as often as not, is some facet of a government project or industrial contract upon which the thesis director is working and for which he is being paid. Inevitably, the Greek and Shakespearean scholars and the historians and sociologists on the faculty look with mingled feelings of dismay, contempt, and jealousy upon the vocational cast of scientific training; the larger enrollments in science fostered by the lure of scholarships, fellowships, and highly remunerative employment following graduation; the auxiliary income of the science staff; the superior equipment of science departments; and the abandonment of pure, or scholarly, research in favor of applied research.

In view of these trends, there is an only too human tendency on the part of German and English and art professors on faculties to unite against the scientists, and to reduce the science requirements or to limit the kinds of courses that will meet the broad cultural objectives for graduation. Several factors aid and abet them in this procedure. The poor preparation of entering students has compelled colleges to relax entrance requirements and to broaden the freshman-sophomore curriculum to cope with a lower common denominator of precollege training. Mathematics and science have followed Greek and Latin, first as electives, and then as discards, among the courses our educationists deem essential in the so-called life-adjustment programs in many secondary school systems. To solve the problem of nonpreparation of entering freshmen, and in the hope of reculturizing required science, colleges have tended to imitate the example of the secondary schools, where "general science" has displaced physics, chemistry, and earth science. Today the college freshman ordinarily finds himself with a choice—or a requirement—of introductory physical science or introductory biology, in which he is exposed to scientific principles but is rarely trained in the rigorous methodology and precision that comprise the essence of science.

Enter General Science

Science faculties initially resisted the introduction of general courses, which brought them few majors and little pedagogical satisfaction. The resistance has waned—in the liberal arts colleges because the general science course is a simple device to get the poorly prepared student out of the way, and in the larger schools because the staff is far more interested in the training of graduates than in struggling with undergraduates. A great deal has been made of the recent discovery that the small liberal arts colleges produce a much larger proportion of the nation's scientists than the undergraduate schools of large universities, but little attenion has been paid to the significance of this fact: Institutions with large graduate schools commonly attach no importance to undergraduate training and provide, at best, mediocre and uninspired instruction at the college level.

During the chaotic war years, the question of college science seemed academic, and after the war, with classes bulging, the science departments were not interested in measures that would add to their enrollments. Since 1950, however, the tide has turned, and only the impending population increase promises to stem ebbing college interest in science and mathematics. The beach at ebb tide is not entirely a thing of beauty, but it brings the viewer face to face with some of life's (and death's) homely realities. By analogy this is the time to take stock of some of the realities in the situation confronting science and scientists. . . .

Lack of Well-Rounded Science Teachers

A demand from nonacademic sources for scientists in nonacademic fields of activity has had at least one disastrous consequence, with others imminent. College and university staffs have grossly neglected the training of well-rounded, cultured scholars whose sole or primary interest lies in teaching and/or in pure (i.e., nonapplied) research. The result of this neglect is now rearing its ugly head in the secondary schools. Since 1950 the number of college students training for careers in teaching science and mathematics has dropped 50 per cent, and half this dwindling supply is lured into industry. Forty per cent or more of the secondary school vacancies that must be filled in so basic a subject as mathematics are being filled by teachers who lack the qualifications to teach it. This is the situation despite the fact that modern educational theory has reduced the need for mathematics instructors by turning from solid instruction in a few fundamental subjects to mass education by way of a bewildering assortment of electives, many of extremely dubious value for any purpose. Under this theory, only one quarter of our high school students are taking two years of algebra, and fewer than 10 per cent manage to acquire the mathematical background that qualifies them for college work in science and engineering. Low salaries and unsatisfactory working conditions in the public schools further complicate the problem created by scientists' neglect of their source of student supply and by the "life-adjustment" theory of mass education. In prospect, therefore, it is by no means certain that science and engineering will get their proportionate share of the large post-depression crop of students. . . .

There is something strangely familiar about the problem confronting science. Just as the American people found themselves unprepared to assume the role of leadership thrust upon them during and after World War II, so with the scientists. Hailed and damned for the release of atomic energy, they are doing too little too late to publicize the vital role it can play in promoting social welfare and progress. With the national security and economy virtually in their hands, they have made belated protests against the waste of scarce scientific and engineering brainpower and have left the power of decision entirely in the hands of uninformed legislators and government administrators who seek guidance on this moot subject as avidly as they seek votes. With the key to modern civilization and to future progress in their formulas and instruments, scientists have stood idly by while educators have trimmed science and technology to a bare minimum in school curricula that are supposed to "adjust" young people to life in an age of science and technology. And now, when their birthright in the field of education is threatened, they remain passive, although the creative imagination of scientists who gave us the principles of evolution and genetics, the law of gravitation, and the periodic table must be ranked with the inspired contributions of Shakespeare, Goethe, Beethoven, Kant, and Herodotus to our culture.

Although the remedy for these deficiencies and outright failures lies in education, education cannot begin without communication. At present communication seems to end, instead of begin, in the classroom. In most of our state and large private universities, the instruction of teachers is scorned. The task is left to the ill-equipped and underfinanced teachers colleges. Yet scientists are loudest in their condemnation of the school systems that deliver to them poorly prepared freshmen. They too often consign these beginning college students to the tender but unseasoned care of a young instructor not far enough away from the technical minutiae of his dissertation, or to an overworked graduate student in training for his orals. Most beginning students acquire a quick and lasting immunity to the mental DDT contained in this kind of instruction, and to the subject matter of the course; whereas the few who are affected become the same kind of scientists as their instructors. Yet here is the place to present an inspiring canvas of earth history, or evolution, or nuclear energy; to stimulate the thirst for more, equally inspiring knowledge in the same or related fields; to encourage the dissemination of the knowledge gained, in other classrooms, in the press, or in the lecture hall. Specialization, when it comes, should be relegated to its proper place in the field and should be kept in perspective. And it should never be permitted to destroy or impair the art of communication. . . .

The Root Evil—Specialization

Specialized science moves farther away from the public and from that stream of public consciousness on which it ultimately depends for its existence. Only through a handful of interpreters does it maintain communication with the rest of the world. Its lack of concern about communication is already evident in the diminishing supply of teachers, and this will be followed by a shrinking pool of students, in a descending spiral leading toward technical competence but to cultural extinction.

It is easy to rant about the defects of a system but difficult to prescribe correctives. In a recent book dealing with the secondary school problem, Arthur Bestor describes the corrective as "the restoration of learning." No better label could be devised for the needs of the moment and of the future, but the situation in the sciences is more involved than Bestor recognizes. The Congress and the Administration are aroused to the dire need for more scientists and engineers if we are to maintain our national security and economy at their present relative level. Industry, in general, is so absorbed in meeting its contractual obligations that it still lacks a conscious concern—or a conscience—about the future source of trained personnel. (Witness the case of the aircraft company that, last summer, hired six of the eight physicists from the faculty of a small engineering school, thus wrecking the physics curriculum for the entire student body.) With a few noteworthy exceptions, our science faculties have yielded to the pressures of industrial demand for their product and to student demand for good jobs and high salaries, and have vocationalized their instruction.

Here is an aggregate of forces that need not necessarily be countered. On the contrary, it appears feasible to organize and direct them into the one essential goal that is being neglected—that of self-preservation. Nature's chief concern is reproduction, and it must be made a primary objective among scientists. Reproduction takes place at every level of instruction, and only through instruction. It demands, first, good teaching, which can come only from broadly trained scholars in our universities and colleges. This good teaching must be employed, among other objectives, to inspire more students to enter the teaching profession, particularly at the secondary school level. It should also be directed toward effective communication that will reach the public and impart a knowledge of science, its aims, its methods, its achievements, to every segment of a nation that has risen to greatness through science and the applications of science. Self-preservation does, indeed, require the restoration of learning, the resurrection of scholarship, the re-entry of science into education.

SEPARATION OF CHURCH AND STATE [10]

We are not concerned in the testimony we shall offer to favor or oppose any particular program of Federal aid to education. We are concerned only, as our name suggests, that in any program of such aid which may be approved, the principle of the separation of church and state shall be meticulously respected. This principle is set forth in the First Amendment to the Federal Constitution. We accept that enunciation of the principle given by Mr. Justice Black in the prevailing opinion in *Everson v. Board of Education* . . . (1947):

> The "establishment of religion" clause of the First Amendment means at least this: Neither a state nor the Federal Government can set up a church. Neither can pass laws which aid one religion, aid all religions, or prefer one religion over another. Neither can force nor influence a person to go to or to remain away from church against his will or force him to profess a belief or disbelief in any religion. . . . No tax in any amount, large or small, can be levied to support any religious activities or institutions, whatever they may be called, or whatever form they may adopt to teach or practice religion. . . . In the words of Jefferson, the clause against establishment of religion by law was intended to erect "a wall of separation between church and state."

Not only is church-state separation contained in the Federal Constitution, . . . it also appears in the constitutions or statutes of at least forty-six of our states. Here it has been carefully spelled out that no aid from tax sources is to go to the support of sectarian worship or sectarian educational enterprises. We believe that the First Amendment and these state constitutions should be diligently respected in any program of Federal aid to education. Our testimony will bear directly upon this concern. . . .

[10] From statement filed by Protestants and Other Americans United for Separation of Church and State. In *Science and Education for National Defense*; hearings before the Senate Committee on Labor and Public Welfare. 85th Congress, 2d session. Superintendent of Documents. Washington 25, D.C. 1958. p 1350-3.

H.R. 10763, the Murray-Metcalf bill, appears to be unexceptional. It does not attempt to bypass state laws as others do. It would seem to be the bill which most nearly embodies the American tradition of public money for public education. It is significant, we think, that this bill is being actively supported by the men and women who know at first hand the problems of our schools—the educators themselves. We refer to the Council of Chief State School Officers and the National Education Association.

In regard to the other bills we have certain apprehensions. Let us consider, first, the scholarship grants which are provided in both the administration bill and in the Hill-Elliott bill. We understand that these scholarships provided at public expense would be usable in sectarian colleges as well as in public and private, nonsectarian colleges. We do not oppose scholarships usable in sectarian colleges as such at the present time—provided that there is a fair and genuine system of examinations to determine recipients.

Our apprehension about these grants is prompted by the fact that they will assuredly be cited as precedent for similar scholarships in lower schools operated by sectarian groups. We believe that the scholarship grants should be safeguarded against such misuse by specific language inserted in any Federal aid bill.

Strong demands for scholarship aid at the elementary and secondary level have already been voiced. John Francis Cardinal McIntyre, of Los Angeles, speaking at Dallas, Texas, December 9, 1956, urged a program of public grants to all pupils in sectarian schools with the aid "to all children directly as it did to our returned heroes" under the GI bills. In the October 25, 1957, issue of *U.S. News & World Report,* Father Virgil C. Blum, of Marquette University, set forth a program calling for scholarship certificates issued by the Federal Government that would be cashable for education in sectarian elementary and high schools [See "A Catholic Viewpoint" in this section, below.] The plan of these two ranking churchmen has been widely publicized and inserted in the *Congressional Record.* Their plan repeatedly cites as precedent the scholarship grants in the GI bills. We cannot doubt that the scholarship grants contemplated in the legislation before us here would provide additional precedent and stimulus for sectarian demands at the elementary and secondary level.

We should like to delineate and underline our stand on this issue since it represents the focal point of our concern. During the ten years of its existence POAU has diligently sought to educate the American public as to the dangers of any program which would divert tax dollars to sectarian schools. The charge has been made that we are discriminating against such schools when we urge that they be denied tax funds. The fact is, however, that such discrimination is simply the historic public policy which, under our laws, denies tax funds for the support of church enterprise, and carefully relegates all churches to the status of free and voluntary societies. It is a far more serious discrimination against taxpayers to use their funds to support sectarian enterprises in which they do not believe. There is no difference either in principle or in practice between tax support of a school integrally related to a church and tax support of the church itself. The school exists to teach and propagate the doctrines of the church which operates it. The school exists by and for the church. The school is the church; the church is the school.

We have consistently opposed tax support of sectarian schools at the lower levels because of the inevitable proliferation of our educational system that is bound to result should Congress or the states commence such support. Dr. Rolfe Lanier Hunt, executive director of the department of religion and public education of the National Council of Churches, in an address in Omaha, Nebraska, February 11, 1958, has, we believe, accurately forecast the kind of chaos that will obtain in education should we resort to tax support of sectarian schools. A former superintendent of schools in Mississippi, Dr. Hunt points out that in a nation of 250 religious denominations, a small town with 2,000 population might be called upon to support a dozen sectarian school systems, while in a large city like New York or Los Angeles there could conceivably be a couple of hundred. "Ardent teachers would teach that only in their schools was the truth," Dr. Hunt said. "Would we wish our tax money to support these schools?" In his address Dr. Hunt also warned the nation that sectarian segregation of school children could do more damage to American unity than has been done by racial segregation in public schools.

We concur in these statements . . . and we believe that the Congress concurs in them. We do not believe that it is the intent of the Congress to give the remotest encouragement to any course which might result in the weakening . . . of our system of public education. We respectfully suggest, therefore, that a section of any Federal aid bill providing for a scholarship program should be written to include an explicit denial that such legislation is intended in any sense as a precedent to scholarship aid for private or sectarian schools of less than collegiate rank, and also reasserting our constitutional provisions on this issue.

We are apprehensive, also, about those sections of the Hill-Elliott bill and the administration bill which would make possible other forms of aid to sectarian institutions at the college level. For example, in section 552 of the Hill-Elliott bill we find that Federal funds for certain teaching, equipment, and materials would be made available to sectarian, higher institutions of learning. Again, under section 1031 of this bill we find a provision of Federal funds for certain materials and equipment for sectarian institutions. The administration bill, while less objectionable at this point, also contains provision for such aid to sectarian institutions at the graduate level. Our feeling is that direct grants of the kind envisaged here would constitute far too dangerous a precedent for the complete public support of all sectarian schools.

According to our information, no previous bill—and this includes the GI bills—has ever appropriated Federal funds for equipment for sectarian institutions in the direct manner contemplated in these bills. Both the Hill-Elliott and the administration bill go farther in the direction of sectarian grants than any previous legislation. In the past, all appropriations of this nature for equipment have been under specialized headings such as research in diseases, atomic energy, and military work. They represented a specific grant for which there was to be a specific return. There is no such pledge or safeguard in these bills. For these reasons, we suggest elimination from Federal aid of expenditures for equipment, teachers' salaries, materials, or buildings in sectarian institutions of higher learning.

The administration bill has one provision which we find particularly ominous so far as the maintenance of church-state separation is concerned. The bill provides in section 103 (1) that funds shall be provided for a testing of students in private elementary or secondary schools. There is, of course, always the danger that any such grant of public funds to sectarian schools will be made to serve as precedent for more substantive grants. But our especial concern here is the stipulation in section 103 (b) that where the state is not permitted by its law to provide its half of the expense for the program in private or sectarian schools, the Federal Government shall, in effect, override the law of the state by setting up and carrying out its own program in such states. We feel that this provision of the bill is inconsistent with others which seem to indicate a determination not to override state and community control of education. We believe, as most of these Federal aid bills declare, that state and community control of education is desirable and should be preserved. We believe that such a conspicuous violation of this principle should not be included in any Federal aid legislation. We respectfully suggest its elimination from this program. To state our conviction positively, we believe that all Federal legislation in aid to education should observe state laws and constitutions in the matter of church-state separation.

We should like to consider, next, the matter of definitions in the bills before this committee. We believe that the American tradition of public funds for public education makes it highly desirable that the word "public" as referring to tax-supported, community-controlled schools shall be used consistently throughout the legislation. We consider the administration bill faulty at this point since it defines "elementary school" and "secondary school" so loosely that the terms would include private and sectarian schools. In this respect the Hill-Elliott bill is superior since it defines the terms as applying specifically to public institutions. Wherever there are to be exceptions in the practice of tax support for public schools only, then these exceptions should be carefully spelled out. There should be at all times meticulously clear semantics on this point so that no aid to sectarian institutions contrary to the original intent of the Congress can be provided.

The wise churchmen who founded POAU more than a decade ago believed that the arrangement of separation as between church and state was a happy one and should be continued. This is the key to understanding and cooperation among the churches in our common culture. These churchmen have on many occasions made clear what we state today—that the holding of the present money barrier against subsidies to any church, is basic to the preservation of the entire principle of separation. We urge the careful consideration of that principle in connection with this and all Federal legislation.

A CATHOLIC VIEWPOINT [11]

Educational problems are clamoring for solution throughout America. Public educators are demanding more classrooms, more teachers, and more money. Parochial-school educators are building more classrooms, seeking more religious teachers, and hiring more lay teachers in the expectation that parents of parochial children will continue to be both willing and able to support two school systems.

Many parents of children attending church-related schools are finding this double burden excessively heavy. Besides the double tax, they do not like the crowded facilities that are all too common in our parochial schools. Furthermore, our educators and parents alike are disturbed by the all-too-persistent statements, even by Catholics, that we shall soon be forced, for want of sufficient money, to drop either our high schools or the first four years of our elementary schools. This suggestion is a purely negative approach to a difficult problem, and in such an approach there is no hope of finding a solution. . . .

The right of parents to control and direct the education of their children is, as our American bishops so well pointed out in their statement of November 17, 1955, based in nature and

[11] From " 'Freedom of Choice' in Schools," by Virgil C. Blum, S.J., assistant professor of political science, Marquette University. *Homiletic and Pastoral Review.* 58:27-33. October 1957. Reprinted by permission.

guaranteed by the Federal Constitution. This is a right that American parents will never willingly surrender. Upon the continued exercise of this right depend freedom of thought and freedom of religion. For, if government can dominate and control the processes of education, it can control thought and belief. Witness the totalitarian governments of yesterday and of today. . . .

Do children attending parochial schools have any claim to public educational benefits? May government impose a condition for sharing in educational benefits which demands the surrender of the most fundamental of all constitutional rights—religious freedom? The answer to these questions is fundamental to the solution here proposed.

Children attending church-related schools are American children. They have liberties and rights under the Federal Constitution. One of these rights is freedom of choice in education. Children who exercise this choice may not be deprived of other constitutional rights *because* they have exercised this right. Among such constitutional rights is the right to share equally with other children in welfare benefits. Education itself is one of these welfare benefits.

The Supreme Court of the United States has repeatedly declared that government cannot demand the surrender of a constitutional right as a condition for sharing in welfare benefits. The Court enunciated this principle, for example, in the Frost case of 1926, in the Terral case of 1922, and Justice Frankfurter expounded this doctrine in his concurring opinion in the Douds case of 1950.

Hence, government cannot demand that a child *not* attend a church-related school as a condition for sharing in the state's educational benefits. When government does this, it imposes an unconstitutional condition on the exercise of a constitutional right. That is to say, when a child exercises his constitutional right to attend a parochial school, government may not deny him a share in educational funds. To do so is to penalize him for his exercise of religion.

In the distribution of its benefits, government must be objectively indifferent to the religious beliefs of its citizens. When government conditions its educational benefits on the surrender of freedom of choice in education, it violates freedom of religion. Such a condition constitutes economic coercion to conformity in conflict with religious belief.

A government may no more force all children through economic coercion to conform to the philosophical and theological orientation of the public schools than it may force all citizens to conform to the religious doctrines of a state-established and state-controlled church. Without freedom of education, every other liberty is in danger of being lost.

How can this freedom of education be achieved? This is imperatively necessary: Government must make educational benefits available to all children without demanding the surrender of religious freedom. How can this be done? This presents a difficult problem, but for a liberty-loving and fair-minded people the problem is not beyond solution. The problem, however, must be solved on the basis of constitutional guarantees of religious liberty and equality before the law.

Possible solutions to the problem are limited by the fact that forty-six state constitutions, directly or by interpretation, prohibit the use of public funds in aid of denominational institutions. In view of these prohibitions, perhaps the simplest solution to the problem is either a tax credit for parents of nonpublic-school children or the direct subsidization of the individual child. The latter plan follows the precedent established by the Federal Government in the education of veterans who served during the Korean conflict, and in the education of war orphans.

The Certificate Plan

This plan is the certificate or voucher plan. Under such a plan, the state government gives parents of nonpublic-school children certificates of money value for their children's education in the school of their choice. The role of the government is limited, as it is under our present system, to that of inspection to make sure that minimum standards are met.

There are many things to recommend a program such as the certificate plan. What is said here of the certificate plan is equally valid for the tax-credit plan. And what is said of state educational benefits is equally true of Federal educational benefits.

Seven more or less distinct advantages of the direct-grant method for securing equality and religious liberty in education may be considered here.

1. The certificate plan of direct state educational grants to the individual child does not raise constitutional questions.

The plan does not violate state constitutional prohibitions against aid to denominational schools. The grant is a subsidy of the individual child to enable him, under the direction and control of his parents, to purchase his education in the market place of elementary and secondary education. In this respect the certificate plan incorporates the same constitutional principles that underlie the educational provisions of the GI Bill of Rights. . . .

2. The certificate plan secures freedom of choice in education.

This freedom is essential to democracy. Nothing is so incompatible with the democratic ideal as enforced conformity. Yet our children are forced to conform to the philosophical and theological orientation of a single educational system as a condition for sharing in the state's educational benefits.

In human affairs freedom without alternatives is not freedom. America's educational policy, in fact, penalizes nonconformity and independence of thought, and rewards conformity and orthodoxy. It is based on the principle of conformity. It aims to dress thought in uniformity. This policy violates freedom of mind and freedom of religion, and thus undermines the very foundations of democracy. These fundamental constitutional liberties demand freedom of choice in education.

The proposed plan applies the principles of democracy to education. No child is forced to conform to a *mass* pattern. Each child is individually considered, and his parents, in whom the prime responsibility for his education rests, can choose the kind of education best suited to develop their child's character and talents.

Such individual freedom and diversity are essential for the preservation of democracy. Democracy, if it is to remain free, must rest on individuals who are free to exercise their rights and responsibilities as individuals. Enforced conformity creates an undifferentiated mass. Such a *mass* is the foundation, not of democracy, but of the totalitarian state.

3. The certificate plan protects the religious liberty guaranteed by the Federal Constitution.

The Supreme Court of the United States has asserted on a number of occasions that parents have a constitutional right to send their children to parochial schools. This right is grounded in the religious liberty guaranteed by the First Amendment. The Court so declared in the Prince case of 1944, in the Everson case of 1947, and this is the meaning of the Pierce decision of 1925.

Parents have an inviolable right to direct and control the education of their children consistent with their religious belief. Yet, when they do exercise this right, their children are deprived of all state educational benefits. This is to penalize parents because of their religious belief.

Under the certificate plan the individual child receives equal educational benefits regardless of his religious convictions. This plan, moreover, enables the state to fulfill its educational obligations to all its children in accordance with the commands of the First Amendment to the Federal Constitution. And children who are today forcibly denied the opportunity of attending a God-centered school would be *free* to choose such a school.

4. The certificate plan ensures the personal right of the individual child to share equally in the educational benefits of democratic society.

The state's purpose in education is to secure the good of the individual child and the good of the entire community. With respect to this purpose, all children are alike. That is to say, with respect to this purpose, children cannot be classified on the basis of religious belief. Consequently, every individual child has an equal right to share in state educational benefits regardless of his religious convictions and practice.

The constitutional doctrine of legal equality would be meaningless unless it presupposed individual differences. The state, while recognizing its citizens with all their individual differences, must yet treat them alike. For the state to demand conformity as a condition for sharing in welfare benefits is to negate the whole intent and purpose of the equal-protection clause of the Fourteenth Amendment.

And, more important still, for the state to demand the surrender of a First Amendment right as a condition for sharing in such benefits violates a most fundamental constitutional principle —the principle of the liberty and integrity of the human person. The state, in the distribution of public funds for the education of its children, must, therefore, treat all children alike regardless of their religious belief and practice.

The denial of such benefits, furthermore, forces parents, because of their exercise of religion in the choice of school, to support a second school system. This imposed burden is a tax on the exercise of religion. As such, it is unconstitutional; it does the very thing that the First Amendment forbids: it prohibits the *free* exercise of religion.

5. The certificate plan enables society to pay for the benefits which society itself derives from the education of children in parochial schools.

The only legal justification for the spending of public money for the education of children in *public* schools is the good that society derives from an educated citizenry. But society likewise derives advantages from the education of children in nonpublic schools. For these advantages and benefits society should pay.

Hence, society has a twofold interest in education. First, the benefits that are conferred on the individual who receives the education. Second, the benefits which society itself derives from an educated citizenry. These benefits are political, spiritual, moral, material and cultural. This is to say, simply, that education is a necessary condition for democratic society; it serves to maintain the spiritual and moral foundations of our democracy; it is essential for our highly technical, industrial economy; it is prerequisite for cultural and social intercourse.

Since American society derives these benefits from parochial education, no less than from public, it has an obligation to pay for them. It is unjust and discriminatory to *force* parents of parochial-school children to pay for these benefits which redound to the advantage of American society as a whole. It is doubly unjust and discriminatory to force them thus to subsidize society because of their exercise of a constitutional right.

The certificate plan enables society to pay for the benefits which parochial education confers upon it, thus removing both a grave injustice and a serious violation of constitutional rights.

6. The certificate plan would moderate the trend toward the complete socialization of primary and secondary education; it would restore free enterprise in education.

In a nation that is dedicated to free enterprise, education below the college level has, nonetheless, been almost completely socialized. It is almost completely state owned, operated and controlled. Public schools are government schools. This nullifies the advantages of free enterprise in education. State monopoly in education, as in business, destroys that initiative, ingenuity, imagination and enterprise that, in the American competitive system, has satisfied the wants of such a diversified people.

In our American economy, we do not think that monopoly—state or otherwise—is capable of producing the best commodities. We think that competition is essential . . .

7. The certificate plan would help to preserve our other highly cherished liberties.

Since the plan would ensure freedom of choice in education, it would reduce the power of government over the minds of our nation's children. The independence of our private and church-related schools would be maintained and their number probably increased.

Today a relatively small group of officials are in the position to determine the political, the economic, the philosophical and the theological orientation of government schools throughout the nation. Such a high concentration of power in the hands of so few individuals in an area so all-important as education is undemocratic and dangerous.

Liberty is an essential ingredient of democracy. This liberty demands that the individual person be free, particularly in those things that determine what he shall think and what he shall believe. But this freedom of mind and freedom of spirit cannot be achieved if children must conform to a particular kind of education as a condition for sharing in state educational benefits.

Freedom of thought and belief demands diversity in the field of education.

Diversity is the distinguishing characteristic of a free pluralist society; enforced conformity is the distinguishing characteristic of a totalitarian society.

In the final analysis, the only internal force that can destroy our liberties is government. A wise people will not permit its government to become too powerful, particularly not in those things that touch the mind and spirit of man. The best defense against the gradual encroachment of government is freedom of mind and freedom of religion secured by freedom of choice in education.

IN FAVOR OF FEDERAL AID [12]

This hearing extends to all proposals for science and education for national defense now pending before the Senate Labor Committee and it is with that understanding that I wish to bring out a few points I feel have not yet been sufficiently emphasized.

Most of the testimony we have had so far has involved higher education and most of that has emphasized higher education aimed at improving our standing in science and technology vis-à-vis the Soviet Union.

I do not quarrel with the need to improve the use we make of our intellectual resources in these fields. But I would warn this committee against stopping there. We need a national scholarship program, and we also need grants to the states for education at the elementary and secondary levels. At all levels, aid must not be confined to any special fields of study, and that is true even if our sole purpose is to raise our standards in terms of the progress being made in Soviet Russia.

It is quite true that action by Congress in this field has been stimulated by the Russian Sputniks.

But while Soviet achievement with satellites and missiles presents a challenge to us in these fields, we must not react so

[12] From statement by Senator Wayne Morse (Democrat, Oregon). In *Science and Education for National Defense*; hearings before the Senate Committee on Labor and Public Welfare. 85th Congress, 2d session. Superintendent of Documents. Washington 25, D.C. 1958. p 1137+.

defensively that we meet only one challenge. We know enough about communism to know that it menaces Western civilization as a whole, not just our scientific and technical capacity. It will not confine its assaults upon us to these fields. It is a challenge to our entire culture, to our political, economic, and social systems, to our religions, and to our creative arts. The Communist system will seek by any avenue it can find to overthrow our own. Therefore, we must develop our intellectual resources in all fields of endeavor—in the humanities, the arts, and the social sciences, as well as in the physical sciences and mathematics.

For Communist advances are not made only via modern transportation. They are made through literature, through all kinds of propaganda, and through subversion. Its appeals are made to the sympathies and aspirations of mankind. It attacks any weakness that appears in a national society, and cannot be guarded against just by putting a rocket on the moon ahead of Russia, as important as that is.

We must remember that it is all the intellectual power and talent of our youth that must be mobilized. I think this must be the framework of the legislation that is developed from these hearings.

That is why . . . we need to watch out that we do not waste brainpower in our country. I do not think we have any right to deny to a boy and girl a college education if he or she has the mental potential to do satisfactory college work. We need to follow various criteria for admission to college. A high school transcript is one, but it must not be made an exclusive one. . . .

The major premise on which I approach this problem is that I want to see the maximum education benefits given to every boy and girl who wants to go on and develop his or her mental potential. That means I want whatever facilities are necessary to save the brainpower of American youth. . . .

Financial Assistance to States

I think we must start meeting our national responsibility by providing financial assistance to the states for their elementary and secondary schools. No American program that deals only with the final stages of our educational system, as the Eisenhower Administration's program does, is going to restore America to an equality with Russia even in the fields of science and technology.

In my judgment, any legislation that comes out of the Eighty-fifth Congress on education that does not deal with this part of the educational system will not meet the real need.

We know from many estimates, including the White House Conference on Education and the President's Committee on Education Beyond the High School that educational expenditures must be increased at least 75 per cent within the next fifteen years, just to stay where we are now.

With half of our public elementary and secondary school revenue tied to local property taxes, there is little hope, in my opinion, that local governments can double their contributions to education. We should be improving our educational system in that time, not just maintaining what we have now.

As a matter of fact, just what do we have now? First, we have 840,000 boys and girls attending classes only part of the time because of classroom and teacher shortages. I respectfully ask what good we can do these youngsters by offering them scholarships to attend colleges and universities? They are being penalized right now, and the penalty will be felt again when they compete with full-time students for financial assistance to go to college which so many of us think necessary and desirable.

Second, we have 87,391 emergency teachers. I do not intend at all to disparage these men and women by pointing out that they do not have minimum requirements for teaching in their states. We can be thankful we have them at all in the teaching profession. But their continued employment means that our boys and girls are not getting the standard of instruction that each state has fixed for itself. Interestingly enough, the United States Office of Education does not seem to regard these emergency teachers as replaceable, but includes them in the figures for the entire teaching staff in American schools. The skill of our teaching staff as a whole will not rise to where we want it unless salaries are raised to a level in keeping with what these men and women can earn outside the profession. That is one of the primary reasons why I believe Federal grants to the states are essential.

Third, we need more classrooms and other school facilities. As we cast about for construction projects to stimulate our sagging economy, I can think of no more useful and timely program than one of school construction. . . .

Just last year, the Administration was agreeing with us about the classroom shortage to the extent of giving half-hearted support to a construction bill. Now it has abandoned that program, without, of course, giving any indication that Federal assistance is no longer needed. It did not because it cannot. At the opening of the school year, the nation required about 200,000 new classrooms to meet new enrollments and replace obsolete buildings. The states are building about 60,000 new classrooms a year, thereby keeping up with new enrollments but making only a small dent in the backlog of construction needs.

School Construction—Public Works Program

I can think of no more worthwhile public-works program than one of school construction. The bill I sponsored last year with Senator Clark (S. 1134), and the new bill (S. 3311) introduced by Senator Murray and cosponsored by myself and many others would include school construction among the uses to which the Federal grants could be put. Senator Proxmire of Wisconsin, this year joined us as a cosponsor of S. 1134.

To those who still cling to the old notion that Federal assistance would lead to Federal control, I remind them of the history of Federal school construction. A great many people have forgotten that school buildings were among the major projects built by the Federal Government during the depression of the thirties. In the 1955 report on Federal aid for school construction by the Library of Congress, there is contained a summary of activities of the Public Works Administration and the Works Project Administration. PWA made its grants to the localities to use for the construction they needed most. From 1933 through 1942, PWA made allotments for 6,687 elementary and secondary schools costing over $979 million. Every state of the Union participated in this program. School buildings comprised 40 per cent of all non-Federal projects for which PWA made allotments.

Every senator, in other words, has schools in his state that were built with Federal grants in the 1930's. Can any one of them show where any Federal control of teaching methods or curriculum has resulted? Can anyone point to a single school in this country built with PWA funds and say that it fell under Federal domination because Federal money helped build it?

Then we have WPA schools. The WPA did not make grants to the localities or states, but built its projects directly. Over a period of eight years, more than 5,900 new schools were built, and more than 33,000 others were modernized under WPA, at a cost of $466,700,000. Can any senator, who is opposing Federal aid because of fear of Federal control point to any WPA-constructed school and say that it is now being run or dominated by the Federal Government? . . .

I think the record already made on Federal funds for school construction puts to rest these fears of Federal control of the schools of America.

In fact, I digress to point out that millions of dollars have poured into the states over many, many years for the so-called land-grant colleges under the Morrill Act. . . .

Does any senator want to tell me that any state college in his state is dominated by the Federal Government because it has been the recipient of great sums of money over the years?

Of course, the answer is that such a charge is nonsense. It is pure nonsense. It is a fear argument. It is a scarecrow that is being built up in the communities of America, with the result that timid politicians too frequently are following this propaganda line, and unwittingly, I am sure, but nevertheless effectively, denying to American boys and girls the educational opportunities that I think are their heritage.

AGAINST FEDERAL AID [13]

The National Association of Manufacturers appreciates this opportunity to offer its views on Federal aid to education for the record of the Senate Committee on Labor and Public Welfare.

[13] From statement by the National Association of Manufacturers. In *Science and Education for National Defense*; hearings before the Senate Committee on Labor and Public Welfare. 85th Congress, 2d session. Superintendent of Documents. Washington 25, D.C. 1958. p 1335-7.

The association, which has a membership of some 22,000, 83 per cent of whom employ less than five hundred employees, is genuinely concerned with the adequacy of the nation's schools, and the contribution they make to our nation's well-being. The association has and will continue to work in the nation's best educational interests. But it cannot believe that the nation's interests in education, or in other domestic programs, is a mandate for action by the national government.

Numerous proposals have been brought before this committee for programs which claim to strengthen the country's educational system. The approach, emphasis, or specific aspect involved differs from bill to bill, but one characteristic is constant. This is the assumption that Federal aid to the states, in one form or another, and for one purpose or another, is the solution to the problem at hand, whether it be better schoolrooms and better teachers, or better courses and better sudents. The chronic answer to more and better education seems to be more and better forms of Federal aid.

The National Association of Manufacturers takes vigorous exception to Federal aid as a basic answer to problems in our educational system, regardless of the particular pattern of the proposed aid. Fundamentally, the association believes that public education is the direct and exclusive responsibility of each state and its own communities, that the financial position of each of the states is adequate to fulfill this responsibility, and that failure of some of the states to meet this responsibility can be rectified by the states themselves through changes in statutory provisions and through improved foresight and leadership. The association also believes that the best help which the Federal Government can offer the states is not an aggressive aid policy, but abstinence.

There are several aspects to a pertinent policy of restraint, abstention: (1) do not open new doors to Federal aid; (2) firmly close those already in use; and (3) unblock the basic tax-rate barrier to adequate state-local and private financing of education.

This committee is considering, among other proposals, S. 3187 and S. 3163, both of which open new doors to Federal aid to education which should not, and need not be opened. Where the emphasis in past years has been on Federal aid for school construction, the essential characteristic of these bills is Federal aid for school instruction. The framework is one of providing scholarships and fellowships for students, and institutes for teachers; testing and counseling of students, and training and counseling of teachers; equipment or facilities improvement for instruction in science, mathematics, or modern languages; and grants to help state educational agencies in their supervisory and consultant relationship to local schools.

The content of S. 3163 was previewed in outline in the President's budget message this January. Comments were made on these proposals in the National Association of Manufacturers' publication, *Federal Expenditure Control and the 1959 Federal Budget,* and are appropriate here:

> In all of the proposals for Federal aid to education heretofore advanced, vigorous disclaimers have been made to emphasize that there is no intention of exerting Federal control over curricula, school management, or other aspects of local responsibility. These assertions have always been open to challenge on the grounds, first, that "he who pays the piper has the right to call the tune," and second, that there would be neglect of Federal responsibility in the failure to exercise supervision over the way in which Federal grants were used. These grounds lead to the unavoidable conclusion that there will be, and in fact must be, controls by the Federal Government to the extent that it provides funds. Obviously, the more money it provides, the more control it will exercise.
>
> This year, there is a frank assertion of intent to control. In the budget message it is said, that a major objective of the new programs will be to provide matching grants "to strengthen state departments of education and local school systems, particularly in the administration and teaching of science and mathematics." The new grants are also to be used to "strengthen graduate schools and expand the teaching of foreign languages."
>
> The direction of this control is pointed up in the President's special message to Congress, in these words:
>
> "Because of the national security interest in the quality and scope of our educational system in the years immediately ahead, however, the Federal Government must also undertake to play an emergency role. The Administration is therefore recommending certain emergency Federal actions to encourage and assist greater effort in specific areas of national concern. These recommendations place principal emphasis on our national security requirements."

In other words, a condition of the Federal grant will be that the states and local school districts expecting to receive Federal money must introduce and emphasize the subjects and courses of study which fit into a Federal determination of "national security requirements."

This study pointed out our specific opposition to grant-in-aid programs. The minimal first-year cost of such was recognized. But, the study says:

Grant programs have a habit of being started on a temporary or emergency basis, and then, as Senator Byrd has said, "growing to the size of elephants." The President's special message says "this is a temporary program and should not be considered as a permanent Federal responsibility." However, all the special interest pressures which were brought to bear for passage of the grants proposed last year for general aid for school construction would undoubtedly be summoned to expand these beginnings. Already the National Education Association has said: "You can't meet a great challenge with a small and restricted program"; and it has asked for a program starting at $1 billion and going up to $5 billion in four years.

The only way to prevent the spending of Federal billions for state and local responsibility is to stop at their inception, programs with so obvious a future. These grant proposals are new doors to Federal aid for education which should not be opened. The case made in 1956 by the association in opposition to Federal aid to education is applicable in this instance, too. And the concluding paragraphs of it are equally pertinent here:

"We agree with the President that the fundamental responsibility for education is state and local; but we do not share the view that Federal assistance will help these governments do their job nor spur them in it; on the contrary . . .

"We believe that a clear statement by the Federal Government of disinclination to participate in financing the public school system in any of its aspects would provide the sharpest spur for the full discharge of state and local responsibility."

But it is not simply the form which the proposed Federal aid takes that is at issue. The question is one of perspective and fundamentals. In these regards, the association's study of the 1959 budget makes the following points:

1. There should be more effective utilization of available scientists and engineers. When this has been done, it may appear that no special inducements are needed to increase the supply.

2. As the budget message admits, the basic responsibility for science education and training as well as for conduct of research in this country

depends primarily on non-Federal support, and requires a thorough understanding of the problem by all citizens. But experience with other grants has shown that a Federal grant tends to prevent the states, local units, and private institutions from fully facing up to their own responsibility. It is not likely to be otherwise in this case.

3. No one should be led into thinking that just by spending money, scientists can be turned out overnight, or even in a year or so. A long period of study and training is required. For this reason, and since there is general agreement that the responsibility rests on the states and localities, and on private educational institutions, these agencies should not be even temporarily distracted from their task by so-called stimulative grants. The budget message recognizes this danger by cautioning against overemphasis on the grants. Contrary to all of the evidence, a belief is indicated in the message that these grants can and will be terminated after a few years.

4. As to the specific case of the science education grants, it must be kept in mind that science, however important, is not the whole of education. Again quoting the budget message: "The national needs require the development through a strong educational system of a vast number of aptitudes and skills." The proper way and the best way to provide better education for more students is to concentrate on the home-town and the home-state obligations to assure that the job is done.

5. In further support of the preceding point, there is a danger that too great emphasis on specialized programs which may be popular at the moment may upset the balance needed in a well-rounded educational program.

All of these reasons connect back to the fundamental truth that in the American system, education is not a function of the Federal Government, but a clear responsibility of the people, whose children are to be educated, acting through their local and state agencies in this field. It is dangerous for the institutions of a free society to let either policy or financing of education out of their control. The menace of Federal grants, regardless of the merit or urgency of particular reasons, is that local control is to some extent weakened and may be lost entirely.

The obstacles to adequate financing of our educational system are several: a too ready acceptance of Federal aid as the necessary or only answer, special-interest pressures for such aid inside and outside the Government, state statutory limitations—many of them archaic and inappropriate today—and the Federal monopoly of tax resources which leads to a vicious circle of Federal fiscal supremacy increasing and supporting state dependency. The excessive rates of Federal income tax constitute a major obstacle to more adequate state-local financing of our public-school system, and to more generous support by individuals of the private higher educational system. As our association's budget study says:

> A cardinal point of NAM policy for years has been the proposition that more of the people's resources must be left at home if the job of providing governmental services is to be done there. The President's strong emphasis on the task of education as a state and local responsibility, a viewpoint that is very generally accepted, adds great strength to the case that can be made of many other grounds for a reform of the tax-rate structure.

In putting our views on this important subject before the Senate Committee on Labor and Public Welfare, the National Association of Manufacturers urges consideration of the whole complex of problems involved. We firmly believe that whatever needs exist for better students, better courses, and better teachers can and will be better met by Federal tax-rate reform and Federal forbearance from grant programs than by the Federal Government with new forms of dependency allotments to the states.

III. LESSONS FROM ABROAD

EDITOR'S INTRODUCTION

Can American education at this juncture in our history learn from abroad? This is a question which would have seemed almost ridiculous to most Americans, including educators, as recently as the inter-war years. Today, as evidenced by many references in this volume, it appears to be of great concern. Here the Russian advances in education, unknown to the general public and also most educators until the Soviets orbited their Sputniks around the earth, have had a telling effect. It has now been realized that not only have the Soviets attempted to provide universal education—the only other country to do so aside from the United States—but that they have built on a pre-Soviet, Czarist Russian educational base which was European in outlook. As a result many critics of American education, impressed by Soviet educational feats, have taken a look at both Western European and Russian educational systems.

The following articles do just this from various points of view. At the outset, the former president of Harvard University and former American Ambassador to West Germany surveys broadly the educational ferment in the Western world. Rear Admiral Rickover plumps almost completely for the Western European system in the next article (see "U.S. Education: an Indictment" in Section I, above, for his condemnation of the American system). Following this a scientist, Professor R. E. Marshak, chairman of the Department of Physics and Astronomy of the University of Rochester, undertakes a critique of Soviet science. He dwells on science education in both the U.S.S.R. and the United States. More important he states categorically that scientific inquiry and research in Russia today have become virtually free of political fetters. This represents the formidable challenge of an otherwise highly regimented society. More than most other articles in this book, this selection points up the challenge—whether the free educational system of America, without controls from state authority, can compete in a race of intellectual achievement. Part of the answer may be found in the next selection by Andrew R. MacAndrew, student and reporter on Russia, in which he surveys more broadly the total picture of Russian education.

From the next article—an official British statement about education in England, Scotland and Wales—a comparison with our own schools may be made. In two short pieces following, the changes now taking place in European and Russian schools are outlined; significantly, it would appear, they may be moving closer to American ideas than is suggested by some of the articles in this book which criticize education in the United States. Last, a view by a Britisher who knows American education well and a view by an American who knows European education equally well are included. Both authors are aware of our educational faults; both on balance favor the American way.

EDUCATION IN THE WESTERN WORLD [1]

To one interested in comparative education, it is fascinating to see how, today, many nations are struggling to solve the basic problems connected with the selection and education of future members of the professions. To a comparative educationalist, many questions about the selection and training of doctors and lawyers in different countries are questions almost without meaning. Asking whether European schools are better than schools in the United States is like asking a comparative anatomist whether a whale is a better mammal than an elephant.

The comparative anatomist is interested in examining the similarities and differences to be found in animal or plant organs which carry out the same function; he is very cautious, however, about proclaiming the virtues of a device found in one particular species over a device for a similar purpose found in another. Of course, the anatomist knows that mammals are

[1] From article by James B. Conant, former president of Harvard University and former ambassador to the Federal Republic of Germany. *Atlantic Monthly.* 200:73-7. November 1957. Reprinted by permission.

modified only slowly by changes in environment; unlike schools or colleges, no man-made decisions will radically alter the structure of the functioning organism he is examining.

Some will argue that this vitiates my analogy; they may claim that the essence of human organizations lies in the fact that conscious acts of men and women can change them, and as history shows, overnight if need be. "But wait a moment," the student of the comparative anatomy of schools will say, "not overnight surely, except at the point of a bayonet or in our time under the shadow of armored vehicles and tanks." And such changes, he will argue, are the equivalent of pathological alterations.

History shows that, except under conditions of duress brought about by external forces, schools and colleges have developed gradually in different parts of the world in response to a variety of different conditions. They are a product of the society they serve and they also influence the future of this society. Reformers who have sought to change education have had to be content with minor alterations or else have had to devote a lifetime to their task.

It is clear that various educational devices have in the past been outmoded by social changes. The situation of Oxford and Cambridge during the first two thirds of the nineteenth century is a case in point. For two generations many leaders of public opinion argued for the need of either establishing modern universities in England or reforming the two ancient seats of learning. Eventually both courses of action were followed; the modification of Oxford and Cambridge by successive royal commissions was so radical as to constitute the equivalent of a series of drastic biological mutations. By the end of the century English universities were once again well adapted to the tasks at hand.

I should like to approach the subject of education for the professions in the mood of the comparative educationalist. I should like to examine in particular the way the future members of the professions are recruited, selected, and educated in certain European nations and the United States.

For a number of professions one phase of professional education—the final stage, so to speak—is essentially identical in all countries. There is little to be gained by noting the minor differences to be found in various nations. This is true of medicine, of engineering, and of the natural sciences; it is likewise true to a lesser degree of certain areas within the social sciences and the humanities. It is possible to pass judgment on the work of the medical faculty of a university, for example, almost without taking into account the traditions of the institution or its surroundings. Considering the training of a medical man only from the standpoint of professional competency, it would not be too difficult to classify all the medical schools of Europe and America into groups according to their degree of excellence. The same would apply to the training of engineers and research scientists.

It is not so much professional education as the education provided *prior* to professional studies that varies from nation to nation. This is particularly true if one directs attention to the way the future members of the professions are recruited and selected. Nowhere on the European continent will one find the equivalent of the American four-year liberal arts college. The European youth, unlike his American contemporary, passes directly from a university preparatory school to professional training.

Americans find it difficult to imagine an educational system without a college; Europeans find it hard to imagine what sort of an institution an American college can be. And the task of explaining the situation in the United States to a German, for example, is not made easier by the fact that there are over 1500 four-year colleges in our country, some part of a university, some not; their curricula and criteria for admission and graduation vary enormously; the one thing they have in common is the right to award a bachelor's degree, an academic symbol derived from the Middle Ages which has completely disappeared in German-speaking nations, though not in France.

One sometimes hears it said that the characteristic feature of American education is the proportion of our youth attending a university. So phrased, this is a completely misleading statement.

What is characteristic is the very large proportion of our youth from eighteen to twenty years of age who are engaged in full-time studies; the fraction is something like a quarter to a third; in Great Britain, France, Germany, and Switzerland not more than a tenth of the youth are so engaged. Equally characteristic are the figures for school attendance at the age sixteen to seventeen; in America more than 75 per cent of those of this age are in school full-time; in European countries and Great Britain the corresponding figure is less than 20 per cent. Some Europeans have said that only a rich nation could afford to keep so many of its youth in school so long. But with the increase in automation, it is a question whether the withdrawal of a considerable fraction of youth from the labor force is a luxury. The type of training needed in the distributive industries more and more requires considerable "book learning."

At all events, when we consider the proportion of youth engaged in *professional* studies, the position of the United States is not so different from that of the rest of the world. Perhaps it is fair to compare the proportion of young men enrolled in the first year of a university in Europe or Great Britain to the proportion in the United States entering engineering, law, and medical schools and starting in the graduate schools of arts and sciences. Taking the figures for young men, the proportion in the United States seems to be something like 6 per cent; surprisingly small, many would say. But what is equally surprising is that similar figures represent the situation in all nations for which I have seen statistics. Therefore, one could say that the proportion of youth studying *professionally* in a university is about the same in the United States as in other nations. What *is* different between America and Europe is the method by which this very small percentage is selected and educated prior to engaging in professional studies.

Today, unlike the situation of a hundred years ago, the education of members of the professions (particularly natural scientists and engineers) is a concern of statesmen; public opinion has an interest in hearing the answers to such questions as the following: Are we including in our education for the professions a large fraction of those who have the requisite ability, or are we overlooking many with high potentialities?

In a totalitarian state these questions lead directly to a control of the entire educational process; the capable are to be sorted out and educated for the different professions according to the nation's need for these professions. This is essentially the directive of the Party Executive Committee to those in charge of schools and universities in the Soviet Zone of Germany. In a free country the political situation is, thank God, very different, not only because of the impossibility of governments ordering youth into different educational channels but because of the freedom of parents to express their desires to school authorities and, if need be, to politicians.

National concern with the number and quality of scientists and engineers is clearly a result of the last phases of the industrial revolution which started two hundred years ago. Parental concern with education as a way by which a son may better himself economically and socially is a consequence of the spread of that spirit of democracy of which Tocqueville wrote more than a century ago. It has taken time for the equalitarian doctrines of the French Revolution reinforced by American notions to affect European education; but there is no doubt that the problem of selecting future university students is becoming more rather than less difficult in England and a number of European states. The question of social prestige is becoming involved, as it has been involved with us in America for at least fifty years.

Let me give a few concrete examples. During the Second World War the British Parliament made certain changes in the English system of tax-supported schools. Among the objectives which the new legislation sought to achieve was the widening of opportunity for children of the less well to do; another was an elimination of the great difference in prestige that in the past had characterized one type of tax-supported school as compared to another. The traditional view of the content of a school program was, however, not modified. A long course was held to be necessary; and selection of those capable of entering those schools which provided this course was to be made at the age of eleven to twelve.

From the point of view of a parent with a low income and a talented child, the new arrangement must appear to be better than the old. But parents of medium income view the altered situation highly critically. In the past the "grammar schools" had provided excellent roads to the universities open to those who could afford to pay a moderate fee. (For well-to-do families the usual road to the university is provided by the famous "public schools.") The new regulations abolished the fees and made the admission of *all* children subject to a competitive examination. And to make matters worse, so some parents have said, a new type of examination is employed—so-called psychological tests—that has no apparent relation to school work! As a result the whole subject of selection at age eleven-plus is a topic of heated discussion among educators and laymen.

In one county in England the experiment is being made of abolishing the examination in two selected geographic areas and sending all children from eleven to fifteen to one school and then providing grammar school places for those whose parents are willing to keep them in school until at least sixteen. Presumably ability to handle the work in the grammar school will be the determining factor in deciding who goes on to the university. The article in the London *Observer* reviewing the experiment carries the heading "Eleven-plus Condemned." This caption corresponds to the sentiment expressed in a number of articles and letters to the editor that have been appearing in British journals and papers in the last few years.

On the European continent, too, difficulties have arisen in regard to the process of selecting those who are to attend the *Gymnasium* in preparation for a university education. Each one of eleven states in the Federal Republic of Germany has complete authority in educational matters; so too have the twenty-five cantons in Switzerland (with a few exceptions). A comparison of the roads to the university in each of these states is interesting; it shows how different local conditions have modified to a certain degree the European pattern. The points at issue are often the exact length of the pre-university school course and the methods by which pupils are selected for the special pre-university schools.

The parental pressure varies greatly from place to place and reflects differences in tradition and economic circumstances. Sometimes the selection can be made solely on the basis of advice given by teachers and accepted by parents. Sometimes examinations are required in order to decide who should start on the road to the professions. If so, parental protests frequently arise. In one German state I heard a mother complaining that the entrance tests for the *Gymnasium* were so foolish and arbitrary that many of her friends could not get their children admitted; as a consequence the parents were pressed into the expense of sending them to private schools. In France, where the road to the professions has been studded with stiff competitive examinations, anguish over the selection process has been particularly acute. The entrance examinations for the pre-university schools (*lycées*) have just been abolished and the program in these schools lightened. Selection of the pupils who head for the university is now to be made on the basis of the primary school record. In Switzerland, the psychological effect on the child of failure in the pre-university school (in some cantons a half to two thirds drop out) is giving concern to the school authorities.

In several German states, parents have brought suit against the government because a child had been barred from a pre-university school. The matter has even become a political issue. It is not the method of selection but the length of the pre-university school course that is in controversy. If the course is nine years, then selection must be made at the age of ten to eleven; this was the usual pattern in Germany, I judge, some years ago. But in the postwar years in some states the pre-university course was shortened and the time of selection correspondingly postponed.

The arguments in favor of keeping all the children together in one school as long as possible are familiar to Americans; an additional (and for Europeans more weighty) argument for a shorter pre-university period of schooling is that it may be easier to select those suited for university work at twelve or thirteen rather than ten or eleven. The abbreviated course has been attacked, however, on the grounds that nine years is necessary if the pupil is to master the subjects required for later university work (particularly Latin). The differences of opinion on the matter seem to run along the usual lines of political cleavage in both Germany and Switzerland; in general the moderate right favors the longer course, the moderate left the shorter.

In one state election in Germany the issue was of major importance. This is hard for Americans to understand, since the difference of opinion appears to be relatively slight and the educational question involved touches the schooling of not more than a fifth of the children. It is interesting to us as evidence of the intimate connection between school problems and sociological questions.

From what I have already reported, it is clear that the age at which selection is made and the time it is made is intimately associated with the content of the pre-university course of study. And here we meet the second major difference between the road to the professions in Europe and in the United States. In Europe, the state determines the requirements which must be satisfactorily fulfilled in order to obtain, on finishing school, the necessary credentials which will enable the holder to enter a university. In Germany and Switzerland, for example, the certificate which a youth obtains after passing a set of final examinations in the last school year is an admission ticket to any university. The absence of any such uniform requirements in America astonishes and perplexes the European observer of our chaotic system.

Though each state in the Federal Republic of Germany is autonomous, the standards throughout are essentially the same. Certain variations in the subjects on which a student is examined are permitted, but one may say that the essential subjects are languages and mathematics. In the classical *Gymnasium* (in Germany called the humanistic school), Latin and Greek are obligatory; in most of the others, Latin and at least one modern foreign language; in a few schools, exposure to a heavy dose of modern languages, mathematics, and natural science is considered a substitute for Latin. A European university is not an American college, and language instruction is not one of its functions; scientists, lawyers, medical men, economists, and historians, therefore, have no opportunity for studying any language after they leave school. With this in mind, one realizes why a long school course is believed necessary for future university students. The central position occupied in the curricula of pre-university schools by foreign languages is a reflection of the role played by both tradition and geography in educational matters. As far as future professional men are concerned, Europeans are convinced that the traditional education in language, literature, mathematics, and European history comprises the best general education.

For the 75 or 80 per cent who have no ambition or no opportunity to head for a university, formal full-time education ends at fourteen or fifteen; further educational development in part-time courses will depend on the occupation of the young man or woman in question. The apprentice system together with continuation schools takes care of industrial workers, it may be said. For apprentices with special mechanical aptitude, technical schools are available. For the 10 per cent or so who must drop out of the pre-university schools, some type of education with more emphasis on practical business affairs is needed. This the European would grant, but the idea of a general education for a large proportion of adolescents aged sixteen to twenty-one is unheard of on the continent of Europe.

How is it at the end of the road, one may ask. Are those Europeans who complete the hard journey and arrive at a university and later become professional men (some 6 per cent of the young men) better educated than the corresponding Americans? This is the type of question a comparative educationalist refuses to answer. For so much depends on your standard of judgment, on what basis you evaluate the nonprofessional knowledge, ability, and attitude of a professional man or woman.

One thing is certain: the average American medical man, lawyer, chemist, physicist, or engineer has acquired a quite different store of general knowledge from that of his European counterpart. If command of foreign language is the test of a well-educated man or woman, relatively few Americans can claim to be well educated. If knowledge of European literature and art is taken as a measure, there again the average American professional man will fail in comparison with the Europeans. European pre-university education is in essence literary education; American college education can rarely be so described.

On the other hand, every American in school and in college will have sampled at least a bit of some of the social sciences. Indeed, perhaps the majority of those whom we are here considering will have acquired a considerable knowledge of economics and political science; a large proportion will have studied psychology and sociology. With rare exceptions these disciplines are only available to a European in a university; and while the student enrolled under the law faculty may find time to listen to some lectures in these fields, the medical man and natural scientist will not.

In other words, those Americans who complete at least three years of a four-year liberal arts college course will have had a kind of academic experience unknown on the continent of Europe. (A possible exception to this statement is the education provided for the future teachers in the pre-university schools who are educated in the famous École Normale in Paris and in the philosophical faculties of the German universities.)

But it is not only the content of the program which characterizes the American college. The whole atmosphere is different from either a European school or a European university. There is far more freedom for the student than in a school, of course, and there is far more personal instruction of the student by the professor than is possible in a university of the European type with its relatively small staff in proportion to the size of the student body. The American student is ready to express an opinion to anyone; discussion is encouraged at every turn. Student activities ranging from dramatics through debating and journalism stimulate student independence; there is no parallel to these expressions of student initiative in Europe. All of which, of course, reflects what Americans have come to believe are important aspects of college education.

Indeed, one can sum up the comparison I have been making by saying that the leading citizens of Europe and the United States have quite different aims in mind when they talk about education as apart from professional training. And the difference reflects the different social histories on the two sides of the Atlantic.

As a first approximation, one may say that Europe adjusted its education to modern times nearly a hundred years ago. A period of rapid educational change on the Continent took place in the middle of the nineteenth century; this reflected the first impact of industrialization. The pattern thus established has persisted to the present with relatively few changes; it is obviously intimately associated with the apprentice system of training industrial workers and a relative lack of geographic and social mobility. It also reflects the powerful influence of the university faculties which were well entrenched when the educational changes were in progress—particularly the influence of the professors of the classics.

During the period of change in the United States in which we are still living, traditional academic forces have played a far less important role. But such social factors as the raising of the school-leaving age in the United States and the near disappearance of the European apprentice system were of more importance in determining the shape of the new educational system which is now emerging.

I have written "emerging" because it is clear that in this country we are still in process of adapting our schools, colleges, and universities to the current needs of our society (and trying to adapt to future needs as well). In England, too, a process of change has been and still is at work. In the nations of Western Europe, on the other hand (with the exception of Scandinavia), few alterations in the systems have been made in the last fifty years; though there are many educational problems similar to our own and England's, a period of reform has not yet begun.

An American observer cannot help wondering if such a period is not considerably overdue. It may well be that the more immediate political and social issues in France and the urgent task of reconstruction in postwar Germany have merely pushed aside consideration of educational changes. I seem to detect signs of dissatisfaction in the Federal Republic of Germany which may be the prelude to important actions; in parts of Switzerland the road to the professions is being resurveyed. In France a few important changes have just been made, and a bill providing for a drastic alteration in the French system has been introduced into Parliament by the Minister of Education.

We here in the United States are still engaged in remaking our educational roads; the nature of the task varies considerably from state to state, from community to community. Pedagogic devices and plans for the organization of schools and universities are not always transferable across state lines; they are almost never exportable to foreign countries. But nonetheless the exchange of ideas and blueprints is always helpful because it stimulates and arouses discussion.

We may watch with interest, therefore, the new developments in those Western nations from which came originally our cultural traditions and our ideas about education. The free nations of the world in planning for their youth, as in many other matters, must be in constant communication, for however diverse their methods their fundamental aims remain the same: the preservation and extension of personal freedom.

IN FAVOR OF EUROPE'S SYSTEM [2]

I have long felt that we erred grievously when we set up our own public education system without first making a thorough study of what at that time were the best foreign educational systems; that is, those of continental Europe. England, whose educational experiences have in many ways paralleled our own, showed greater wisdom. Though then the premier nation of the world, she was not too proud to profit from the experiences of small countries like Holland or Switzerland; or potential enemies like France and Germany.

Matthew Arnold, the poet, equipped with that curious versatility so noticeable in England's educated men, spent most of

[2] From "Education in the Nuclear Age," address delivered December 6, 1957, by Rear Admiral H. G. Rickover, USN. Text from press release issued by United States Atomic Energy Commission. Washington 25, D.C. 1957. p6-10. mimeo. Reprinted by permission. (For another excerpt from this address see "US. Education: An Indictment" in Section I, above.)

his life as a government school inspector; and in that capacity he wrote several reports on European educational methods which proved most useful when England finally established her own public secondary school system. We might profitably study those reports ourselves today.

The significant aspect of the continental educational system is that it is efficient and inexpensive when measured against the results obtained. That is not surprising when we consider that in its basic form it was invented by Prussia after her defeat by Napoleon in 1806. At that time, the country lay prostrate under the heel of the conqueror; her richest lands torn away; her treasury empty. Poor though she was, Prussia had to bring the entire country rapidly from the seventeenth to the nineteenth century, or forgo all hope of ever rising again. A small band of devoted men did the country over from top to bottom, including a thorough and rapid reform of her educational system which had deteriorated badly.

Prussia was one of the first countries to recognize that a modern state must have a citizenry with at least an elementary education; that she must have leaders sufficiently educated to deal with the problems of the coming industrialization. She was one of the first to make elementary education compulsory and free, and to put all of education under state control. Being a poor country she could not afford the leisurely, luxury education for her leaders which wealthy England had developed in the closed circle of (privately endowed) "public school"—Oxford and Cambridge. "Public school" students were taught by Oxford and Cambridge men and then themselves went to Oxford and Cambridge if they wanted more education. This closed high quality educational circle was run by Anglicans, and non-Anglicans were barred from it by law. It was confined to the old upperclasses and to the newly rich middle classes on their way up into the upperclasses; others were excluded by the high fees.

Prussia, too, had privately endowed boarding schools for the nobility, resembling somewhat the eighteenth-century English "public schools." But when she set up public secondary education she realistically cut out all features not necessary for education per se. Because the people were poor, fees had to be kept low; so a large part of the cost of education fell to the state. Hence the carefully thought-out businesslike way in which she worked out a two track system, one track designed for the mass of children, the other for those destined for the higher professions.

The rapid rise of Prussia to industrial and military power and the excellence of the scientific research done at her universities—to which students flocked from all over the world—led to widespread adoption of her basic educational system by most of Europe. Her lightning victories in 1864, 1866 and 1871—a mere half century after she had been soundly beaten by France—were recognized everywhere as a victory of the Prussian schools and universities. To defeated France the lesson was plain; she took energetic measures to modernize her own educational system.

Other European countries also adopted the basic principles of this system. These were:

First, that elementary, secondary and university education be devoted solely to developing the intellect of the student to his greatest capacity. All vocational training must be done in special schools set up for the purpose.

Second, that the secondary schools give a broad general education in the shortest possible time, so that professional study can begin no later than age eighteen. This was necessary both for reasons of economy and in order to find time for compulsory military training.

Third, to get youngsters ready for professional study at age eighteen, serious study of foreign languages, higher mathematics, literature, geography, and history must begin no later than age nine, at which time the fast learners begin to be separated from the slow learners.

Fourth, to complete this broad general education in nine years requires carefully thought-out courses for each subject, advancing in logical sequence, year after year, from the simple to the complex. Thus, elective subjects can have no place in such a comprehensive and well-balanced program. Only at the university level is selection of subjects left to the student.

Fifth, three basic types of secondary schools gradually evolved and are now provided—the classical, the semiclassical and the mathematics-scientific. Each of these three types provides a broad enough general education to permit the student to take almost any professional university course. For example a graduate of the classical secondary school can become an engineer by taking additional mathematics and science courses.

Sixth, considerable latitude was allowed in each school as long as national standards were met. These standards governed the qualification of teachers and the competence of the graduates. Tests of graduates to prove their competence were conducted by authorities external to the school itself, through very comprehensive examinations without which no diploma or degree was granted.

Because of the class distinctions dividing nineteenth-century Europe, this educational system tended in all countries to separate the lowest class—which sent its children to the elementary school—from the middle and upper classes whose children went to secondary school and thereafter to the university. The class character of this system made it anathema in the United States. But it is usually forgotten that Europe, too, has moved towards greater democracy, and that application of the six principles I have mentioned can be varied in many ways.

The European education system has now been democratized by abolishing school fees and by subsidizing the education of able students through scholarships. This is done extensively in England where, for example, three fourths of the students at Oxford are on government grants. Russia has gone furthest in this respect by paying complete living expenses to able students. Opportunities have also been developed which permit the late blooming child to catch up or shift from one educational track to another.

Also European secondary schools now have so-to-speak junior partners, i.e. schools giving the same type of education but stopping at age fifteen. These prepare for various subprofessional careers.

This whole system is flexible and can be adjusted to different national aims. It has the great advantage that it allows children of diverse mental capacities to move forward at their own speed in classes which are homogeneous in intellectual requirements. While she has opened all her educational institutions to all children, Europe has held fast to the fundamental requirements of good education: a high standard of professional competence for teachers, and a firm adherence to the principle that the secondary school educates; that it develops the powers of the mind; that vocational training or the teaching of social graces must be obtained elsewhere.

Moreover, democratization has not meant the lowering of academic standards. Examinations weed out those who cannot absorb further education. And yet the system is, in fact, less rigid than ours when circumstances require emphasis on certain professions. Thus, it permits changes in the demand and supply of the several professions to be effected rapidly.

It is this continental European system which the Soviets reintroduced twenty years ago and which has enabled them to forge ahead at an astonishing rate. There is nothing specifically Russian or communistic in their system, except that they have stripped all the "nonessentials" from the European model—they have stripped everything that develops independent thought and a cultivated mind—and that they have introduced as much political indoctrination into the curriculum as they consider necessary. By paying the living expenses of most students, by putting large sums into construction and equipment of superb laboratories and libraries, and by offering their children no other road to success but education, the Soviets have been able to get a larger percentage of their students—almost twice the number in Europe and America—into professional university level study.

It is this tremendous increase in Russia's professionals which threatens our technological supremacy today.

The method is simple. Combine the European educational system with adequate funds, and motivate children by offering the highest material rewards for hard mental study and you can get the same result anywhere in the world. There are the beginnings of this in China, too.

NATURE OF THE SOVIET SCIENTIFIC CHALLENGE [3]

On August 6, 1945, an atomic bomb was dropped on Hiroshima. Within days, a second A-bomb was dropped on Nagasaki to persuade the wavering Japanese government to surrender. The war was over and the United States was master of the world. To the public everywhere, this was the hour of triumph for American science, climaxing a long series of successes such as radar, the proximity fuse, and other developments. For American scientists, who had urged our military leaders not to drop the A-bomb on inhabited areas, the hour of triumph had come in a harmless test several weeks earlier when the first A-bomb lit up the heavens above the New Mexico desert. Be that as it may, the end of World War II saw the United States in a position of world leadership and American science the mighty bastion of a victorious and powerful nation.

Twelve years later the U.S.S.R. hurled its first Sputnik into outer space. Within a month, a second and larger Sputnik was fired. From a state of devastation and inferiority in 1945, the Russians had forged ahead of us in the very important field of missiles. This is an extraordinary development and the fact that it is not suprising to some of us scientists does not make it any less remarkable or challenging.

Why the Change?

What has happened during the short span of twelve years? How have the Russians made such rapid progress? The first point is that the Russians are determined to outstrip the United States in science and in all the arts of peace and war which are based on modern scientific developments. When my colleagues and I toured the nuclear research laboratories in the U.S.S.R. in May 1956, we noted the same personal dedication to the task at hand, the same emphasis on speed rather than cost, the same unlimited financial support for facilities and equipment which we ourselves had known at Los Alamos during World War II.

[3] From article by R. E. Marshak, chairman of the Department of Physics and Astronomy, University of Rochester, New York. *Bulletin of the Atomic Scientists.* 14:83-6. February 1958. Reprinted by permission.

It was clear that scientific research in the Soviet Union was being pursued with an urgency which was reminiscent of a wartime operation and that the objective was to overtake American science in its great diversity, its high quality, and its magnificent sweep. If this great sense of urgency prevails in such basic research fields as high energy nuclear physics, with which I am connected, how much more intense must be the crash programs in the atomic weapon and missile laboratories?

Lavish provision for new up-to-date laboratories and the most modern experimental equipment is essential but it will not guarantee scientific research of high quality. It is also necessary to attract talented persons into the fields of science and engineering, to insist on high educational standards, and to inculcate the proper attitudes toward basic research.

The U.S.S.R. is certainly sparing no effort to induce the most talented youngsters to prepare for scientific and engineering careers. The stipend of a Russian university student equals the salary of a worker. All students who show talent in the sciences are encouraged to receive more advanced training. Those who become professional scientists are handsomely rewarded both with material benefits and status in the community. As a result of such a policy, Soviet scientists form an elite whose scale of living stands in extreme contrast to the still low living standards of the general populace. It is therefore not surprising that of the 16,000 students at Moscow State University, 2,000 are majoring in physics. It is also not surprising that in the five-year period from 1951 to 1956, for which statistics are available, the number of graduate students in physics has tripled. This is in contrast to the United States where the number has remained stationary. It is probable that the number of doctoral candidates in physics is now greater in the Soviet Union than in the United States.

Quality as Well as Quantity

Granted that the Soviet Union is turning out large numbers of scientists and engineers, how good are they? The answer is that their quality is generally high and, in certain fields, superior to the United States. The Soviet Union has developed an educational and technical training system which maintains high standards. It must be realized, of course, that the strong emphasis on science and mathematics in Soviet education and the strictness of the high school curriculum are not Russian innovations. In most European, as well as non-European, countries the high-school curriculum is equally exacting. We Americans must realize that our schools are departures from the norm and differ from those throughout the rest of the world. Somewhere along the line, the American people were persuaded that a system of free and universal education can only be implemented by a lowering of academic standards, by hiring some teachers who have a superficial knowledge of the subject matter which they are supposed to teach, by allowing students to eliminate science and mathematics from their curriculum, and by permitting the parents to interfere with the development of special programs for talented children.

There has always been a strong engineering tradition in Russia and at the present time, in some areas, the educational standards in engineering are higher than in the United States. For example, the average Russian electrical engineer takes more mathematics and basic physics in his curriculum than his American counterpart, and as a result appears to be more independent, creative, and critical than the average American electrical engineer. Moreover, these highly talented engineers receive higher salaries and enjoy more prestige in laboratories where basic research is carried on than in industrial laboratories. In my own field, physicists must design and construct the large cyclotrons, synchrotrons, and other types of high energy accelerators because engineers with the necessary training do not exist or, if they do exist, they are employed in more lucrative industrial positions. Is it then surprising that Russian engineers have constructed the largest accelerator in the world, and that they have achieved the technological breakthrough in the missile field?

Science Mobilized

It is evident therefore that the Soviet Union is not only providing new up-to-date laboratories and the most modern experimental equipment for its scientists and engineers. It is also insisting on high educational standards and, by multitudinous devices, attracting persons of the highest intellectual caliber into the scientific and engineering fields. Superimposed on this is a political dictatorship which is intent on rapid industrialization of the country and on the development of a modern technology which is superior to that of the United States. This mobilization of scientists and engineers achieves results in the absence of political freedom and, under Stalin's regime, even in the absence of scientific freedom.

In Stalinist Russia, technological advance was extremely rapid for at least two reasons. The first reason is that large technological developments depend almost as much on organization and mobilization of resources as on the application of scientific brainpower. Stalin did not allow himself to be disturbed by interservice rivalries, by conflicting claims of industrial and government laboratories, nor by division of authority at the highest government level. The second reason is that sciences like physics, mathematics, and chemistry which are at the basis of modern technological development, were allowed some freedom, even by Stalin. The biological sciences and, even more, the social sciences were badly damaged by the Communist party line imposed by Stalin. However, the natural sciences, which include mathematics and physics, while not completely immune to political pressures under the Stalin regime, enjoyed some measure of intellectual freedom. . . .

Importance of Freedom

And now we come to the crucial point. Basic research in science cannot flourish without full scientific freedom. Scientific freedom implies that the scientist is free to choose the subject matter of his own research and is not compelled to work on problems in which he has no interest. Scientific freedom means that the scientist can draw the conclusions to which his investigations lead without subjecting them to the requirements of some nonscientific authority. Scientific freedom requires openness of communication, through books, periodicals, and personal contacts. Now the interesting thing, and in many ways I consider this the most challenging of all the developments which have taken place, is that scientific freedom has essentially been reestablished in the Soviet Union since Stalin's death.

We obtained direct evidence for a marked improvement in the scientific climate in the Soviet Union during the course of our visit last year. The first and obvious change was that all scientists formerly in disgrace or under arrest had been rehabilitated and that all the brilliant scientists who had been in trouble had been returned to positions of leadership. The second change was that the rigid mobilization of Russian scientists to work on war projects had apparently been discontinued. We were told that since 1954 Soviet physicists were no longer required to work on radar, rockets, or nuclear weapons, and it was evident that many of the luminaries in Russian physics were working on the basic problems at the frontiers of our science. It was also evident from our discussions with the Russian physicists that not even lip service was being paid any longer to the role of dialectical materialism in the development of modern physics. Finally, insofar as openness of communication is concerned, it was clear that a very liberal policy of declassification of basic research had been adopted, that the usual exchange of scientific and technical information with foreign scientists was allowed, and that freedom of scientific criticism was regarded as a virtue. Indeed, we were amazed at the vigorous and uninhibited discussions which took place at the Moscow Conference which we attended where young Russian physicists did not hesitate to call to task distinguished academics if points of difference arose.

On the basis of our visit to the Soviet Union and of our personal and scientific contacts with Russian physicists since that visit, it seems safe to assert that Russian physics is now almost as free as American physics. This newly established scientific freedom is not to be confused with political freedom which is still essentially nonexistent. . . .

A New Challenge

It is this fundamental change in the scientific climate in the Soviet Union which is the most challenging aspect of the entire situation. Suddenly to be given the moral and spiritual conditions for independent and creative research has filled Russian scientists with optimism and self-confidence for the future. It is the combination of his post-Stalin reemergence of scientific freedom plus the continuation of strong financial support for scientists and engineers, their laboratories, and their education which constitutes the nature of the Soviet scientific challenge. In the absence of scientific freedom, it is possible to bring to a successful conclusion a Sputnik or an A-bomb project provided a sufficient effort is made and the raw materials, the industry, and a corps of well-qualified scientists and engineers are in existence. It is much more difficult to make the basic scientific discoveries which underlie these applied science and engineering developments. Basic research is a much more delicate flower and can only flourish under proper conditions of light, air, and absence of external compulsion. In the long run, applied science and engineering will become repetitious and second-rate if they are not vitalized by the new discoveries of basic science. We have clear evidence that the Soviet government now understands that genuine scientific progress demands scientific freedom.

How are we to meet this Soviet scientific challenge within the context of our American democratic society? There would be little point in exerting ourselves if the Russian challenge could only be met by surrendering our democratic values and adopting the totalitarian way. I believe that the massive Russian challenge can be met in our own American way, but before suggesting concrete remedial measures, it is necessary to make a frank appraisal of the scientific picture in our country at the present time. The picture is far from black. One measure of the strength of basic science in a country is the number of Nobel prizes awarded to scientists in that country. Since World War II, American scientists (including those who have taken up American residence) have won 17 Nobel prizes whereas the Russians have won 1. It would be wrong to deduce from these figures that American basic science is 17 times as strong as Russia's, since the gap is narrowing so rapidly. However, neither is it justified to suddenly acquire an inferiority complex as a result of Sputnik and to assert that Russian basic science has surpassed ours on an over-all basis. [For additional comment see "U.S. Education: An Indictment" in Section I, above.]

The American lead in basic science, precarious as it has become, has been due to a long tradition of scientific freedom in this country as part and parcel of our democratic heritage. There have been occasional lapses like Secretary of Commerce Weeks' dismissal of Dr. Astin, Director of the National Bureau of Standards, for his adverse scientific recommendations on battery additives; and former Secretary of Health, Education and Welfare Hobby's withdrawal of funds from medical researchers in whose files some derogatory information was found. And, of course, there was the brief but terribly disturbing era of mistrust when the Oppenheimer case was a *cause célèbre* and the late Senators McCarthy and McCarran rode roughshod over scientists and intellectual "eggheads" in general. But, by and large, the American scientist has been free for a long time, except during war emergencies, to choose the subject of his own research and to publish his results without approval by a nonscientific authority.

Material Support Necessary

Indispensable as is scientific freedom for the development of a healthy science, basic research will not prosper in the present day and age without powerful material support for laboratories and equipment, without the existence of an educational system of top quality, without the willingness of highly talented persons to engage in the pursuit and creation of basic science, and without the proper appreciation by the public of the value of science. The first obvious weakness which has developed in this country is that the financial and prestige incentives are not such as to persuade the scientist or engineer to remain at the university where most of the basic research is done and where all the training of new scientists and engineers takes place. Increasing numbers of scientists and engineers are leaving their university posts to accept more lucrative positions in industry.

Another weakness which has developed is that while the quality of scientific training in our graduate schools is high, the same cannot be said of the training of our engineers nor scientific training in our high schools and colleges. A third weakness is that many of our universities do not have sufficient funds to provide the new up-to-date laboratories and the latest equipment which are needed for modern scientific training and research. Many colleges and universities are now faced with the problem of inadequate laboratory facilities to train the additional science and engineering students. A fourth weakness is that many young people with the necessary talents do not embark on scientific and engineering careers for financial or other reasons, because the American public is not sufficiently well informed on the importance of science and engineering for the national welfare and security. At least one third of the upper quarter of the students graduating from high school do not go on to college, and many of these are certainly potential scientists and engineers.

A fifth weakness is that government laboratories, where certain coordinated research projects must be carried out, are in a poor competitive position with respect to industry in terms of attracting scientific manpower. The rigid Civil Service System prevents most government laboratories from recruiting the top scientific talent which they need to head up their research projects. A sixth weakness is that in many instances American industry is not fully utilizing its scientific and engineering manpower. Russia is training five times as many engineering aides, laboratory assistants, junior draftsmen, and designers as we are in the United States, and until more of these men are available, we can hardly blame a company for relegating a highly trained engineer to the role of a draftsman. And, last but not least, sufficient funds are simply not being provided for basic research in the sciences and engineering. I have personally served on national advisory committees during the past year which have approved excellent plans for research which are being held up for lack of funds.

What Can We Do?

It is clear that the weaknesses which have developed in the scientific and technological picture within the United States are so formidable that all levels of government, industry, education, and the general citizenry will have to undertake a coordinated and sustained effort in order to correct the situation. It will be necessary to raise the salaries of the science and engineering professors so that they will stay at the universities. It will be necessary to train better teachers of mathematics and science and to keep these teachers in the high schools and in the colleges by financial and other inducements. It will be necessary to re-examine and strengthen our scientific and engineering curricula and to provide special training and opportunities for the young people who are talented in mathematics and science. It will be necessary to provide funds to colleges and universities so that they may enlarge and improve scientific and engineering facilities in the form of buildings, laboratories, and equipment. It will be necessary to provide large numbers of scholarships for science and engineering students on the undergraduate and to a lesser extent on the graduate level so that all young people who desire, and are qualified, to embark on scientific and engineering careers, may do so. It will be necessary to set up more government laboratories on the pattern of the Los Alamos Scientific Laboratory (which is run by the Atomic Energy Commission through a contract with the University of California), so that Civil Service regulations will not interfere with the recruitment of the necessary scientific personnel.

It will be necessary to set up a reasonable number of technical institutes (in the form of junior colleges or through other mechanisms) which will train the many students with science aptitudes who, for one reason or another, either do not wish or are unable to undertake a four-year curriculum. This additional technical manpower will release a sizable number of more highly trained scientists and engineers for more responsible positions. And finally it will be absolutely essential to provide the increasingly large sums of money which are required to carry on basic research in the sciences and engineering. This means at least doubling the annual operational budget for basic research in science and engineering. In addition, capital expenditures must be made for some rather large facilities in science and engineering such as high energy accelerators, astronomical observatories, computational laboratories, specialized engineering laboratories, and so on.

But apart from the measures which must be taken in order to maintain our scientific and technological supremacy over the Soviet Union, we must realize that there are bigger issues at stake. Scientific supremacy or even the maintenance of substantial scientific equality is only a means to an end. It will not secure the peace, guarantee the survival of our democratic institutions, nor assure our moral leadership of the world. Wise political, economic, and human decisions will still be required to achieve these desired goals. And so let us get on with the task at hand. The early American pioneer had a sense of high adventure, but he was of a practical bent. Let us inculcate in our people a new pioneering spirit, a sense of novel and exciting intellectual domains to conquer, and we shall not have to fear for our scientific, cultural, or political leadership. It is only by rededicating ourselves to the values of the mind and spirit that we shall be equipped to achieve our true national destiny.

ARE SOVIET SCHOOLS BETTER THAN OURS? [4]

Like so many facets of Soviet society, educational policy has followed a series of spasmodic oscillations between unbending dogma and frantic improvisation.

Just after the Revolution it was all dogma. The traditional concepts were stigmatized as bourgeois and enthusiastically thrown out. Along with the gilded epaulets of army officers, Victorian architecture, conventional literary forms, and the old family structure, out went the rigid curricula of the Russian schools, the classical *gimnazia* and even the *realnoye uchilishche* [non-classical schools], despite the latter's emphasis on science.

So broke the first emancipatory wave, carrying off, amidst the flotsam of czarism, the compulsory hours of mathematics and Latin, of physics and religion, of Russian grammar and modern languages, carrying them off wholesale along with the bourgeois

[4] From article by Andrew R. MacAndrew, student and reporter on Russia. *The Reporter*. 18:10-14. February 20, 1958. Reprinted by permission.

idea of discipline and the school uniforms made of stiff cloth with brass-buckled belts and military-style caps.

The experiment in "proletarian" education meant complete permissiveness, an absolute trust in the spontaneous blooming of the individual in a free society. All formal scholarship, which was thought to perpetuate class distinctions, was to be replaced by the Marxian concept of "polytechnicism," which condemns all theoretical learning unless accompanied by practical working experience.

But what was not left to spontaneity was the acceptance, by both students and teachers, of the regime's current political dogmas. This led to the characteristic duality that to this day is found in almost every Soviet institution: the division of power between the executive head and the party representative.

Just as in every Red Army unit authority is divided between the commanding officer and the political commissar (the center of gravity shifting from one to the other according to the national state of political balance), so in every classroom the teacher has to share his authority with the chairman of the Komsomol (Young Communist League) or the Young Pioneers (the organization for children nine to fourteen).

Theoretically, the role of the Komsomols is to watch over the individual's behavior in that particular unit of the Soviet structure which is the classroom. Naturally, the organization and its young officers have great influence: they can praise or reprimand a fellow student publicly, at class meetings or via the school wall newspaper, and they have the power, among other things, to allow or bar his participation in an extracurricular activity.

During the 1920's and into the early 1930's, academic teaching was reduced to a mere trickle and the Komsomols behaved like schoolroom vigilantes. The easiest and often the only way for a student, and even a teacher, to get by was to play along with them. Teachers often ended by surrendering all their privileges, including the right to grade according to standards other than those of the Komsomols. The diplomas obtained in that epoch are still looked upon with suspicion.

Meanwhile, the entire country was shivering and hungry in the aftermath of the Revolution, through reconstruction and on into the industrialization, electrification, and collectivization of the first Five-Year Plan. As the demand increased for literate officials and technicians, it became apparent that the polytechnically trained students, who had been spending their school time working at anything from lab experiments to ditch digging, had not picked up enough fundamentals to be of much use even on the lower levels of responsibility. Loyalty to the regime was not enough. An emergency was proclaimed. To cope with the emergency, a new "polytechnical" phase was introduced, which became, in fact, monotechnical. Soviet education was narrowed down to mere vocational training under the slogan "The school is nothing but a branch of the factory." Life itself was declared to be the best school, and no less an authority than Shulgin, the director of the Marx-Engels Institute of Pedagogy, prophesied that the school as such would eventually "wither away." Everything was about to wither away in those days, from the state on down.

Soon, of course, this system too was found wanting. It could produce nothing beyond low-grade specialists, so one-sided that they could not even be transferred to an understaffed production line slightly different from their own. Moreover, they were still illiterate. Lenin himself had once admitted that there was something to be said for bourgeois schooling, some parts of which should be adopted, as he put it, "to beat the bourgeois with his own stick." It was the usual Soviet habit of allowing temporary requirements to smother those of Marxist dogma.

As the years went by, more and more "bourgeois" subjects found their way back into the schools. Between 1931 and 1934 a series of government decrees and party resolutions introduced compulsory school curricula, timetables, achievement tests, and a grading system that did give a measure of achievement. All this made the Soviet school very much what it is today. . . .

Some of . . . [the] spirit [of today's Soviet education] can certainly be found in the Russian Republic Ministry of Education's guides to the teacher for the current school year. For each subject, a booklet of about fifty pages details how much ground has to be covered in what time and what should be taught before or after what. But this does not convey an idea of totalitarianism, nor is there anything necessarily undemocratic in such thoroughness. The reason for all these minute directions seems not to be interference with the freedom of the teacher but, as is explicitly stated, to coordinate the acquisition of knowledge, especially in interrelated branches. In the math teacher's guide, for instance, he is constantly reminded that by such and such a date he must have explained such and such a particular point of geometry to his pupils, who will otherwise be quite unable to grasp certain aspects of optics upon which his physics colleague is about to embark. . . .

The position of the present Soviet educational authorities is that the study of various subjects should be properly coordinated and that the delicate matter of determining the amount of fundamental general knowledge a student should have before he specializes cannot be left to the whims of immature youngsters. Although this stand may be debatable, there may also be some discussion about how an extremely elective system in which one is allowed to study optics without geometry, electricity without trigonometry, and journalism without spelling can be either effective or necessary for the maintenance of a democratic form of government.

The adherence to a prescribed, coordinated curriculum is by no means a Soviet monopoly. Such countries as France and Sweden, for example, seem to be in agreement with the principle. Indeed, many democratic nations have insisted on such practices in their schools longer than the Russians have.

The Ideological Spectrum

Nevertheless, there is one trait in the Soviet educational system that is unique. After reading the whole set of Soviet guides for teachers (about four hundred pages), one discovers that under the dulling uniformity of Soviet pedagogical jargon, they are not all quite the same; that some contain more "political message" than others (e.g., there is more in "Literature" than in "Chemistry"); and that, as the message grows louder, the teacher's guide begins to sound like a soapbox oration.

In arranging the books in a sort of spectrum according to their emotional intensity, one finds, as might be expected, the math book at one end and the history book (completely rewritten again last year) at the other.

On the whole, the math teacher is guided very discreetly by such reminders as that the subject matter of the problems "should be given in the context of" that vague activity which is usually translated as "building socialism." The physicist and the chemist are also reminded to set their problems in a properly constructive background and are further told to "emphasize the achievements of our national genius."

But as soon as the subject begins to touch upon living matter, scholarly restraint goes out the window. Even in its programmatic presentation, the biology teacher's guide . . . is an irate diatribe against certain Western ideas.

Moving even farther away from light toward mere heat in the Russian educational spectrum, one comes to literature, which, needless to say, is a very political subject. And although the history syllabus, like the others, is prepared at the Ministry of Education, the history teacher is an exception among his colleagues in that he does not come under the jurisdiction of the ministry but directly under the party central committee.

Now the "political message," which is less likely to affect a more precise science at an elementary level, can still damage it badly at a level where the logical development becomes less cut and dried. . . . The Soviet elementary physics teacher . . . has . . . been luckier than the university physics professor. Until 1952, advanced physicists had to reckon with the official condemnation of Einstein's special theory of relativity as "idealistic and bourgeois," and even today they must exercise discretion toward the implications of quantum mechanics because its reactionary uncertainty principle in the realm of the infinitely small unsettles their indispensable determinism. The secondary-school physics teacher has been spared . . . [that blow]; it came at too high an altitude to affect him. Of course, no one can tell where the next blow will come. This phase of the Soviet educational approach is indeed an outgrowth of totalitarianism: an attempt to prevent teacher and student from freely seeking their own interpretation of the facts; a bullying insistence by the state on its ready-made interpretation.

At the age of seventeen or eighteen, those who have completed ten grades of this coordinated but dogmatic schooling are ready for the state-controlled assessment of their achievements. This consists of three written and four oral tests, after which, if successful, the students will receive a sort of state-sanctioned intellectual coming of age, the "maturity certificate." Perhaps a look at some of the questions that were asked last summer may help in assessing the academic standards of Soviet secondary education as a whole.

The first written test the candidates had to pass satisfactorily in order to take the next involved writing a composition on a selected theme. They could be eliminated by bad spelling, poor grammar, or an improper application of the "socialist-realistic" critical approach. If they avoided all these pitfalls, the students then faced two more written tests, geometry and trigonometry, before reaching the oral examinations. In both fields, they were asked to establish formulas or demonstrate a theorem and to solve a problem. In geometry, they had studied as far as polyhedrons and solids of revolution, and in trigonometry as far as oblique-angled triangles and inverse trigonometric functions. Then, if still successful, they had to answer more questions on Russian literature, and others in algebra, physics, and chemistry.

An average American high-school graduate trying to cope with the Soviet tests would almost certainly be helpless. But a French boy of the same age who had prepared for his *bachot* [academic diploma] in a *lycée* (no tuition fees for the last twenty years) would have been quite agreeably surprised if his math tests were on the Soviet level. Furthermore the French student undergoes a test in physics, in two languages (ancient or modern), and writes a dissertation that, like the Russian, would eliminate him altogether if he was unable to spell. On top of all this, the French student takes orals in all these subjects as well as in biology, geography, and history. In the case of history, for the last couple of years the Soviet boy has been spared both classes and tests in this most fickle of all his subjects.

Of course, if the French candidate had to apply socialist-realist criticism to Victor Hugo the way his Soviet counterpart applies it to Pushkin, he would surely flunk.

Assuming that the Soviet "maturity certificate" is proof that the bearer has an acceptable command of general knowledge, the next question is, What proportion of those who enter the ten-year schools actually reach that cultural plateau?

Statisticians call this ratio the "success rate," and we find that in the early 1950's, when the Soviet school system hit its academic peak, the diploma was won by only forty-nine tenth-graders out of every thousand students who had started in the first grade. Since then, however, with the yearly lightening of the program, the success rate has increased to about 125 per thousand, far ahead of that in countries like France, Germany, Italy, Sweden, and Denmark.

The only schools in the world that top the Soviets in success rate are those of the United States, and the two giants have left the other competitors far behind in the dust. This would seem to indicate at least one important similarity between the American and the Russian systems. Both are attempts at mass education, in which the emphasis tends to be placed on the "mass" rather than on the "education." Whether this is done by easy aids to learning or by the hard Soviet way of learning by rote, the result, good or bad for the child, is certain to keep the success rate high.

High as the Soviet success rate may be, the picture of a country in which almost everyone ends up with a solid educational grounding is somewhat exaggerated. We know now that out of every thousand children entering the Soviet first grade, 875 will at some point fall by the wayside. But the actual proportion of educational have-nots is even greater than this figure indicates.

The fact that the Soviet government plans to have enough ten-year schools available to accommodate all its schoolchildren by 1960 is an admission that there are not enough of them today. . . .

While the Soviets were the first to send up satellites, and although they have first-class scientists like Fock, Kapitsa, Tamm, and Blagonravov, it is far from certain that these distinctions reflect the general level of their secondary education. After all, not so long ago the United States enjoyed an undisputed lead in technology as symbolized by the first nuclear bombs, and American education then was just about what it is today.

Of course it may be argued that whereas most of the American technological lead in nuclear weapons didn't have much to do with U.S. education—Einstein, Fermi, and so many others being foreign-trained—the Soviet scientists, with a few exceptions like Kapitsa, were trained wholly in Russia, and thus may indeed reflect the excellence of the Soviet schools. But the quality of today's Soviet secondary education could hardly have affected any of today's outstanding Soviet scientists. The older ones must have attended the pre-Revolutionary schools, and most of the rest belong to the generation that was subjected to the worst excesses of polytechnicism. There seem to be no hard and fast rules about the way in which superior talent flourishes.

The Russians' scientific success may owe less to the excellence of their education than to their efficiency in processing and distributing all available scientific data from all over the world. And if one or two particular institutions of Soviet society are to be given most of the credit, it should go not to the secondary schools but to the universities and to the impressive chain of research institutes that are more and more becoming sanctuaries from narrow dogmatism for a new intellectual elite.

Be that as it may, on January 16, 1958, *Pravda* announced proudly in its front-page editorial that Marion B. Folsom, the U.S. Secretary of Health, Education and Welfare, "had to admit that the Soviet schools had outstripped those of the United States in scientific education." *Pravda* went on to urge Soviet teachers to "struggle harder for the revelation of the whole beauty of the Communist idea to the new generation."

If we restrict ourselves to scientific education, Secretary Folsom's alleged evaluation is probably accurate. The Soviet schools, although they are not streamlined education plants mass-producing future scientists and technicians, do have a better science curriculum than that of U.S. public schools. But France, Germany, Italy, and Denmark have even better ones. So if a model is needed, why choose the Soviets? Because of the Sputniks? Why not choose Denmark because of Niels Bohr?

EDUCATION IN BRITAIN [5]

Every boy or girl in Britain must by law attend school (or receive efficient education in some other way) from the age of five up to the age of fifteen. A small proportion of children start school at two, three or four in a nursery school or class. About 7 out of 10 leave school at fifteen, others stay on till sixteen, seventeen, eighteen or nineteen. The number staying beyond the minimum leaving age is increasing. The usual age of entry to the universities is eighteen or nineteen and the length of course for a first degree is three or four years.

Responsibility for providing school education and further education outside the universities is shared by the central department (Ministry of Education, Scottish Education Department, or Ministry of Education for Northern Ireland) and local education authorities. The universities are self-governing institutions, although nearly three quarters of their income now comes from public funds. . . .

More than 90 per cent of children attend schools that are maintained by the local education authorities out of public money. Education in these schools is free. In England and Wales some of the schools maintained by local education authorities are provided by them—these are called county schools; the others, called voluntary schools, are provided by voluntary bodies, usually a church or religious denomination. County schools outnumber voluntary schools. In addition some schools (mostly grammar schools) not financed by local education authorities receive direct grants-in-aid from the Ministry of Education; they charge fees but must provide a proportion of free places.

[5] From articles in *Fact Sheets on Britain.* "Education in Britain." April 1958. p 1-2; "Universities in Britain." July 1956. p 1-2. British Information Services. 45 Rockefeller Plaza. New York 20. Reprinted by permission.

Independent schools must be registered and are subject to official inspection. Fees are charged in these schools but, in many, some scholarships and free places are available, either from endowments or, through the local education authorities, from public funds.

The schools maintained by the local education authorities are divided into primary schools or departments for children up to eleven (twelve in Scotland) and secondary schools for older boys and girls. In Scotland, boys and girls are taught together in almost all schools; in England and Wales this is usual in the primary schools but boys and girls more often than not attend separate secondary schools. Secondary schools are of different kinds: in England and Wales there are grammar schools for boys and girls who hope to go on to a university or to enter a profession, or whose abilities would fit them to do so; there are secondary modern schools for a larger proportion of children; and technical schools for a smaller number. In the technical schools, there is greater emphasis on practical and commercial subjects. Some schools provide more than one kind of secondary education and in some areas there are comprehensive schools providing all types of secondary education. Each local education authority plans its own schools, subject to the Minister's approval, and arranges how the children shall be allocated between them. In Scotland, there are two main types of secondary school, the junior secondary school providing a three-year course and the senior secondary school with five- or six-year courses.

"Public" Schools

The largest and most important of the independent schools are known in England as "public" schools, although some schools classed as public schools are not independent (most of these are direct-grant schools) and public schools form only a minority of all independent schools. The public school has made a notable contribution to English education. Many public schools date from the sixteenth century, some are older (e.g., Winchester, 1382, and Eton, 1440). All are controlled by their own boards of governors. Public schools have emphasized the importance of character-building, and in these schools were developed the prefect system, whereby day-to-day discipline is largely maintained by the pupils themselves, and the house system, whereby a school is divided into groups of about 50, each under the care of a housemaster. The public school is also characterized by a high staffing ratio and a high proportion of pupils doing advanced work. A public school is often, although not necessarily, a boarding school. The usual age of entry to the independent public schools for boys is thirteen and the leaving age about eighteen. There are some girls' public schools modeled to a certain extent on those for boys. . . .

Teachers

Teachers are not employed by the central government but by the local education authority or the management of the school. They are not in general bound by official instructions as to syllabuses, textbooks or methods. There are some 150 teachers' training colleges in England and Wales giving a training usually lasting two years to students aged eighteen or over, and twenty-three university education departments providing a one-year course for graduates. The two-year course will be superseded by a three-year course in September 1960. In Scotland courses normally last one year for graduates and three years for non-graduates. In Northern Ireland also the basic course in the general training colleges lasts three years. The Education Departments, the universities, local education authorities and other bodies provide a variety of short courses for practicing teachers.

Teachers from schools in the United Kingdom go to a number of overseas countries each year under interchange schemes or schemes for temporary overseas posts.

Further Education

Increasing numbers of young workers are being released by their employers on one or two days or half-days each week to take classes in trade subjects or general educational subjects. All local authorities and some other bodies provide technical colleges which offer full-time and part-time courses, some of university degree standard. Some, such as colleges of art, are specialized institutions, others are polytechnics. Fees at grant-aided establishments are moderate and many students pay no fees, for all local education authorities grant scholarships to qualified students.

Evening classes are organized by the universities, local education authorities and voluntary bodies, notably the Workers' Educational Association, and are aided by government grants. Almost any subject can be studied in these classes, whether it be academic, cultural or practical, and vocational or non-vocational. Six grant-aided residential colleges provide one-year courses for adult students, and, since the second world war, more than twenty residential colleges have been established where adult students can take short courses lasting from a few days to a few weeks.

Technical Education

The British system of technical education is very flexible. A boy leaving school at fifteen, by part-time study at a technical college and practical experience in industry, can achieve professional qualifications in technology from the age of twenty-five. Alternatively, a would-be technologist may go from school to university, or he may take a full-time course at a technical college. Technical colleges, in cooperation with industry, provide courses at craftsman level, at intermediate or technician level, as well as at advanced level. One form of advanced course is the sandwich course which lasts four or five years and involves alternate periods, usually of three to six months, of education in a technical college and training in industry A big expansion of technical education is in progress.

Universities in Britain

There are sixteen universities in England and Wales, four in Scotland and one in Northern Ireland. Oxford and Cambridge, unlike most of the other universities, are mainly residential. London, the largest university in Britain, also has separate colleges, as has Durham. The other English universities are Birmingham, Bristol, Exeter, Hull, Leeds, Liverpool, Manchester, Nottingham, Reading, Sheffield and Southampton. There are also smaller university colleges at Leicester and North Staffordshire. The University of Wales consists of the university colleges of Cardiff, Aberystwyth, Swansea and Bangor and the Welsh National School of Medicine. Scotland has its four ancient universities of St. Andrews (which includes Queen's College, Dundee), Glasgow, Aberdeen and Edinburgh. Northern Ireland's university is Queen's University, Belfast. The present number of full-time students in all these institutions is about 84,000, of whom over 4,000 come from Commonwealth countries overseas and nearly another 4,000 from foreign countries.

Over two thirds of university income is now provided by the national Exchequer, but the universities have always been independent of State control. . . .

Government financial aid is in the form of direct grants from the Treasury on the advice of the University Grants Committee, a committee of individuals with experience of university administration and education, appointed by the Chancellor of the Exchequer. In 1939 the Treasury grant was a little over £2 million; in 1956-1957 the total grant-in-aid for universities in Great Britain comes to £34.5 million, including £7.2 million for nonrecurring grants for development.

Admission to the universities is by examination and selection; there is no religious test and no color bar. Women are admitted on equal terms with men, but at Oxford and Cambridge their numbers are limited by statute.

All universities in Britain limit the number of undergraduates which they will accept; and in spite of the increase in these limits which has taken place since the end of the Second World War, the demand for places continues to be very keen and many candidates are unable to gain entrance to the university of their first choice.

Nearly three quarters of the full-time university students in the United Kingdom are aided by scholarships or other awards of which a large number are granted by the State or by local education authorities in addition to those offered by the universities and colleges from their own funds. . . .

Nearly all the universities and colleges have to some extent developed a tutorial system to supplement the mass lecture, particularly for the benefit of their senior students. The individual tuition provided by the Oxford and Cambridge colleges is one of the main reasons why admission to those universities is so eagerly sought after.

Research is one of the main functions of a university. Most members of the academic staffs devote some time to research and at all universities there are postgraduate students engaged in research. There has been an expansion particularly of research and study in science and technology in recent years.

The social life of universities in Britain is characterized by the existence of a large number of students' societies and clubs, which are organized by the undergraduates themselves. Some of these societies have an athletic purpose; others are concerned with topics of professional, religious or cultural interest such as politics, drama, music, modern languages, literature or science. (Political societies in universities in Britain do not take a direct part in national or local politics. They exist only for the study of politics and for the cultivation of the arts of public speaking and debate.) In many universities, there is an all-embracing Students' Council or Union which has the oversight of all these extracurricular activities and which, in addition, provides cheap meals, common rooms, reading rooms, libraries, games rooms and a hall where dances, debates, concerts and lectures may be held for members and their friends. Universities in which such unions exist recognize their position and frequently provide them with premises for their activities.

CHANGES IN EUROPE'S SECONDARY SCHOOLS [6]

Educators from twenty-six European and Mediterranean countries agreed at a two-weeks conference . . . concluded

[6] From "European Educators Discuss Secondary School Revolution," UNESCO press release. United Nations. New York. April 23, 1958. p 1-3.

Saturday, April 19 [1958] at Sèvres, France, that the traditional pattern of European secondary education has been disrupted by the pressures of population increase and technical change, and that further modifications of the system are needed.

The conference, organized by the French National Commission for UNESCO in cooperation with the United Nations Educational, Scientific and Cultural Organization, heard papers from leading educators in several countries on all aspects of curriculum problems, and on the purposes and methods of secondary school education.

Summarizing some of the findings in an address to the closing session, Louis François, Secretary General of the French National Commission, reported a consensus of the delegates that the traditional classic study course of European secondary schools should be broadened, and that the exacting comprehensive written and oral examinations should be abolished. Mr. François told the conference in a round-table on examinations:

> We have come to an almost catastrophic situation in France. During the *baccalauréat* examination in June parents, grandparents, great-grandparents and children all go into a fever. It's worse than a national election. The number of students sitting for the *baccalauréat* has trebled in ten years. Subjects are crammed, and then forgotten three weeks later. What we need is an examination system that takes into account the aptitudes and ability of the student to solve problems, not the testing of encyclopedic knowledge. (The *baccalauréat* degree is an oral and written examination which French students take at the end of the *lycée,* or classical high school.)

Soviet delegates said that the U.S.S.R. has gone far to eliminate the tension and exhaustiveness of final examinations and, between grades, had eliminated year-end examinations, except for one examination between lower and upper school.

Other subjects on which educators were in general agreement, although application differed depending on the country, were:

1. In order to teach students at a time of tremendous increase in specialized knowledge and science, the schools should not attempt to teach a little bit of everything, but should limit

and correlate subject matter so that the students could have a deeper understanding of subjects.

2. All participants were agreed that the goal should be a basic course for all students, up to around fifteen years of age Union in 1960). They said they favored prolonging the ten-of high school, at which time students could specialize to a greater degree.

The Soviet delegates, however, stated that the U.S.S.R. favored a common course for all until the age of seventeen (their present ten-year school course from seven to seventeen years of age will be completely in effect throughout the Soviet Union in 1960). They said they favored prolonging the ten-year school to twelve years, or to nineteen years of age.

3. History courses should be revised to make room for the main currents of thought of Eastern countries, and not to mention them only occasionally in connection with invasions, crusades, trade or colonial ventures. History courses should stress the interdependence economically and culturally, of all nations. In some areas history and geography courses should be revised to introduce material on economics and sociology.

4. All delegates were agreed on the necessity of moral and civic education by the school itself. Ways of providing for this instruction varied among countries. Some, like the Federal Republic of Germany favored civic instruction through activities like childrens' parliaments, others preferred adding a course in civics to the curriculum, while still others like the U.S.S.R. believed that civics should form an integral part of all teaching.

Among the statements made during the course of the conference were these:

Dr. J. A. Lauwerys, Professor of Comparative Education, University of London:

It would be a mistake to give the impression that in Western Europe and in Great Britain the state of education is standing still. The wind of reform, on the contrary, is being very strongly felt. Let us take, for example, the famous institutions known in England as our "Public Schools." In the nineteenth century, they were supposed to form the social and political elite, who were to rule England and the Empire. Technical knowledge was considered less necessary than the quality of character. Essential characteristics were will power, determination, energy, loyalty, an effortless assumption of superiority . . . tough-minded courtesy . . . and fair play. These qualities were acquired on the playing-field and in the chapel just as much as in the classroom. But today, the Public Schools rely more and more on the teaching of organized knowledge by specialists. Success in a university today is much more important than success on a playing-field, at a time when knowledge of the interior structure of the atom counts more than a good physique or a charming manner.

Roger Gal, educator and adviser to the French Ministry of Education:

In some countries, there is a tendency merely to add new subjects or new branches of education to the existing curriculum. In other countries, notably Sweden and the U.S.S.R. traditional types of education have been scrapped and a completely new approach attempted. Still other countries, like France and Italy, are in an in-between stage. . . . One of the difficulties in French education at present is that the small percentage of students who are trained in the *lycée* (French high school) form an elite who are extremely adroit at verbalizing, but not equipped for action. . . . The ideal falls somewhere between the U.S. system and the present French system. We do not wish to destroy what is worth while in our culture; but on the other hand, I hope that the pendulum in American education does not swing back too hard towards traditionalism."

Eugen Loffler [of] Stuttgart, Federal Republic of Germany, said that students of *Gymnasia* (German high schools) are complaining that the work-load is becoming too heavy. Compulsory courses in the *Gymnasium* include: religious teaching, German history, geography, civics, at least two foreign languages, mathematics, science (physics, chemistry and biology), fine arts, music, physical culture, and for girls, sewing.

If we add to this the numerous extraneous distractions which occupy the child mentally, morally and physically, we are faced with the problem of overloading, deplored by teachers, parents and children. To remedy this situation, we have tried to sift the curriculum, accenting only the essential elements, and reducing or even eliminating traditional matter, while introducing modern teaching methods. We have also increased the number of optional courses.

[Mr.] E. I. Monoszon, corresponding member of the Soviet Academy of Pedagogy, said that heavy scholastic schedules are also characteristic of Soviet schools. The basic aim of the secondary school system in the Soviet Union is to give children both general and technical education, and to assure their harmonious development as future builders of Soviet society. Besides close attention to the social, physical and esthetic development of the child, courses like physics and chemistry are essential to the training of technicians. The relationship between schools and practicing scientists and technicians is very close, and meetings are constantly being held to keep the scientific and technical curriculum up to date. Adoption of such innovations as automation and electronics by Soviet industry requires a constant renewal of technical material taught in schools.

LATE REFORMS IN RUSSIA [7]

Soviet educational authorities plan a major revision of the school system to spur practical education in industry and specialization in science.

Nikolai K. Goncharov, vice president of the Academy of Pedagogic Science of the Russian Republic, outlined the proposed reforms of the educational pattern in a program on the Moscow radio [on May 18, 1958].

The plan reflects ideas voiced recently by Premier Nikita S. Khrushchev for greater attention to practical experience in education and for removing class distinctions between educated citizens and workers.

The new system would provide for eight years of formal schooling. For most students this would be followed by three or four years of further study and work in big industrial enterprises and collective farms. Others would spend the three or four years of further education specializing in physics, mathematics, natural science or humanities.

At present, Soviet students in cities spend ten years at school, while in rural areas they attend elementary schools for seven years.

Mr. Goncharov said the plan still was only in the draft stage and must be discussed by "millions of teachers, trade unionists

[7] From "Moscow Outlines School Reforms." New York *Times*. p 6. May 19, 1958. Reprinted by permission.

and Komsomol [young Communist] organizations before any action can be taken to put it into force."

The change is designed to eliminate what Mr. Goncharov called the main shortcoming in education at present—a gap between theory and practice. He said it would also aim at promoting a belief in the dignity of labor among students.

Both these points were made by Mr. Khrushchev in a speech last month to the Communist Youth League Congress. . . .

The Premier criticized agricultural institutes for turning out graduates who were "frightened by cows" when they went to work on farms. He also scored Soviet citizens who consider manual labor "good only for second-grade people." Too many Soviet youths want to get a university education without having worked in factories or on farms, he said.

A BRITISHER'S VIEW [8]

Like most outsiders, I find a great deal to admire and envy (and much to deplore) in American education. Above all, I am impressed by the enormous energy which goes into it, the interest it arouses at all levels and in all sections of the community. By contrast, the British attitude is relatively lukewarm. It is true that many distinguished critics, Dr. R. M. Hutchins among them, would have us believe that America has become rich and powerful not because of its educational system, but in spite of it. I respect, and see the force of, their arguments: nevertheless I believe they are mistaken. The shortcomings and the vices of the Big Business approach to education are only too apparent, but if we ask how it comes about that education in the United States is big business, the answer can only be because it is felt to be everybody's business. Basically, the difference between the one-track system which America favors and the two-track system which prevails in Britain is the difference between

[8] From article by W. Kenneth Richmond, senior lecturer in education, Glasgow University, and author of books on education. *Nation*. 186:411. May 10, 1958. Reprinted by permission.

an education that is provided *by* the people and one that is provided *for* them.

Since 1890, the American high school has been called upon to fulfill a dual function: providing a sound general education for the mass of nonacademic pupils, while at the same time offering courses for the minority (substantial and growing but still a minority) who go on to college or university. It is not surprising, therefore, that in assuming this difficult rôle, the high school has never quite succeeded in allaying the suspicions of either of the two parties concerned—the so-called academic and nonacademic groups. In opening its doors to all comers, in freeing itself of college requirements, in laying on an *à la carte* curriculum, in adopting a points system which purports to treat Laundry as somehow the equivalent of Latin, the school has gone to great lengths—to cater to the meanest as well as the highest intelligence. Even so, the feeling persists that it is still biased towards the college preparatory side.

The record shows that public opinion has been overwhelmingly against any move which sought to make secondary education more selective or to create special provision for the abler students. It may be conceded that in taking this line, public opinion has as often as not been inspired by motives best described as anti-intellectual, and that its influence has not been altogether for the good. Having said this, I still think that the resolute refusal to have anything to do with policies calling for differential treatment has been based on a sound instinct.

Looking back over the past two centuries, it can be shown fairly conclusively that the upward extension of the educational ladder—through the elementary school, thence through the high school and, currently, through to the junior college—has been nothing if not a popular movement. It can be shown, further, that attempts have been made all along the line to discourage this upward extension—and that many of these attempts have originated in the academic camp. Certainly some of the arguments of this outspoken school of thought are not to be ignored.

No one can blink his eyes to the dangers of an education which is half-way to becoming the slave of public relations. No one should cherish the illusion that excess of quantity ever makes up for deficient quality. When it is known that the average American high-school graduate is nearly two years behind his opposite number in the English grammar school (at any rate so far as scholastic attainments are concerned), there is no room for complacency.

But in recognizing that the prosecution has a strong case, Americans will do well to make sure that a new problem of segregation, no less bedeviling than the one the South already has to grapple with, is not smuggled in by the side door. As things are, the existence of a large and growing number of exclusive, fee-paying schools in the United States, whether or not on the model of the English Public School, indicates that the desire of some to be "more equal" than others is as strong in the United States as it is anywhere else. It may well be, then that behind all the complaints about the existing set-up there is the furtive desire to promote an intellectual elite. If so, the move is retrogressive and needs to be checked.

As England interprets it, equality of opportunity can mean only one thing—finding the best brains and seeing to it that they come to the top. The result is a selective system, the sheep being separated from the goats at the tender age of eleven. Solutions of this sort have their advantages, not least in guaranteeing high standards in the professional cadres, but it may be questioned whether they are quite so happy in satisfying the aspirations of the three quarters who fail to make the grade.

It may be a sorry confession, but the truth is that England has never taken kindly to the doctrine of equality, still less to that of fraternity. Yet the fact remains that the social conscience here is uneasy, if not actually dissatisfied, with the present arrangement; and the signs are that, where she is not entirely bound by tradition, a solution in some ways approximating the American one will eventually be arrived at. It would, I believe, be both tragic and ironic if America were so far to forget her own native tradition as to move in the opposite direction.

IS EUROPEAN EDUCATION BETTER? [9]

Having been out of the country for several years, I have been amazed at the criticism American education has been getting in the public press since Sputnik. . . .

Agreed that we Americans want very much to improve our educational system, does this mean that we should turn to European models? "What then is the American, this new Man," who has made the deserts bloom, who has taken the peasantry out of farming, who has removed the drudgery from factories, whose productivity per worker is by far the highest there is, who is surrounded by the world's best existing systems of communication and transportation. Was this progress made by a people with an inferior educational system? If so, inferior to what? To their own ideals perhaps but to little else. . . .

If observations comparing European and American education are to be useful, then it is of first importance to know something of the scope of what is being compared. If we can assume that the end of the sixteenth year is a good point to compare percentages of young people in secondary school, then we find that at that point approximately 70 per cent of the American age group is in school compared with 10 per cent of the age group in England and France. At college age, about 25 per cent of the American age group is attending, compared with 5 to 6 per cent of the European group.

In other words, in the United States, some seven times as many of the age group attend high school and at least five times as many attend college as in Europe. Or, to think of it in another way, we have almost as many students in the national honor societies in our high schools, and in Phi Beta Kappa, Sigma Xi, and Phi Kappa Phi in our colleges as Europe has in its entire student bodies. If comparisons are to be made, perhaps it is only the students in our honor groups who should be compared with the total European group.

[9] From article by Byron S. Hollinshead, former director of the Technical Assistance Department of UNESCO, now with the American Council on Education. *Educational Record.* 39:89-96. April 1958. Reprinted by permission.

But does this larger quantity of American students in attendance have anything to do with quality, you say. May I give three illustrations to show such relationship. Doubtless there are others. One of the reasons for the establishment of consolidated schools in America was that if you could bring more students together, you could give them more by way of equipment and facilities such as laboratories, libraries, gymnasiums, visual aids, and so on.

A first class illustration of better quality where there is quantity is textbooks. Publishers can afford to produce for many a quality book that they cannot produce, at least without prohibitive expense, for a few. Partly for this reason American textbooks are the envy of the world.

A first class illustration of better quality where there is the selection of quality. Intelligence seems to be distributed fairly equally among social groups and one certainly cannot discover it if members of some social groups have little chance to appear. Furthermore, talent is of various kinds and appears at various stages. One cannot decide for life, at the age of eleven, as the English try to do, who has academic talent and who has not. Therefore, opportunities to display talent must be provided at more than one stage of development. Nor is academic talent the only type to be nurtured. Society has an equal stake in providing learning opportunities for those who have, for example, a high degree of social, artistic, or manual intelligence.

Again, as Sir Richard Livingstone has said, we educate people to use their reason and for the less intelligent this should develop the ability to understand why the more intelligent are saying what they are. The training of the second or third echelon of workers and citizens who can understand what their leaders are saying is desperately important in all fields of endeavor if a civilization is to advance. This means quantity. It is precisely this lack in numbers which retards social, economic, and political development in what we call the underdeveloped countries. The leaders are there. It is the trained followers who are lacking.

Let me turn now to another point. In a sense, about all one can compare in different systems of education is the philosophy, because an educational system illustrates the social, political, and cultural ideals of a nation.

The United States system originally had and still has the general objectives (apart from teaching reading, writing, and arithmetic) of uniting a highly diverse population, mostly of European background. In this respect one of its purposes has been to de-Europeanize the new citizens. Another objective was to give a chance to everybody by equalizing educational opportunity. This provided and still provides a mobility within the population by allowing the bright to rise on the economic and social scale. It means that the school is not only providing a shared experience for everybody, but that it also spotlights talent of various kinds which might otherwise never be discovered. . . .

European education, on the other hand, as one is told frankly in Europe, is to train an elite, usually recruited from the higher social ranks, which will govern social, political, and economic life. To some degree its purpose is to maintain the existing class structure rather than to break it up. . . .

In fact, European aims and methods are so different from ours that the question arises of whether it is even appropriate to try to compare systems which have such different purposes. . . .

To me, an American educator away from his country for over five years, there is an unreal quality to these arguments about returning to an earlier of more restricted curriculum. It is somehow as if the twentieth century had failed to exist. The curriculum of the nineteenth century was possible when our percentages in school and college were more like the present European percentages. At that time the secondary school and college group was fairly homogeneous, representing the so-called "cultured few." In contrast, the present group in secondary school and college represents all social levels, all income levels, a great variety of races and creeds, and nearly all ranges of ability and interest. To serve them there must be comprehensive high schools with all sorts of courses designed for all sorts of abilities.

To serve the college group we need almost the same kind of differentiation. We not only need differentiation within colleges but we need also many types of colleges serving many ranges of abilities and interests. Indeed, this is one of the chief things we have learned in the twentieth century. We could not now go back to the constriction of the old single pattern of courses in high school and college even if we wanted to. The social sciences have given us too much useful information about individual differences to permit us to be so stupid.

Also, we do not now accept, in the same way, the idea of the superior discipline of some subjects over others, nor do we believe any more that there is necessarily a transfer of training that makes the study of one subject the best way to learn another subject. We know all sorts of things about youth development that we didn't know in the Victorian Age. Some of it we don't practice very well, to be sure, and there is still much to be learned about the developmental tasks appropriate for each individual and age group, but substantial progress has been made.

Perhaps the best proof of what I have been saying is the intense dissatisfaction Europeans feel about their own systems. There was such an outcry last winter from the French people about their examination system that a committee of inquiry was appointed to suggest changes. The Butler Report for England and the reforms proposed by the Langevin-Wallon Commission in France are further evidences of their desire for change. The Europeans recognize that they will be having our problems as they widen the scope of their education by increasing their numbers. Our task is to preserve our gains in quantity and develop new means to improve quality.

One way to see by magnification the difference between European and American philosophies of education is to observe these differences when applied to underdeveloped countries. The European system is to try to train an elite. The American system is to try to educate as many as possible. The European system offers a highly traditional curriculum to the few who can qualify by examination. The American system starts where the student is and tries to relate his education to his needs and aspirations. In the unfortunate caricatures of both systems which exist in some of the less-developed countries, one system, the

European, seems to lack relevance, and the other, the American, seems to lack clear standards. Certainly no educational transplant is completely successful. An educational system must be indigenous. But the wider scope, greater variety, and plural control of the American system allow it to be adapted more readily to new situations than can the European.

European belief can be summed up in the syllogism of Hutchins that the truth is everywhere the same; education is to propagate truth; therefore education should be everywhere the same. Most Americans do not accept this syllogism. We do not believe that human truth is always and everywhere the same. We believe it varies and changes with time and place. We believe that truth as we know it changes as our knowledge of reality changes. Therefore, we believe, with Russell and Whitehead, in making education relevant to time and place, and we also believe that education has something to do with preparing the student to be able to adjust (horrible word of the critics).

That today's student lives in a time of tremendous change is almost too trite to say. He must be prepared to shift his occupational moorings, sometimes quite quickly. He must find a way to relate his social and political heritage to the social and political here and now. And, again to be trite, he must be prepared to recognize that some of the clichés which were good guides to social, political, and economic behavior in past days may not guide the future equally as well. However imperfect our teaching may have been about the "brave new world," it has been better than having had none at all. Does anyone seriously contend that the almost amazing lack of development of the social sciences in European schools and universities, except the Scandinavian, is a good thing? Do we want life in America to be as static as that in Europe?

Obviously there is no perfect education to prepare the student for 1960 or 1990. But an education which relates to the abilities of the individual, which relates to his personal and special interests, which tries to explain the modern world in relation to its heritage, and which provides a variety of educational institutions controlled in a variety of ways, seems more likely to meet the requirements than one in which a ministry of education hands down a traditional curriculum from a central office. It is not an exaggeration to say that in some European countries the minister of education can tell at a given time of the day exactly on what page of what textbook the student is reading. This may provide a common standard but does it allow the diversity and experimentation upon which progress depends?

Finally, may I say that my years abroad taught me many things about America that I might never otherwise have learned. You recall Kipling's saying, "What do they know of England who only England know." So with Americans. If they would see the greatness of their own country they may need to view it from a distance. When they do, I think they will discover, as I did, that the greatest glory of America is its democratic idea: its belief in the value and possibilities of the individual—every individual. It would be strange if an educational system designed to carry out this idea or ideal did not have defects and difficulties. No nation at any time in earlier history has ever tried to give everybody educational opportunity.

But it is not only that we have tried to follow a great ideal. We can be genuinely proud of what our schools and colleges have accomplished, proud of their present efficiency, variety, and scope, and particularly proud that the professional conscience of our educators has given them the humility to see faults and the desire to correct them. In our criticisms let us remember that such faults as our system may have result from the generous grandeur of an idea unique in the world. Our future does not lie in a retreat to lesser ideals. It lies in the enrichment and invigoration of what is already ours.

IV. TOWARD IMPROVEMENTS

EDITOR'S INTRODUCTION

The ferment occasioned by the great debate on education has, of course, led to many proposals for action. In this section only a few of the outstanding plans are reviewed. Comprehensive coverage would include reference to many more undertakings, especially business or corporate aid to education and aid by the great philanthropic foundations. Both these sources of financial support to education are now significant factors for improvement. The vast structure of education within industry, labor, the military forces and other segments of our economy should also be noted.

Plans for Federal aid to education, both for school construction and through various scholarship plans and further aid to science education constitute the most promising new development. Following the convening of the White House Conferences on education after 1955, Congress has been engaged in determining what aid should be given to education. Support for school construction has, however, never been passed and current bills for scholarship and other aids are only now being considered.

Some of these matters are dealt with below. In the first selection the National Education Association's Policies Commission surveys the whole field, recommending various steps for improvements. The summary proposals of the White House Conferences are noted next, followed by the President's message to Congress on education of January 1958.

A report on Dr. James B. Conant's work in surveying the needs of secondary education, sponsored by the Carnegie Corporation of New York, follows. Information about special programs for advanced high school students is sketched by Mr. S. A. Kendrick. Dr. James R. Killian, Jr., the President's Assistant on Science and Technology, then gives his views on the need for emphasis on science education. Next, two articles take a look into the future. In the first, John L. Burns, president of the Radio Corporation of America, outlines some of the unusual possibilities open through the use of television in education. The second describes the rapid growth of junior colleges and predicts that they may relieve the mounting enrollments and costs of four-year colleges. Next, the superintendent of a city school system gives his views on the controversy over educational theories, dealt with at many points in this book. He also tells of developments within his own school which typify to some extent the steps toward improvement which are being taken in practice in many schools throughout the country. In closing, excerpts are given from the significant report of one of our important private foundations, the Rockefeller Brothers Fund. Ranging over all of the problems which now confront education in America, the report recommends drastic changes but favors more balanced views than some of the extremist critics of our schools today.

CHANGES WITHIN THE DEMOCRATIC PATTERN[1]

Educational Needs of the Times

As the White House Conference on Education so clearly demonstrated more than two years ago, responsible Americans want good education for their children and recognize the efforts they must make to obtain it. In every state there are public schools with high-quality educational offerings and well-qualified teaching staffs. Graduates of such schools make excellent college and university records. But the quality of American public schools is uneven. Differences in ability to pay for education and in quality of leadership, coupled with differences in belief as to what schools should accomplish, have led to wide variation in the quality of schooling. . . .

Every major study of the status of American education tells the same story of neglect. It is a story of crises in education, of teachers poorly paid and in inadequate numbers, of poor com-

[1] From "The Contemporary Challenge to American Education," official statement by the Educational Policies Commission of the National Education Association. *NEA Journal.* 47:188+. March 1958. Reprinted by permission.

munities struggling to pay mounting school bills, of classroom shortages, of colleges and universities contending with overenrollment and undersupport, of limited programs and limited opportunities for learning, of waste of human talents. These problems are not entirely monetary, but lack of money is the major element. Where support is adequate, the schools are usually of high quality, with broad and diversified programs and excellent teaching staffs. There is little teacher shortage where schools are well supported. Where communities struggle to meet school requirements far beyond their means, where the citizens neither understand nor seek good education, there one finds a compounding of deficiencies.

The major needs of the present can be defined. They involve finding ways to improve those schools and colleges where, for lack of support, lack of public understanding, or lack of professional leadership, deficiencies exist. The deficiencies are most urgent in the following areas. There must be better educational opportunities for the academically able students; there must be better counseling and guidance; there must be improvement in the selection and education of teachers; there must be improvement in the working conditions of teachers and in their social prestige and economic status; there must be more and better equipped school and college buildings; and there must be improvements in instruction in all subjects, including mathematics, sciences, and languages. To bring about these improvements there must be a substantial breakthrough in educational finance; and programs which will contribute to the solution of all these problems must be developed at all levels of government.

Education of the Gifted

American leaders in public life or in private occupations come not from one class or one economic level; they rise from every section of the people and possess widely varied talents. The country needs an educational system which attracts leaders from every source and provides for the talented without divorcing them from the greater society.

Gifted pupils should be identified early and given early opportunities to challenge their powers and develop their talents to the fullest. . . .

In making plans for the education of the gifted, it is important to realize that giftedness may be difficult to recognize. Far more is involved than merely testing verbal abilities and equating them with intelligence. Talents lie in many areas and are of many types. Pupils who rank low by one set of standards may rank high by another. Wide and flexible programs are needed to identify talented students and to plan for them that combination of general studies which will develop them as good citizens and advanced courses which will develop their talents to the fullest. . . .

Guidance

A variety of resources should be utilized to supplement teachers' judgments in discovering the abilities and aptitudes of all students as early as possible, certainly before the end of the eighth year of schooling. This is essential to planning programs of study suited to individual talents.

The failure of this nation to develop fully its intellectual potential underlines the importance of guidance programs for all youth. Among high-school graduates qualified to profit from higher education a tragically large number—in some places as many as half—do not go to college. Lack of money accounts for an important share, but not for all, of this failure. Among the other factors which permit the undereducation of the able is lack of motivation. This results not only from their failure to understand their abilities and the advantages which will accrue to themselves as well as to the nation if they will seek the opportunities open to them, but also from lack of encouragement in the home. This problem should be attacked at the secondary level or earlier.

Guidance of gifted students should not be permitted to detract from equivalent services for all students, for the obligation of the school is to all students. Also it must be recognized that a student's gifts may lie in areas other than the academic. Artistic and creative talent must also be sought out and developed.

Guidance should also involve the cooperation of parents, for parental attitudes strongly influence the school plans of all students.

There is an urgent need to foster in both parents and children a fuller appreciation of the values of intellectual endeavor. Some study of mathematics and science for example is needed for all. The basic findings of the scientific revolution and their implications are essential ingredients in the general education of a modern people. Furthermore, these subjects must be taught before the high-school years in order to stimulate and discover talent.

Advanced study of mathematics and science in the senior high school, however, is appropriate for those who have the particular aptitudes to profit from such study.

The present practice of universal study of mathematics through the ninth year should be continued, and after that year more of the abler students should be encouraged to study both mathematics and science. At the same time the need for other learnings should not be obscured. In advising students, guidance counselors should keep in mind both the changing demands of society and the importance of balance in programs of study.

Through good guidance programs educators can bring the major needs of the society to the attention of students, and this will make possible the meeting of these needs in ways consistent with democratic freedom of choice.

To motivate and guide all students to fulfillment of their promise, guidance programs must be expanded to include all who teach, and reach all who learn.

Improvement of Teaching and Educational Programs

The quality of learning in schools and colleges depends upon skillful teaching. None of the other needs of education can be met without a substantial increase in the number of competent teachers. Yet the evidence continues to accumulate that many American schools are unable to employ well-qualified teachers.

According to data from the Research Division of the National Education Association, American high schools employed about

5,000 new teachers of mathematics in 1956-1957. For these positions, the institutions in which teachers are educated had graduated some 2,500 persons qualified to teach mathematics, of whom only about 1,700 entered teaching. In 1956-1957, 5,500 new teachers of science were employed by American high schools, although the higher institutions had graduated only 4,320 qualified to teach science. On the whole, the best prepared gravitated to the schools which offered the best salaries and best working conditions. The underprepared will doubtless be found in schools which already suffer from other educational deficiencies.

Equivalent figures exist for other areas; the teaching shortage is not confined to mathematics and science. It is most acute, in fact, in elementary education, where 78,938 new teachers were employed in 1956-1957, although higher institutions graduated only 37,922 prepared as elementary teachers.

In the present school year, well over 80,000 teachers in American public schools have substandard or emergency credentials.

These facts reveal both a serious shortage in the number of qualified teachers graduated from those institutions in which teachers are educated and a willingness to certify and employ in professional positions those who lack adequate professional qualifications.

The conclusion is inescapable that hundreds of thousands of American children at every level of education are denied competent teaching.

The highest single priority, therefore, in responding to the contemporary challenge to American education is the recruitment, education, and retention in the profession of qualified teachers. . . .

Substantial improvement in the financial status of education is clearly called for. This must involve greatly increased support at all levels of government and bold attacks on the problem of paying for education.

Small, weak school districts must be consolidated into larger, more effective units. There are many such districts. Half of all American high schools have fewer than 175 pupils. In one state half of all the high schools have under 70 pupils and four or fewer teachers. In such schools the diversified program necessary to meet the varied needs of students is impossible of achievement. High priority should be given to speeding the process of consolidation.

If American education is to be improved, opportunities for schooling throughout the nation must be more nearly equalized than they are now. Some states lack sufficient wealth to provide their young people with even a satisfactory minimum educational opportunity, with the result that many of their youth and adults are tragically undereducated.

Yet the undereducated exact a high price that goes beyond individual unhappiness and undeveloped talents. The cost of unemployment, public assistance, relief, disease, mental illness, crime, delinquency, and the institutions needed to deal with them, are occasioned largely by undereducated persons—the educational derelicts of the United States. It costs far more to correct the damage done by the ignorant than it would have cost to educate them.

Programs which will enhance the capacity of education to serve the national interest can be outlined. Included would be provision for both short-run improvement in scientific capabilities and long-run improvement in educational capabilities. The following would be the major elements:

For the short run the emphasis should be on higher education, particularly at the graduate level, including opportunities, as appropriate, in the fields of mathematics, science, and technology. As this commission has stated in its recent publications, *Manpower and Education* and *Higher Education in a Decade of Decision,* the needs at this level are for teaching staffs, laboratory and bibliographic equipment, and scholarships and fellowships. Activities to meet needs in all these areas should be expanded and the responsibilities of the three levels of government as well as of individual initiative should be more fully met.

Intermediate-range programs are needed at both the secondary and the higher level in the area of recruitment, training, and retraining of teachers in most subject-matter fields, including mathematics, science, and languages. Such programs would involve assistance both to the training institutions and to the students. There is also need for expansion of post-high-school education of less than degree grade for technicians.

In planning intermediate-range programs, it is unwise to assume that merely shifting salary levels of teachers of particular subjects will improve instructional performance. For example, the proposal has been made to raise the salaries of teachers of science and mathematics only. This step would cause serious deterioration in staff morale and in the quality of teaching in many schools.

The long-term need is for improved underpinning of the entire enterprise of American education, beginning at its foundation point in the elementary schools.

It is futile to expect that a multitude of small, limited projects can do much lasting good for American schools and colleges. The real need is for an infusion of public and private support on a massive scale.

At the minimum, expenditures on education should be doubled within a decade, as proposed by the White House Conference on Education. Realistic programs which will bring about such levels of spending should be developed without further delay.

Called for are important increases in teachers' salaries, in school construction and equipment, in financial assistance to students and prospective teachers, in funds for the general support of free, public higher education, and in the professional services of public agencies and professional organizations. The challenge now before the American people demands recognition of these needs and resolution in facing up to them on all levels. . . .

Conclusion

The challenge before the American people calls on them to evaluate their schools and to help improve them. There is no reason, however, to abandon the basic democratic pattern in which they have developed. The strength of this nation will continue to be found in the talents and spirit of individual Americans. President Eisenhower, as a member of this commission in 1949, helped to prepare a report which reads, in part,

Our system of universal education provides a means of developing individual capacities. It strengthens the stamina and value of the individual citizen. It possesses a far greater potential for future development of America's strength than has yet been realized.

These words continue to represent the opinion and faith of this commission.

The challenge before American education ought not, therefore, to be regarded as a matter of competition with Soviet science, technology, or education. The real challenge to America is to fulfill the great potential of her own ideals. . . .

Let no one doubt that this will require sacrifice from every American. Today, more than ever before, the survival of this nation depends on the success with which the schools and colleges accomplish their task. When the American people realize what is at stake, and when they understand what must be done to ensure the national future, they will respond with that massive support—enthusiastic and hopeful—which alone can develop and channel the powers of a free people to build a safe and free world.

WHITE HOUSE CONFERENCE REPORT [2]

From the work of the Committee for the White House Conference on Education, one fundamental fact emerges: schools now affect the welfare of the United States more than ever before in history, and this new importance of education has been dangerously underestimated for a long time.

Some of the reasons for the rapidly increasing importance of the schools have been often noted. Ignorance is a far greater handicap to an individual than it was a generation ago, and an uneducated populace is a greater handicap to a nation. This trend is obviously going to continue and quicken.

An equally important and less frequently mentioned reason for the growing importance of education is the plain fact that the schools have become the chief instrument for keeping this nation the fabled land of opportunity it started out to be. In

[2] From *A Report to the President,* by the Committee for the White House Conference on Education. Superintendent of Documents. Washington 25, D.C. April 1956. p 4-7.

other decades, the opportunities of America lay primarily in escape from the rigid class barriers of Europe, the availability of free land at the frontier, and the excitement of a violently growing nation, where farms often became villages and villages became cities within the span of one human life. When the frontier was closed, it would have been easy for opportunities to dry up in this nation, and for rigid class barriers to develop. It has been primarily the schools which have prevented this from happening. As long as good schools are available, a man is not frozen at any level of our economy, nor is his son. Schools free men to rise to the level of their natural abilities. Hope for personal advancement and the advancement of one's children is, of course, one of the great wellsprings of human energy. The schools, more than any other agency, supply this hope in America today. By providing a channel for ambition, they have taken the place of the frontier, and in a highly technical era, have preserved the independent spirit of a pioneer nation. The schools stand as the chief expression of the American tradition of fair play for everyone, and a fresh start for each generation.

It is this fundamental conception of schools designed to give a fresh start to each generation that has broadened the ideals of education in America so much in the past twenty-five years. It is no longer thought proper to restrict educational programs to the skills of the mind, even though those skills remain of fundamental importance. Schools also attempt to improve children's health, to provide vocational training, and to do anything else which will help bring a child up to the starting line of adult life as even with his contemporaries as native differences in ability permit. . . .

It is, of course, obvious that much progress has been made toward realizing this new educational ideal in the United States during the recent past. It is the belief of this Committee, however, that improvement has been nowhere near fast enough. The onrush of science has outstripped the schools. What is even more important, ideals of human conduct have in some areas advanced as rapidly as technology. Many a school which seemed good enough a generation ago now seems a disgrace to the community where it stands.

The schools have fallen far behind both the aspirations of the American people and their capabilities. In the opinion of this Committee, there is growing resolve throughout the nation to close the gap between educational ideals and educational realities. This Committee therefore makes the following fundamental recommendations:

1. We recommend that school authorities emphasize the importance of priorities in education. This Committee has embraced with enthusiasm the concept of schools which provide a great variety of services designed to do all that is possible to fit children for fruitful adult lives, but there is real danger that in attempting to do everything a little, schools may end by doing nothing well. At present, school funds are limited, and the student's time will always be limited. It is essential that schools pursue a policy of giving children first things first. In the rush for a great quantity of courses, quality must not be lost. The desire to provide education for all American children need not be inconsistent with the need to provide full opportunity for the gifted.

2. We recommend that the American people study carefully their systems of school organization and consider measures to deny funds, other than local, to districts which do not, after reasonable time, organize on an efficient basis. If the American people are asked to make sacrifices for better education, they deserve to have their funds used as efficiently as possible. . . .

3. We recommend that local boards of education quickly assess their school building needs, and give this information to their state departments of education, and that the chief state school officers quickly relay this information to the United States Office of Education. Responsible estimates place the nation's school building need at from less than 200,000 to nearly a half-million additional classrooms by 1960. Inadequate communication between local school districts and state departments of education is the chief cause for these contradictory figures. This Committee also recommends that every community and every state do all that is economically possible to construct the buildings required, and that during such emergency periods as now

exist, Federal funds also be used wherever shown to be necessary. In the richest nation in all history, there is no valid reason for the grimy, dilapidated, and overcrowded school buildings which too many children now occupy. It is an ironic truth that most Americans would not permit their children to live in a house which is as bad as the school buildings which many pupils are forced by law to attend.

4. We recommend that greater inducements of all kinds be offered to attract and retain enough good teachers, and that during the coming decade of teacher shortages, every effort be made to utilize the services of available teachers more effectively. Practical steps must be taken to change the concept of teaching as an impoverished occupation. Teaching must be made a financially comfortable profession. Every effort must be made to devise ways to reward teachers according to their ability without opening the school door to unfair personnel practices. Present salary schedules have the effect of discouraging many able people from entering the profession. Teacher preparation programs have the reputation of requiring needless and repetitious courses. This reputation has the effect of deterring brilliant young people from becoming teachers. Salary schedules and preparation courses should be reexamined and changed where necessary to make the teaching profession more attractive to the most able young men and women. This Committee believes that the next decade and possibly two decades will be emergency periods during which the teacher shortage will grow more acute, but that there is ample reason to hope for sufficient supplies of good teachers in the long run.

5. We recommend that a new look be taken at the entire question of how much money this society should spend on education. In view of the recommendations of this Committee concerning the objectives of education, teachers, and buildings, it seems obvious that within the next decade the dollars spent on education in this nation should be approximately doubled. Such an increase in expenditure would be an accurate reflection of the importance of education in this society. The exact sources of the necessary funds will be determined more easily when there is

more public agreement that the funds must be provided, and more vigorous determination to do something about it. In the opinion of this Committee, money for schools must continue to come from all three levels of government, with a portion of funds for school buildings being made available by the Federal Government on an emergency basis. Good schools are admittedly expensive, but not nearly so expensive in the long run as poor ones.

6. We recommend that every possible step be taken to encourage the interest and activity of all citizens in school affairs. Citizen advisory groups, organizations of parents and teachers, education conferences, and all other means at the disposal of the people of a democracy should be utilized to keep the schools in close contact with the people. In the final analysis, it is only the public which can create good schools and nurture them. In the long run, schools must do what the public wants, and if no strong public will is made known, schools falter. Public interest in education is aroused only by knowledge of problems and intentions, and can continue only if the public can play an active role in school affairs.

7. We recommend that a White House Conference on Higher Education, similar in scope to the program just concluded on the needs of elementary and secondary schools, be held promptly to consider the many complex problems facing, or soon to face, the nation's colleges and universities. . . .

ON HIGHER EDUCATION [3]

Revolutionary changes are occurring in American education of which even yet we are only dimly aware. This nation has been propelled into a challenging new educational era since World War II by the convergence of powerful forces—an explosion of knowledge and population, a burst of technological and economic advance, the outbreak of ideological conflict and the up-

[3] From *Second Report to the President,* by the President's Committee on Education Beyond the High School. Superintendent of Documents. Washington 25, D.C. 1957. p 1-5.

rooting of old political and cultural patterns on a world-wide scale, and an unparalleled demand by Americans for more and better education.

These forces have created enormously increased educational challenges of which we have not yet taken full stock and which our educational institutions as a whole are ill-prepared to meet. The gap between this nation's educational needs and its educational effort is widening ominously. . . .

World peace and the survival of mankind may well depend on the way in which we educate the citizens and leaders of tomorrow.

Four Educational Complexes

Without realizing it we have become a "society of students." More than 40 million of us—one quarter of the nation—are enrolled in formal education programs. Millions more are involved in less formal educational efforts.

No longer is there a single "American educational system." Four major educational complexes have evolved—our traditional system of schools and colleges, an elaborate educational program under the military, a mushrooming system of education operated by private business for its own employees, and a great variety of programs of continuing education under the broad title of "adult education." In addition, every individual's environment is crowded with powerful educational forces—newspapers, books and magazines, radio and television, libraries and museums, concerts and art galleries.

Strictly speaking, of course, no one of these is a system in the sense of being unified, closely coordinated or centrally directed. Moreover they are interlocked because the colleges and universities provide extensive services to all the others. No one knows their full dimensions, but the educational programs run by the military and by business are approaching in total expenditures all of our college and universities combined. Most of the military programs are 100 per cent federally financed, and business firms recoup at least half their educational costs as deductions under the Federal income tax, whereas the heavy dependence of colleges and universities upon private funds and state and local tax revenue places them at a competitive disadvantage in the scramble for scarce resources, especially teachers.

In a recent year 400,000 armed service personnel received training in civilian-type specialties; 230,000 took a variety of correspondence courses; nearly 200,000 had college-level courses in the Resident Center Program, and 200,000 more received classroom instruction under the Group Study Program.

The number of students in business-sponsored educational programs now equals the total enrollments of all colleges and universities. Almost 90 per cent of the 500 largest corporations have entered the field.

One out of every three adults, an estimated 50 million, participates in various sorts of adult education programs, some primarily vocational, others primarily recreational or cultural.

The rapid and parallel growth of these four educational areas reveals the enormous demand for education in our society and raises serious questions. To what extent do they overlap, or complement, or remedy one another's defects? How well are they coordinated, and what can they learn from each other? What total economic resources are devoted to all four, with what efficiency and effectivensss and how is the total divided?

Answers to these and many other questions are needed, but we have no answers now because crucial facts are lacking and the Committee was not equipped to gather them. Accordingly, the Committee has found it impossible to appraise systematically the total field of "education beyond the high school" or to make meaningful recommendations for certain important sectors, including that burgeoning but amorphous field called "adult education." Hence this Report focuses largely upon colleges and universities, about which more is known and more can be clearly foreseen.

The Committee is acutely aware that the strength of education beyond the high school depends heavily upon the strength of our elementary and secondary schools. Much of what is said in this Report, therefore, concerning the needs of higher education applies with equal force to the lower echelons of education.

Demands of the Next Fifteen Years

Our colleges and universities are expected by the American public to perform something close to a miracle in the next 10 to 15 years. They are called upon to provide education of a continually improving quality to a far larger number of students—at least 6 million by 1970 compared to 3 million now. The sharp rise in births which began in the 1940's and which has already overcrowded the schools will shortly begin to strike the colleges. Meantime, with the college age group in our population at its lowest point in 25 years, enrollments in higher education are at the highest level in history because a steadily increasing proportion of young people are going to college.

This great expansion of capable young people seeking education beyond high school represents an enormous opportunity and challenge for our society. But our institutions of higher learning, despite their remarkable achievements in the past, are in no shape today to meet the challenge. Their resources are already strained; their quality standards are even now in jeopardy, and their projected plans fall far short of the indicated need.

No good would come, the Committee is convinced, from presenting a softer picture of the hard difficulties faced by our colleges and universities in the years ahead, but these difficulties are not so great that they cannot be overcome by the American people if they set themselves to the task.

Economic Realities

A stern reality to bear constantly in mind is that our colleges and universities must operate within the limits of the economic and educational resources available to them.

In round numbers colleges and universities are presently spending a little over $3 billion a year on educating students and on physical facilities—about three quarters of 1 per cent of the gross national product. (This excludes board and room, auxiliary services and special research projects, most of which are or should be self-financing.) If in 1970 the United States should devote to these same purposes the same proportion of its increased gross national product—estimated moderately at $630 to $650 billion—the colleges and universities collectively would still have less than $5 billion per year with which to educate at least twice as many students and to expand facilities.

This increase would scarcely provide for the top priority need of insuring an adequate supply of good teachers. Nothing would remain, then or in the meantime, for new buildings, for strengthening services and for a host of other important needs.

To pay adequate faculty salaries and accommodate twice as many students—at present student-teacher ratios and with present amounts of building space per student—would require something like a trebling of the current level of expenditures. With greater efficiency this requirement can undoubtedly be reduced, but even then it will call by 1970 for half again the present percentage of the gross national product devoted to higher education.

Even if this many dollars were available, it is doubtful that enough top-quality teachers could be obtained to maintain present student-teacher ratios in view of the physical limits between now and 1970 upon the nation's over-all supply of highly trained manpower, the mounting demands for such manpower from all directions, and the difficulties of expanding the capacity of graduate schools to prepare more college teachers.

Findings

These considerations concerning the next 10 to 15 years lead the Committee to the following conclusions:

1. If the United States is to become increasingly a society of students it must also become increasingly a society of teachers. Ways must be found to harness into the service of education a far larger number and variety of people, organized around a highly skilled group of professional teaching and administrative personnel.

2. The quantity of students and the quality of education cannot rise together unless basic educational resources also rise with sufficient speed. The American people must be willing to devote a significantly greater proportion of the nation's rising income to higher education or else colleges and universities will

be forced to choose between poorer quality and sharply restricted enrollments. In either event hundreds of thousands of able young Americans would be deprived of the opportunity to develop their full capabilities.

3. If an unwelcome choice were required between preserving quality and expanding enrollments, then quality should be preferred, because it would do neither individuals nor the nation any good to masquerade mass production of mediocrity under the guise of higher education. But the choice between quality and quantity is not mandatory. The nation needs more of both, and it can have more of both if it decides to do so. The decision rests much more with the public than with the educators, and the public's decision must be expressed in terms of greatly increased financial support for colleges and universities.

4. The educators in their turn have a heavy obligation to put these increased resources to their best use. Money alone will never be sufficient. Teachers must be enabled to increase their effectiveness, and buildings and all other educational resources must be used more efficiently, through improved management and more effective academic procedures.

5. By dint of strenuous effort by all concerned, the resources available to higher education can be greatly enlarged. Yet even then they are unlikely to be sufficient to meet in full measure every need and every desire. Therefore it is of the highest importance that priorities be wisely established and firmly adhered to, that careful and comprehensive planning be done, with a high degree of lay participation, and that the efforts of neighboring institutions be better coordinated than ever before. There will at best be much unfinished business in 1970—but meantime anything short of maximum efforts could place the long future of our democratic society in serious jeopardy.

6. The coming years will require greater public understanding and support, a strong and sustained effort to enlarge and improve higher education, a burst of imaginative experimentation and many changes in our conventional educational practices—changes comparable to the technological revolutions in industry and agriculture.

THE PRESIDENT'S MESSAGE [4]

Education best fulfills its high purpose when responsibility for education is kept close to the people it serves—when it is rooted in the home, nurtured in the community and sustained by a rich variety of public, private and individual resources. The bond linking home and school and community—the responsiveness of each to the needs of the others—is a precious asset of American education.

This bond must be strengthened, not weakened, as American education faces new responsibilities in the cause of freedom. For the increased support our educational system now requires, we must look primarily to citizens and parents acting in their own communities, school boards and city councils, teachers, principals, school superintendents, state boards of education and state legislatures, trustees and faculties of private institutions.

Emergency Federal Role

Because of the national security interest in the quality and scope of our educational system in the years immediately ahead, however, the Federal Government must also undertake to play an emergency role. The Administration is therefore recommending certain emergency Federal actions to encourage and assist greater effort in specific areas of national concern. These recommendations place principal emphasis on our national security requirements.

Our immediate national security aims—to continue to strengthen our armed forces and improve the weapons at their command—can be furthered only by the efforts of individuals whose training is already far advanced. But if we are to maintain our position of leadership, we must see to it that today's young people are prepared to contribute the maximum to our future progress. Because of the growing importance of science and technology, we must necessarily give special—but by no means exclusive—attention to education in science and engineering.

[4] From text of President Eisenhower's Message to Congress, January 27, 1958. New York *Times*. p 18. January 28, 1958.

The Secretary of Health, Education and Welfare and the Director of the National Science Foundation have recommended to me a comprehensive and interrelated program to deal with this problem. Such a program contemplates a major expansion of the education activities now carried on by the National Science Foundation and the establishment of new programs in the Department of Health, Education and Welfare. I have approved their recommendations and commend them to the Congress as the Administration program in the field of education. This is a temporary program and should not be considered as a permanent Federal responsibility.

Programs of the National Science Foundation

The programs of the National Science Foundation designed to foster science education were developed in cooperation with the scientific community under the guidance of the distinguished members of the National Science Board. They have come to be recognized by the education and scientific communities as among the most significant contributions currently being made to the improvement of science education in the United States.

The Administration has recommended a five-fold increase in appropriations for the scientific education activities of the National Science Foundation. These increased appropriations will enable the foundation, through its various programs, to assist in laying a firmer base for the education of our future scientists. More immediately, these programs will help supply additional highly competent scientists and engineers vitally needed by the country at this time.

First, the Administration is recommending an increase in funds to support institutes sponsored by the foundation for the supplementary training of science and mathematics teachers and a somewhat larger increase to support teacher fellowships. This will provide additional study opportunities to enable more science and mathematics teachers in our schools and colleges to improve their fundamental knowledge and through improved teaching techniques, stimulate the interest and imagination of more students in these important subjects.

Second, the Administration is recommending an increase in funds to enable the foundation to stimulate the improvement of the content of science courses at all levels of our educational system. The efforts of even the most dedicated and competent teachers will not be effective if the curricula and materials with which they work are out-of-date or poorly conceived.

Third, the Administration is proposing an expansion of the foundation's programs for encouraging able students to consider science as a career. Good teaching and properly designed courses are important factors in this regard, but there are other ways in which interest in these fields may be awakened and nurtured. The foundation has already developed a series of programs directly focused on the problem of interesting individual students in science careers, and these programs should be expanded.

Fourth, the Administration is recommending an increase in the foundation's graduate fellowship program. The enlarged program will make it possible for additional competent students to obtain better training for productive and creative scientific effort.

The Administration is recommending that funds be provided to enable the foundation to initiate several new programs which will provide fellowship support for secondary school science teachers (during the summer months), for graduate students who serve during the school year as teaching assistants and for individuals who wish to obtain additional education so that they may become high school science and mathematics teachers.

Programs of the Department of Health, Education and Welfare

The education programs of the National Science Foundation deal exclusively with science education and operate mainly through scientific societies and science departments of colleges and universities. There is, however, an emergency and temporary need for certain additional Federal programs to strengthen general education and also for certain Federal programs to strengthen science education in our state and local school systems. The Administration is recommending legislation authorizing these additional programs in the Department of Health, Education and Welfare for a four-year period only.

High-quality professional personnel in science, engineering, teaching, languges and other critical fields are necessary to our national security effort. Each year, nevertheless, many young people drop out of high school before graduation. Many able high school graduates do not go on to college. This represents a waste of needed talent. Much of this waste could be avoided if the aptitudes of these young people were identified and they were encouraged toward the fullest development of their abilities.

The Administration proposes, therefore, that the Congress authorize:

(A) Matching grants to the states to encourage improved state and local testing programs to identify the potential abilities of students at an early stage in their education.

(B) Matching grants to the states to encourage the strengthening of local counseling and guidance services, so that more able students will be encouraged to stay in high school, to put more effort into their academic work and to prepare for higher education. The program also would provide for grants of funds to colleges and universities to permit them to establish training institutes to improve the qualifications of counseling and guidance personnel.

(C) A program of Federal scholarships for able high school graduates who lack adequate financial means to go to college. The Administration recommends approximately 10,000 new scholarships annually, reaching a total of 40,000 in the fourth year, to be closely coordinated with the testing and counseling programs. Scholarships should be allotted among the states on an equitable basis and awarded by state agencies on the basis of ability and need. Although it should not be compulsory for students to pursue a specific course of study in order to qualify, reasonable preference should be given to students with good preparation or high aptitude in science or mathematics.

National security requires that prompt action be taken to improve and expand the teaching of science and mathematics. Federal matching funds can help to stimulate the organization of programs to advance the teaching of these subjects in the public schools.

The Administration therefore recommends that the Congress authorize Federal grants to the states on a matching basis for this purpose. These funds would be used in the discretion of the states and the local school systems either to help employ additional qualified science and mathematics teachers, to help purchase laboratory equipment and other materials, to supplement salaries of qualified science and mathematics teachers, or for other related programs.

To help assure a more adequate supply of trained college teachers, so crucial in the development of tomorrow's leaders, the Administration recommends that the Congress authorize the Department of Health, Education and Welfare to provide:

(A) Graduate fellowships to encourage more students to prepare for college teaching careers. Fellows would be nominated by higher educational institutions.

(B) Federal grants, on a matching basis, to institutions of higher education to assist in expanding their graduate school capacity. Funds would be used, in the discretion of the institution itself, either for salaries or teaching materials.

Knowledge of foreign languages is particularly important today in the light of America's responsibilities of leadership in the free world. And yet the American people generally are deficient in foreign languages, particularly those of the emerging nations in Asia, Africa and the Near East. It is important to our national security that such deficiencies be promptly overcome. The Administration therefore recommends that the Department of Health, Education and Welfare be authorized to provide a four-year program for:

(A) Support of special centers in colleges and universities to provide instruction in foreign languages which are important today but which are not now commonly taught in the United States.

(B) Support of institutes for those who are already teaching foreign languages in our schools and colleges. These institutes would give training to improve the quality and effectiveness of foreign language teaching.

More information about our educational system on a national basis is essential to the progress of American education. The United States Office of Education is the principal source of such data.

Much of the information compiled by the Office of Education must originate with state education agencies. The Administration therefore recommends that the Office of Education be authorized to make grants to state educational agencies for improving the collection of statistical data about the status and progress of education.

This emergency program stems from national need and its fruits will bear directly on national security. The method of accomplishment is sound: The keystone is state, local and private effort; the Federal role is to assist—not to control or supplant—those efforts.

The Administration urges prompt enactment of these recommendations in the essential interest of national security.

CAN OUR HIGH SCHOOLS DO THE JOB? [5]

What educators know as "comprehensive" high schools are known to most of us simply as the Abraham Lincoln or Washington and Lee or Thomas Alva Edison High School we went to in our home town. But educators call them "comprehensive" because they offer, under one administration and under one roof or series of roofs, secondary education for almost all the high school age children of one town or, in a big city, of one neighborhood. They are responsible for educating the boy who will be an atomic scientist and the girl who will marry at eighteen; the prospective captain of a ship and the future captain of industry.

Is it really possible to provide appropriate and adequate education within one school for the bright and the not so bright, for children with various motivations, for many with different vocational or professional ambitions? Does not the attempt to

[5] From *Carnegie Corporation of New York Quarterly*. 6:1-4. April 1958. Reprinted by permission.

do so result in a mishmash of educational fare suitable for no one? And is not the attempt made at the special expense of that 15 or 20 per cent of the intellectually most able from whom our future leaders must be drawn?

Some leading public figures say the answer to these questions is "yes." They believe that the high schools, as they are now constituted, cannot do the job that needs to be done. But to one distinguished observer and student of American high schools, the answer is "no—if." Not all high schools are now doing the job, but some are, and most *can*.

During the past twelve months James B. Conant has been moving without fanfare (or with as little fanfare as a man of his eminence can move) about the country making a study of our high schools. A chemist, former president of Harvard, former ambassador, lifetime student of American and comparative education, Dr. Conant has by now personally visited some 50 high schools in 18 states, East, West, North, and South. By the end of the year, he and a small staff working with him will have first-hand information about 100 schools in 20 states. The study is being done under a Carnegie grant to the Educational Testing Service.

Dr. Conant asked endless questions of the principals, teachers, and students in the schools he visited, and sat in many classes. He discussed detailed questions of curriculum and organization with more than 500 students in groups of ten to twenty (and points out that the youngsters' views are often expressed in startlingly frank terms in the absence of teachers or administrators). He talked over educational problems with more than 1,500 high school teachers in groups ranging from three to thirty.

He concentrated on schools which may be considered as truly comprehensive—senior high schools of sufficient size (at least 1,000 students) to provide adequate education for all types of youth, located in communities where not more than half the students proceed to a four-year college or engineering school or university, and where the distribution of academic ability corresponds to the national average.

Dr. Conant's conclusions are presented in tones and terms so non-dramatic as to become dramatic by that fact. Always the scientist, he refuses to fall into the error of talking about schools in general terms without reference to the type of community they serve, and insists that one must talk about specific kinds of problems in particular kinds of schools. He is willing, however, to make certain assertions about what can be done in the kinds of schools he is talking about—what can be done for all the students in them, and in particular for the talented ones.

"I am convinced," he says, "that a satisfactory course of study for the bright boy or girl can be offered in the public high school which is of a general or comprehensive type. I am further convinced that the students in the comprehensive school derive certain advantages from their school years which are denied to their contemporaries in special schools."

He doesn't think it is going to be easy, or that easy does it. In fact, he has some firm ideas as to what it takes to make it happen. In the first place, a "satisfactory course of study" for the academically talented would mean that all of the bright youngsters would be studying five solid subjects in each of the four high school years, and by solid subjects Dr. Conant means English, history, mathematics, science, and foreign languages. They should do 15 to 20 hours of significant homework each week. All of them should acquire something like a mastery of at least one foreign language, which will require at least three years of hard work; all of them should complete at least three years of mathematics (and maybe four) ; all of them should take physics or chemistry, or both, as well as a course in biology.

Dr. Conant breaks down the ideal course of study for students with various types of academic orientation or aptitude. Thus, for those who show ability in science, he would prescribe three or four years of one foreign language, four years of mathematics, and three years of science. For those with less interest in science, he would suggest taking perhaps only two years of science and three years of mathematics. This program would make room for three years of a second foreign language.

These courses would be in addition to those which would be required of *all* the pupils in a satisfactory high school: four years of English and four years of history or related social studies. It is here that one of the most controversial questions in

American education is encountered: whether or not, in these required general courses, the students should be grouped according to their ability. Dr. Conant says yes. From what he has heard from administrators, teachers, and particularly from the free expression of opinion by *students,* he has been persuaded that some degree of grouping in terms of ability in the English and history classes is in the best interest of all concerned. The same would be true for the science, mathematics, and foreign language courses if they were elected by students without considerable academic ability, but under a proper counseling and guidance program very few such pupils would take those courses.

Dr. Conant found that the schools he visited which seem to be doing the best job are those in which there are three or four kinds of English sections in grades nine through twelve. One group of sections is for the boys and girls who are particularly bright in English; another accommodates the 10 or 15 per cent of those who, by any test, are not capable of doing work in English at the level of the majority. Another group of sections is composed of those of average ability.

The same kind of sectioning is used in the ninth grade biology or general science course (which he believes should be taken by all students). It applies also to the ninth, tenth, and eleventh grade history or social studies classes. But in twelfth grade social studies, which usually comprises study and oral discussion of American government and contemporary problems, Dr. Conant believes the mixing of students with a variety of vocational goals is desirable.

He is well-versed in the argument most often used against sectioning by ability, namely, that it tends to reduce social cohesion among the student body. He believes that producing such cohesion is a proper function of the school; he agrees that the future factory owner and the future lathe-operator should, in school, learn to know and to respect each other as human beings. It is, in fact, the primary reason why he argues for educating the talented in comprehensive schools rather than in special institutions. He believes, however, that this important aim is not served in any significant manner, if at all, by having students of widely different abilities in the same history or English sections.

How then is social cohesion to be achieved? In several ways. Dr. Conant believes the most effective is using homerooms for this purpose. Homerooms should be assembled from students of all sorts of abilities and interests, kept together throughout the high school years, and should play a real part in student activities through an effective student council. The twelfth grade social studies class will bring all kinds of students together in discussing those problems which they will share as full citizens when they are of age. Finally, there are all sorts of extracurricular activities and sports in which everyone can participate.

Implicit in all of Dr. Conant's recommendations is the assumption that each school will have a good guidance system. It is, he says, "the keystone of the arch of public education." In a free country it is not enough, he reminds us, merely to offer a sound education; boys and girls and their parents must be persuaded to accept the best that is offered, the best in each case being what is the most appropriate to stretch each youngster to the limit of his capabilities. All kinds of pressures—economic, social, and parental—exist, and they vary greatly from place to place and from school to school. At one extreme, for example, is a suburban high school where perhaps 90 per cent of the parents have collegiate aspirations for their children—aspirations which simply cannot in all cases be strictly related to the abilities of the children. In an industrialized section of a big city, on the other hand, only 10 to 15 per cent of the parents may have any idea of sending their boys and girls on to college; yet perhaps 25 per cent of those children should go on. In both cases, Dr. Conant would be the first to admit, it takes a high degree of statesmanship to persuade students to elect the courses most suitable to their aptitudes.

Without minimizing the difficulties, Dr. Conant says: "It can be done. I have seen it done." He offers some advice as to how a guidance system may best be tested. The first and most important step in counseling is to identify each student's particular aptitudes and interests. This can be done in most cases, Dr. Conant is convinced, by the eighth grade. Most academically talented students can be recognized on the basis of what their individual teachers have to say about their ability, what their marks in school thus far have been, and how they perform on scholastic aptitude tests. (You will notice that he says "most." One of the beauties of the comprehensive school, Dr. Conant points out, is its flexibility: the "late bloomer" can easily be shifted to another course of study if previously undiscovered aptitudes become apparent during his high school years.) Once the administrators and guidance people are in possession of such information on each student, they should keep an "academic inventory" of the school. In other words, they should know who is taking what.

At the end of a four-year period, the inventory might show, for instance, that a substantial majority of the academically talented boys in the class just graduated had taken four years of mathematics, or it might show that only 10 per cent had done so. The first result would indicate a good guidance system; the second would reflect the existence either of a poor guidance system or extraordinary parental resistance to good advice.

With respect to the counseling which is now being given the academically talented, Dr. Conant offers two major criticisms. One of the worst practices is the prevalent custom of advising, or allowing, students to take two years of each of two languages. This, he points out, is analogous to drilling for oil and stopping a couple of feet above the pool of black gold. Students should take at least three years, perhaps four, of any one foreign language. His other criticism has to do with the fact that not enough girls are encouraged to take more than a minimum of science and mathematics: the young ladies are not being made aware, he says, of the future waiting them in those fields.

This recital of some of Dr. Conant's opinions is, of course, only partial. It relates only to what he thinks should be done for the youngsters whose talents are primarily academic. He has things to say also about what kinds of programs should be offered those who probably will enter upon vocations shortly after leaving high school; about the small group at the bottom of the academic scale who cannot be properly educated in classes with the middle group; about what might be done for the *really* gifted—the top 2 or 3 per cent. His views on these and other subjects will be made clear in speeches he will be making over the course of the next year to state-wide educational and citizens' groups, and in a final report, the form of which has not yet been decided upon.

The public schools of the United States have been a powerful agent, perhaps the most powerful single agent, for "transforming a heterogeneous selection of mankind into a homogeneous nation," as Bertrand Russell once wrote. They have served certain political and social goals which the American people hold to be of the highest importance. The belief of such a man as James Conant that they can continue to serve these democratic principles without slighting the intellectual goals which are the aim of all education should hearten a people who care about both the minds and the hearts of their children.

THE ADVANCED PLACEMENT PROGRAM [6]

If I read educational literature correctly, the main preoccupations of our profession since World War II have been, in about this order: (1) financial support, (2) teacher recruitment, and (3) better provision for the instruction of the gifted. This third topic, improved programs for gifted pupils, is particularly alive now that the country has been scared out of its wits by tangible evidence that our enemies are not entirely retarded.

In general, there seem to have been three approaches to programs for the gifted. One is an enriched curriculum which keeps the child in that educational unit appropriate for his chronological age but seeks to give him more to do than is provided for or required of the usual student. A second approach has been unadorned acceleration in which the student who is obviously superior simply moves into the next highest grade at an earlier date than is usual. This has included, of course, moving students from the junior year of high school straight into the freshman year of college. A third approach . . . provides that the student

[6] From "Advanced Placement in High Schools," by S. A. Kendrick, vice president, examinations and research, College Entrance Examination Board. In *Science and Education for National Defense*; hearings before the Senate Committee on Labor and Public Welfare. 85th Congress, 2d session. Superintendent of Documents. Washington 25, D.C. 1958. p 1497-9.

be kept with his age group but that instruction at a higher level in the regular school-college sequence be provided for him. In the most typical case, the high school senior is given conventional instruction in conventional courses at a level which is thought to represent that of the college freshman curriculum.

The first two plans are, when well executed, good ways of dealing with the gifted under certain circumstances. When badly done, enrichment turns into a piddling diffusion of the curriculum and acceleration forces students out of their optimum social and emotional climate, often to their disadvantage. The third plan, that of giving college-level instruction in the high school for those students who are prepared to take it, leaves the schoolboy in school and at home but provides the intellectual tasks which he may be ready to master and which otherwise would be available to him only by removal to a college campus. . . .

Because I know it best and because it is the only scheme, I think, which involves multiple relationships among larger numbers of colleges and schools, I shall give most of my attention to the advanced placement program sponsored by the college board. . . .

The college board advanced placement program provides essentially that colleges agree upon a published definition of the freshman course in some twelve subjects. Schools then undertake to teach this course to their more able students. The outcomes of school instruction are evaluated by examinations offered by the board each May. Upon the basis of these examinations and a perusal of the school's experience with the student, cooperating colleges give actual credit for work done in school. This plan, which seems simple enough in brief, requires a great deal of tolerance and accommodations on the part of everyone. Nevertheless, it has proved practical enough for hundreds both in colleges and in schools to accept it.

Any plan for advanced placement involves three essential elements. First, there must be a definition acceptable to schools and colleges alike of the college freshman year. This definition will inevitably involve compromises, especially if more than one college is involved in the plan. No college professor has ever admitted that any other person could teach a course entirely equivalent to his own. Yet this is just what must be admitted if advanced placement is to be practical. The schools, on the other hand, must accept from the colleges a much more definite kind of direction than they can or should accept when the normal secondary program is in question.

Second, any practical plan for advanced placement must include some means of assuring the college that students in advanced courses in school have really attained levels of achievement equivalent to the college freshman course. In the college board program, which involves hundreds of colleges and schools in a single system, quality control is exercised through a set of examinations.

Finally, any advanced placement program must include an arrangement in the colleges to take the student's advanced achievement into account when he actually becomes a college student. This arrangement may be actual college credit, either granted directly or contingent upon later performance, or it may merely be placement in advanced courses. Whatever the arrangement, it should insure, sometimes against the student's will, that work is not repeated in college which has been mastered in school. . . .

There are risks in advanced placement as there are in almost any educational enterprise worth doing. There will undoubtedly be cases where college placement of students, whether advanced or not, will be in error. There will also be instances of school instruction which is in no sense equivalent to the college freshman level. As far as that goes, there is no such thing as the college freshman level and the establishment of a fictional one through the advanced placement program will not fit perfectly with the facts of life in all colleges. It is possible that advanced placement classes will, if badly managed, generate unwise pressures upon students from their parents and other school and community forces. It is certain that some institutions will maintain such impossibly high standards for the granting of advanced placement that students and schools will lose interest in attempting the program. But none of these or any other dangers that can exist in an advanced placement arrangement are inherent in the program itself.

It may be said that advanced placement is inherently expensive and demanding of time and talent from both students and faculty. This is true, but irrelevant unless the money and time needed are stolen in disproportionate quantities from the programs of other children in the school. It may be said that advanced placement requires a high degree of communication and cooperation among school and college teachers. This is true and is one of the greatest of all advantages of such programs. It may, and certainly will, be said of programs using external examinations that tests are fallible. This is certainly true, but it leads merely to the normally sensible provision, in the college board's program at least, that as much information as possible about the student, his school, and the course he has taken, be taken into account with the test score when placement decisions are to be made.

Basically, as I have suggested earlier, advanced placement is merely a special case of the general educational problem of compromising between the necessity for teaching in groups—usually rather large groups these days—and the ideal of tailoring each child's program and instruction to him alone. Advanced placement can be mismanaged but it need not be. It will not remove all the defects of American education and, in fact, may not become important enough to merit the designation "reform." But I know of at least a few high schools in which the initiation of advanced instruction has renewed the zest of the faculty and affected favorably instruction even in the regular courses.

PRIORITY FOR SCIENCE EDUCATION [7]

In speaking as an ardent advocate of better science teaching and greater emphasis on science in U.S. schools, I must start with some personal observations about education. Our overriding objective today must be to elevate standards of performance and enlarge the intellectual content of the secondary school program.

[7] From text of address delivered by Dr. James R. Killian, Jr., Special Assistant to the President on Science and Technology, on leave as president of the Massachusetts Institute of Technology. March 23, 1958. White House press release. Washington 25, D.C.

There needs to be a greater interest in matters of the mind, a weeding-out of the trivial, peripheral, narrowly vocational subjects, and a more general acceptance by parents, teachers and students of the importance of intellectual qualities and high standards in all parts of the secondary school program. If we are to have better science education, we must have better over-all education and if we are to have better education, we must have a shift in values so that intellectual interests and performance are not played down and socially denigrated. We must cultivate in all of our education a distaste for the "take-it-easy" and anti-intellectual attitudes, and a positive taste for what is excellent in intellect and spirit.

These same observations can be made about college education. The emphasis on quality must run through the whole spectrum of education. We need to bring down into the undergraduate college program more of the spirit of independent and creative work that now marks our good graduate schools, and we need to bring down into the high school more of the depth and the sense of individual responsibility for intellectual effort that is to be found in college. In both secondary school and college, we must provide both opportunity and incentive for high talent; especially in the secondary school must there be an unremitting search and enlarged opportunity for talent and intellectual giftedness.

In the development of our public school system, we have concentrated in recent years on making it universally available and of the greatest help to the greatest number. The next phase —the next great mission of our educational system—should be to introduce more extensively into our system of mass education the opportunities and means for differentiation in order to permit the fullest encouragement and development of our high talent.

In emphasizing the importance of intensifying the cultivation of talent and the raising of standards as objectives of top priority, I do not mean to suggest that our great secondary school system should cease to provide effectively for all of the varying needs of our young people. In discussing education, it is a frequent error to think of one's own son and, in the broader sense, of one's own kind of people when discussing school curricula. I am struck by the number of presumably intelligent college graduates who apparently think the sole purpose of the public schools is to prepare students for college. I am equally shocked by enthusiasts of another aspect of education who apparently forget that one extremely important function of schools is to prepare youngsters for college. Too many college professors think of the high school only in terms of its responsibility to prepare students to do well in the freshman subjects they teach.

Our schools must be designed to help all children, and the needs of children of different ability, different background and different aspirations must constantly be kept in mind. The diversity of educational needs in America is very great. Regional differences, economic differences, differences in the desires of the people, all these things and many others make it difficult to generalize about the high school curriculum or dangerous to try to regiment them.

This necessity of thinking of the whole list of things schools should attempt to accomplish brings us hard up against the thorny question of priorities. It is easy to argue that almost any kind of instruction is at least potentially helpful to students—that is one reason why the curricula of schools and colleges, like a perfect gas, seem to have an infinite capacity for expansion. The list of school objectives tends to proliferate almost endlessly.

The question we must ask ourselves is not whether this course or that course of instruction has any good in it; what we must ask ourselves is what school objectives are the most important for a given community, a given time and for the nation. There are limits to what the schools can attempt, but most important, there are limits on the student's time. Time is the most precious ingredient of all in education. The average student has only a few pennies of time to spend on education, and he can't buy everything in the store. It is up to his elders to help him spend his time as wisely as possible—to purchase not just a lot of little educational trinkets, but something that will sustain him all his life. As long as we remain fully appreciative of that, I believe that we will find ourselves thinking in terms of educational priorities, rather than in terms of omnibus lists; of excellence rather than coverage.

With the expression of these general views on education, let me now turn more specifically to the problem of priority for science teaching and science education. During the last quarter century our schools have gone through a phase during which languages, mathematics, and science have been far too generally neglected or ostracized. I think it futile to try to assess blame for this; it has occurred in part because the attitudes and values of the American people resulted in a low value being placed on these subjects. But clearly the time has come for a redress of this imbalance. The needs of the nation today require that these subjects be restored to a priority at least as high as other principal subjects in the high school curriculum, and that they be taught, not superficially, but thoroughly and well—and imaginatively. It is not that we want to make scientists of all our young people—far from it. Rather, it is that science courses have come to be taught much more poorly in many schools than have the humanities and social sciences, and they need to be brought up to par. Up until now, we have done little—save in our best schools—where science is probably taught as well as anywhere in the world. We have been blocked by the baseless fear that if we strengthen our science education, we might run the risk of distorting the emphasis on other subjects. I hold that we have extraordinary opportunity and unique incentive now to strengthen science education, and that in doing so it can serve to strengthen other parts of the curriculum. Science can be the flagship in leading to a deepening and strengthening of the high school curriculum. It also may well do much good by serving as a sorting-out factor of excellence, since scientific courses along with languages are likely to give better mental discipline and a better test of student mettle than descripive courses. In the longer view, it is well also to remember that it is usually easier to make a good businessman out of a scientist than it is to make a good scientist out of a businessman.

At the institution from which I am now on leave, we have been sponsoring an inter-institutional project for preparing a new approach to the teaching of secondary school physics. It early became clear to the teachers conducting this project, after examining extensively the present approach to the teaching of physics, that it has largely failed to keep pace with the progress of physics, and that far too little of the exciting and important new concepts had found their way down into the high school program. It also became clear that too much of the science instruction was either descriptive or technological and that it did not penetrate to the fundamental concepts and views of the universe, which make physics so basic and powerful a subject—both culturally and in terms of science. I cite this as an example of the importance of rethinking the content of our school subject matter at the secondary level, not only in the sciences but in other fields, and of achieving a deeper grasp of the great fundamentals which underlie our culture and our professions. In a subject which changes so rapidly as science, especially is this important. As the Physical Sciences Study Project continues with its tryouts of new materials it becomes increasingly clear that students of more than average ability readily respond to the excitement and invigoration and the penetration that comes from grappling with some of the profound and basic concepts of physics, even though they are intellectually quite demanding.

Another requirement for the improvement of science education is the correction of some of the strange notions about science.

There is a widespread view, for example, that science is "vocational," that it is "black magic," that it is "materialistic," and "anti-humanistic"—that it contributes only to the practical needs and the defense but not to the quality of our society.

It is my own deep conviction that the liberal arts cannot be liberal without including science, and that humanism is an indispensable ally of science in a sound scientific education. In the face of the practical responsibilities which rest in science and engineering for our security and our material welfare it is all too easy for people to conclude that science is inimical to the spiritual ends of life and for them to fail to understand that in reality it is one of man's most powerful and noble means for seeking truth and that its driving force is the thrust of man's curiosity to discover more of the beauty and order of the universe.

Let us not forget this complementary character of science, which deals with nature, and of the humanities which deal with man. The scientist must study nature in a world of men and the humanist must study man in a physical environment dominated by science. Neither can achieve optimum effectiveness without working in harmony with the other and without the benefit of a harmonious and understanding reaction one with the other.

Let it also be noted that we have a far better chance of producing great scientists in the United States if we have an educated community that understands science and values it as well as the humanities and that views them both as essential parts of our common culure and the wholeness of learning.

Our progress in science will be aided by our achievement of a high degree of scientific literacy among the rank and file of Americans. A man cannot be really educated in a relevant way for modern living unless he has an understanding of science. Our young people, whether they become scientists or not, need some of the intellectual wealth of science, a feeling of greater intimacy with its language and concepts, some of its excitement and adventure, some of its special vision for interpreting nature —some of the understanding which our citizens should have if they are to deal intelligently with the great issues of our time arising out of science.

If we fulfill our potential for skill, talent, education, and quality; if we can give full recognition in our national life to the importance of emphasizing quality and of achieving intellectual preeminence, both for our internal benefit and our external position, there would appear to be no real impediment to our steady scientific and technological advance.

With our own American prized pattern of education, with the laboratories and factories and advancing skills and freedom of our industrial society, we may well show the way to nobler level of living for all men and enhanced freedom and dignity for man the individual.

COMMUNICATIONS AND EDUCATION [8]

New developments in electronics should be of special interest to every school board member because they can bring about increased effectiveness in the vital area of communications between teacher and pupil.

I believe that electronics offers a realistic solution to your shortages of teachers and facilities.

I believe that electronics can help strengthen the curriculum by making available to more and more schools expertly-taught courses in such essential subjects as physics and chemistry.

I believe that with the aid of electronics, the talented teacher can do a better job for more pupils in less time and at less expense than ever before.

Tonight, I would like to suggest some of the exhilarating prospects that electronics offers now and for the future.

All over the country, experiments have turned up heartening evidence that electronics can contribute significantly to improved education.

Magnetic tape recorders, with their spinning reels and shiny ribbons, are proving themselves astonishingly versatile teaching tools. Educational tapes are taking distinguished thinkers and scholars and linguists into classrooms everywhere.

The pioneer electronic teaching tool—the sound film—is finding new usefulness in more than half the nation's schools.

Phonograph records of musical masterpieces, Shakespearean plays and great poetry are enjoying increasing popularity in the classroom.

Electronic reading machines—featuring printed cards with special sound tracks—enable a child to see and to hear words simultaneously, and thus learn more quickly.

Other devices such as electronic computers are speeding up the testing and grading of pupils, and keeping school files more efficiently.

[8] From address by John L. Burns, president, Radio Corporation of America, delivered before the National School Boards Association, Miami Beach, Florida, April 19, 1958. p 1-14. 1958. Reprinted by permission.

By far the most significant electronic teaching device—and the one which, in my judgment, can do the most to bring about a massive upgrading of our educational standards—is television.

A comprehensive, nation-wide survey, just completed by the Radio Corporation of America, shows sharply increasing activity in all three forms of educational television—by the commercial stations and networks, by the noncommercial education stations, and by closed-circuit system in schools and colleges. . . .

The closed-circuit method is now used in well over 200 public school systems and colleges to send lessons from one studio or classroom to a group of classrooms or even to several schools. Another 100 school systems are planning to install closed-circuit this year. . . .

"School of Tomorrow"

The potential of closed-circuit television and other new electronic teaching tools is so great that it is fascinating to visualize "the school of tomorrow."

Televised lessons will originate from a central building having perhaps four or five master studios. The lessons will be carried into classrooms all over a city or an entire county.

Because of the television camera's ability to magnify tiny objects, hundreds of students peering at classroom receivers throughout the city will have front-row seats for the demonstration.

Realism will be further enhanced when color television comes into extensive use in the classroom. Color TV's amazing capacity for enlivening educational presentations is being demonstrated right now at the Walter Reed Army Medical Center in Washington. There an RCA system is used to bring both military and civilian doctors up-to-date on advanced medical and dental techniques.

Such are the exciting possibilities for day-to-day use of classroom television. When events justify it, there is no technical reason why all schools throughout the country could not be tied together in one vast educational network to take advantage of television's magic gift for thrusting millions of spectators at once into the lap of history-in-the-making.

Once a televised event or lesson is completed, the classroom teacher will take over for the all-important "follow-up" period. The students will unburden themselves of their questions. Difficult points will be cleared up through discussion. The teacher in the classroom will have additional electronic tools.

On the teacher's desk, the traditional bright red apple will have been replaced by a multiple-control panel and magnetic tape players. The tape machines will run prerecorded lessons especially geared to the level of the students, ranging from the slow learners to those who are highly advanced. Each pupil will follow the lessons with headphones.

Whenever he has a question, he will be able to talk with the teacher directly on his "intercom" without disturbing the rest of the class. In this way, the teacher will actually be able to conduct as many as three classes at the same time.

Lining the sides of this "classroom of tomorrow" will be soundproof, air-conditioned, private study-booths for individual recitation and research. Simply by flicking a switch, the teacher will be able to listen in on a pupil's recitation and offer helpful suggestions.

Not only voice but pictures, too, will be carried by magnetic tape. A small, portable . . . tape player, now under development by RCA, will be able to take a reel of tape and play it back immediately on the classroom television screens. Highlights of current events, explanations of the great mysteries of science, symphony concerts, lectures by world famous figures—all these and more will be available, conveniently and economically, on video tape.

If the classroom teacher wants to refer to a library book, he will simply consult his "television directory" and dial a number. Instantly, a microfilm edition of the book will appear on the TV screen.

I can see from the expression on your faces that some of you think this "classroom of tomorrow" is pretty fanciful and far-fetched. Let me assure you most emphatically that it is not. In fact, many of the techniques are already at hand to provide such a classroom. . . .

In the city of Hagerstown, Maryland, . . . an entire public school system of one county is being taught in part by closed-circuit television in the first full-scale educational experiment of its kind.

One of the major problems in education today, it seems to me, is how to change the keep-in-step-or-be-left-behind pattern of instruction, and reach the child on a personal basis.

I believe that we must deal with both selective education and education of the many. We do not have a choice of one or the other. And, with electronics, we now have at our disposal the means to do something about both.

In the case of classroom television, the TV teacher can reach a large number of students simultaneously. By concentrating on just one phase of teaching, he has a chance to prepare stimulating presentations that will spur the students to greater achievement. This kind of presentation also saves time, so the classroom teacher—with his own burdens eased—can give incomparably greater personal attention to the individual needs of each pupil.

Practically every experiment has demonstrated that the student learns at least as well from televised instruction as from conventional teaching—and frequently he learns much better.

TV students have been able to cover as much as six or eight weeks' more material during the school year than their counterparts in regular classes. . . .

Impact on the Teacher

What about television's impact on the teacher?

I am convinced that, to most teachers, television offers three opportunities.

The first is the opportunity to concentrate on the things for which he is best suited, and thus enjoy the satisfaction of being able to do a better job.

The second is the new opportunity he will have to achieve increased stature and greater dignity in his own community—a stature comparable to that of top-flight individuals in other professions.

The third is the opportunity to attain a higher salary level through what might be termed "increased productivity"—the same factor that has so remarkably raised salaries in American industry over the years.

Many communities are spending 50 per cent or more of the tax dollar on education. For some time now, we have heard talk of giving teachers more money, but not much has come of it. Classroom television, through its more effective use of teachers, can make higher salaries a reality.

Some critics of classroom television have said that it poses a threat of "technological unemployment" for teachers.

Nothing, to my mind, could be further from the truth. Through the years, technological innovation has not only upgraded the work, but has invariably created more jobs in the long-run than it has eliminated. With our exploding school population, the demand for qualified teachers is so much greater than the supply that authorities have all but despaired of ever closing the gap.

The U.S. Office of Education estimates that the nation is short 170,000 teachers in elementary and secondary schools, and another 28,000 in colleges and universities.

The Fund for the Advancement of Education figures that it would take half of all college graduates over the next ten years to meet our need for new teachers. Of course, nothing like this proportion of our graduates can be expected to go into teaching.

Television and other electronic teaching aids will help to meet a need for teachers that can be met in absolutely no other way.

Impact on the Taxpayer

What about the impact of television on the taxpayer?

At Pennsylvania State Uuniversity, a careful cost analysis of four specific courses disclosed that television teaching had saved as much as $40,000. Put another way, the unit cost per student-credit for these four courses was $2.72 for television teaching, against $4.80 for conventional instruction.

In Chicago, education authorities were able to save the cost of a new junior college building when they found that they could broaden their instruction more effectively by television.

In Hagerstown [Maryland] it has been found that a large number of pupils can be handled without increasing the teaching staff. In the case of music and art instruction, the per-pupil cost is estimated at $1.71 by television, compared with $16.78 by conventional classroom methods.

Now if we translate these experiences into terms that apply to your own local situation as school board members, here is what we find:

You are dealing with a communications medium in which the research and basic development work has already been done. For example, RCA alone spent $50 million on the development of black-and-white TV, and more than $100 million on color television. In a sense, the schools are beneficiaries of these investments because they now have a solid foundation on which to advance.

Let me give you some idea of the cost of installing closed-circuit television. If you take an ordinary classroom and convert it into a studio, your cost will run about $30,000 for cameras, lighting and other equipment. Each additional studio you equip will cost about $25,000.

Can we afford educational television? you ask.

I suggest that a more logical question would be: Can we afford to do without it?

Surely there is no reason why our classrooms should not be at least as well equipped as our kitchens. A country which spends billions of dollars a year on kitchen and other appliances can certainly afford the equipment necessary to educate its youth for survival.

Advantages of Educational TV

Summing up the advantages of television, then, we see:

First, that it can raise the quality of instruction by extending the influence of the best teachers in your own school system and introducing—if you prefer—the best teachers in the nation on video tape.

Second, that television enables you to call upon men of specialized talent in your own communities for occasional lectures. And it provides an opportunity for bringing into the classroom—again through video tape—the greatest minds of our times: men like Carl Sandburg and Arnold Toynbee on history, Dr. Jonas Salk on medical research, Wernher von Braun on outer space, Dag Hammarskjold on diplomacy, Frank Lloyd Wright on architecture, and Robert Frost on literature.

Third, that television can extend the classroom to limitless fields. To missile ranges and inside atomic reactors. To planes in flight and legislatures in session. To living bacteria and cells, and to galaxies of evolving stars. To points on and beneath the land and the sea.

Fourth, that television—through more efficient use of teachers and classrooms—can ease the great shortages now plaguing our schools, and at the same time provide more attention to students' individual needs.

Fifth, that television promises great reductions in the cost of education per student and enables schools to match the higher salaries that now lure some of our finest teachers into other fields. I should caution that this will only happen when broad and effective uses are made of television.

A PLACE FOR JUNIOR COLLEGES [9]

As this country heads into a crisis of overcrowding in the colleges, you hear an increasing amount of talk about junior colleges. They are being suggested as a possible answer to the problem of providing enough classrooms for the flood of U.S. youngsters now approaching college age.

Already, junior colleges have had a tremendous and rapid growth. Just 25 years ago there were only about 300,000 junior-college students in the entire United States. As late as 1952,

[9] From "Junior Colleges: Low-Cost Answer to Crowded Campuses?" *U.S. News & World Report.* 44:77-80. May 2, 1958. Reprinted from *U.S. News & World Report,* an independent weekly news magazine published at Washington. Copyright 1958 United States News Publishing Corporation.

there were only 568,000. Today, there are nearly 900,000 enrolled in 637 junior colleges located in every state. . . .

Now, another big boom in junior colleges is seen developing as state after state turns to these two-year schools to help handle mounting enrollments. In 22 states, publicly controlled junior colleges have won financial aid from state governments. Federal aid is also being proposed in a bill now pending.

Just what is it about junior colleges that is attracting so much attention?

To find out what junior colleges offer, *U.S. News & World Report* made a nation-wide survey. Questionnaires were sent to presidents of junior colleges. From their replies you get the following picture:

Junior colleges offer the same courses usually taken by freshmen and sophomores at a university. Their credits usually are accepted by four-year schools.

In addition, most junior colleges offer courses not found at the average four-year college of liberal arts. They train technicians, offer night classes for adults, give job training for young or old. According to the American Association of Junior Colleges, there were 335,000 adults and 106,000 special students in junior colleges last year.

All this is done, junior-college officials say, at a big saving in money. Students save because most of them can live at home. A junior college is usually a community institution, drawing its students from close by. Savings to taxpayers also are claimed by some educators, who say that junior colleges cost less than four-year schools to build and operate.

The growing trend is toward public junior colleges, supported jointly by the community and the state. Almost 90 per cent of the junior-college enrollment today is in publicly supported schools.

The idea, expressed by numerous educators, is that junior colleges can take over the bulk of the task of providing the first two years of education beyond high school. This, it is said, would create more room in universities and let them concentrate on advanced studies. . . .

One big advantage, stressed by educator after educator, in the *U.S. News & World Report* survey, is this: Junior colleges, serving a community instead of a state, bring the opportunity for college training to millions of people who are not reached by universities.

Records are cited to show that, when a junior college is established in a community, a larger percentage of the high-school graduates continue their education beyond high school.

Dean M. F. Griffith of Casper, Wyoming, College reports: "Fifty to 60 per cent of our local high-school seniors are now enrolling in Casper College. Thirty per cent went on to college before the local school was organized."

Educators' reports show how much a student saves by going to college in his home town instead of going away to school, where he would have to pay for room and board.

According to a recent study by the U.S. Office of Education, living expenses represent about five sixths of the total cost of a student's education in a state college away from home, about two thirds of the total cost in a private college.

One junior-college president, Isaac K. Beckes of Vincennes, Indiana, University, summarized it this way:

> Families using a community institution will be able to save some $800 or more each year in costs that are almost unavoidable in an institution away from home. Away from home, the largest cost to the families of the students is not for education, but for board and room.

Economy for taxpayers is claimed on the ground that junior colleges do not require as expensive buildings or equipment as four-year schools. For instance, at a junior college where students live at home, there is no need to build dormitories.

For educating freshmen and sophomores, a school can get along without some of the costly laboratory and research equipment which universities require.

Often, also, a junior college can use facilities that already exist—share buildings and stadiums and auditoriums with the local high school.

On the whole, junior-college officials surveyed estimated their costs of operation as ranging between $300 and $550 per year per student. Many claim that this is less than half the cost per student in most four-year colleges. . . .

Junior-college economy claims are challenged by some officials of four-year schools. They say that it costs more to educate upper-classmen, and claim that four-year colleges can educate freshmen and sophomores just as cheaply as junior colleges.

Economy is not the only advantage claimed for junior colleges. In their survey replies, many educators argued that the education an underclassman gets in a two-year school is as good as the one he would get in a four-year school—and often better.

Records are cited to show that junior-college graduates do at least as well as other students when they transfer to a four-year school. A recent comparison at the University of California showed that grades of junior-college graduates were slightly higher.

It also is argued that it is better for a teen-age student to start his college career in a home environment. President Marvin C. Knudson of Pueblo, Colorado, Junior College explained it like this:

> The first benefit that accrues to most individuals is that the student has two more years to mature under the guidance and leadership of his parents and as a member of his church and other groups. He also frequently has more opportunities to exercise his leadership in social situations, athletics, drama, art, music, etc. . . . because, usually, the junior colleges are fairly small and also because he is not dominated by upperclassmen. . . . Junior colleges can often promote closer relationships between student and faculty member and more help than is possible in larger institutions.

Robert Gordon Sproul, president of the University of California, said recently: "I would today urge high-school graduates to attend junior colleges unless there is a compelling reason for them to go to a four-year college away from home."

For the student who seeks vocational training instead of a college degree, a junior college is pictured as having a value unmatched by the ordinary four-year college or university. . . .

Here are some of the courses junior colleges offer:

Secretarial and business training, nursing, agriculture, auto mechanics, drafting, machine shop, electricity, electronics, household mechanics, painting, decorating, plumbing, printing, sheet-metalworking, woodworking, welding, cookery. . . .

The idea is suggested by several educators that expansion of junior colleges would help fill the shortage of technicians in the U.S. labor force. . . .

There are some things a youngster has grown to expect from college life that he might not find in a junior college. Some of the traditional trappings may be missing.

For instance, most junior colleges surveyed do not have social fraternities and sororities. Many do not have football teams. Some do not have campuses of their own.

Dean L. J. Elias of Olympic College, Bremerton, Washington, suggests that "many of the social traditions that are identified with American university life"—such as football and social fraternities—"will have to be modified in the philosophy of the community junior college." He says "adequate parking space for commuting students" should be of more concern than "rolling acres of lawn." . . .

Junior colleges are financed in a variety of ways. Of the 637 in this country, 371 are public institutions, supported mainly by taxes, and 266 are private schools. Most public junior colleges depend entirely or primarily upon their local communities for support. In 26 states, they get no state aid.

Where state aid is given, communities still contribute heavily to the junior-college cost.

California is perhaps the outstanding example of state-community cooperation in junior-college financing. There, the state contributes $120 or more per pupil, and the junior-college taxing district puts up the balance of the cost. This method has resulted in the largest state-wide system of public junior colleges in the country. There are 63 such schools, with a total enrollment of more than 400,000.

In California, public junior colleges charge no tuition. They are part of the state's system of free education. In most states, however, students pay at least part of the cost of junior-college education in the form of tuition.

The picture you get from this survey is one of tremendous growth in junior colleges—with more rapid growth ahead.

Junior colleges are a comparatively new development in American education. The oldest public junior college in the country—at Joliet, Illiois—was founded in 1901. It was not until World War II that junior colleges became significant in the over-all educational picture. Yet, today nearly one fourth of all American college students attend junior colleges.

Now you find several states planning big expansion of their junior-college systems. Much of a $250 million bond issue recently voted by the state of New York will go for community colleges of the two-year type. Illinois, Florida and Maryland are considering proposals for state-wide networks of such institutions. California and Texas are constantly adding to their already-big networks. . . .

The hope you find among many educators is that junior colleges may provide an answer to this country's problem of mounting college enrollments—and mounting college costs.

THE MIDDLE WAY IS THE BEST WAY[10]

As a former history teacher who later became a high-school principal and eventually a superintendent of schools, I have long been familiar with such complaints as the following:

> Our young people have been corrupted by luxury; their manners are bad and they are contemptuous of authority. . . . They no longer rise when their elders enter the room. They contradict their parents, chatter in the presence of guests, wolf their food and tyrannize their teachers.

The complaint I have quoted was uttered not, as you might suppose, by a contemporary American, but by an Athenian Greek named Socrates in the fifth century before Christ.

Athenian civilization perished for many reasons, including those mentioned by Socrates in the passage I have quoted. American civilization may perish, too, for similar reasons, but I have no fear that it will so long as the American people remain faithful to the ideals embodied in our Constitution. Thus, before

[10] From article by Earl H. Hanson, superintendent of the Rock Island, Illinois, Public Schools, as told to Leigh White. *Saturday Evening Post.* 230:33+. February 22, 1958. Reprinted by permission.

we blame our system of public education for our failure to launch the first Sputnik, it might be a good idea to consider the purpose of our public schools.

In the final sentence of its statement of aims, the Rock Island, Illinois, Board of Education has declared: "It is understood . . . that citizenship and personal effectiveness demand that each child be schooled to his natural limits in terms of his ability to read, write (which includes spelling), calculate, vote, hold office, make a living, keep a home and keep the law."

In other words, the purpose of public education in the United States is to teach the young to cherish the ideals of their elders and to acquire the skills and knowledge that will enable them, in their turn as adults, to defend them. The Declaration of Independence, the Constitution, the Bill of Rights and subsequent amendments to the Constitution stem from the Biblical idea that man was created in God's image. It follows, therefore, that Americans must do everything possible to provide every child, regardless of race, creed or color, with the opportunity to make the most of his God-given abilities, whatever they may be, in the conviction that only thus can we safeguard the future of the United States.

The United States is the first country in history to dedicate itself to such ideals. Our public schools, therefore, must be judged in the light of one criterion alone: Are they or are they not doing the best that can be done to produce new citizens who are both able and willing to defend the principles on which our country was founded? No other criterion is valid. It is not the purpose of our public schools to create an educated elite. It is their purpose to maintain and improve, if possible, the standards of education of the average citizen without depriving either the superior or the inferior individual of his God-given right to self-advancement.

As a school superintendent, I am faced with a continual barrage of criticism from the traditionalists of the Right and the progressives of the Left. The traditionalists believe that what was good enough for us when we were young is good enough for our children—even better, in fact, in view of all the "nonsense" that our children are supposedly being taught today. The progressives, on the other hand, believe that we are still teaching our children subjects that will be of little value to them in later life. As a moderate, I listen as patiently as I can to both sides, and then do my best to follow a middle way between the two extremes.

The traditionalists, in my opinion, pay too much attention to the curriculum and too little attention to the student. The progressives pay too much attention to the student and too little attention to the curriculum. I believe in the Three R's, but I don't believe that they should necessarily be taught by a whack over the knuckles with a ruler, effective though such a method may be on certain occasions. I also believe in Sweetness and Light, but I don't believe that the student should be allowed to tell his teacher what to do. I agree, in short, with my former professor, Thomas H. Briggs, of Teachers College, Columbia University, who once said, "Some say that you need only to teach arithmetic, others that you need only to teach Mary. I say that you need to teach Mary arithmetic."

I think we are doing so today, better than we have ever done before, in spite of antiquated school buildings, overcrowded classrooms and a growing shortage of competent teachers. Investigators have found that bright students can now learn as much at our public schools in six years as they could formerly learn in eight. And there is abundant statistical evidence to support the belief that graduates of public high schools do better at our Eastern universities than do the graduates of private preparatory schools—probably because they have to work harder to enter the Ivy League. . . .

Critics of our public schools will do well to remember that the courses they offer are largely a reflection of popular demand. Professional educators, whether of the Right or the Left, can do little to oppose the desires of their community. Several years ago, for example, I was persuaded to include a course in driver training in the curriculum of Rock Island's high schools. I opposed the idea in the beginning, but later I recommended to the board of education that the course be offered. I am not sorry that I did. Students who have taken the driver-training course have been involved in only half as many automobile accidents as those who have learned to drive outside of school. Death and insurance rates have been correspondingly reduced.

It could be argued, I admit, that teaching a youngster to drive with care is no part of the responsibility of our public schools. Yet who can say that a safe driver is not a better citizen?

In recent years I also have been persuaded to recommend the establishment of special classes for two categories of mentally handicapped children. The first we call "educable"—those who can learn the three R's on a very low level. These children, if neglected, are likely to become juvenile delinquents, but they can be taught to become self-supporting and to lead satisfying, if limited, lives. The second type we call "trainable" because they have such meager mental capacities that they cannot be educated in processes that require reasoning, but they can be trained to perform many tasks for themselves.

Although I agreed that our public schools should do everything possible to teach educable mentally handicapped children to become useful, law-abiding citizens, I was doubtful of the wisdom of making the schools responsible for the training of those lower on the mental scale. Their welfare, it seemed to me, was more properly the responsibility of our hospitals. The fact remained, however, that these sorrowfully handicapped children could be trained, and their parents wanted the schools to do the job. In the end I was forced by popular pressure to make the schools responsible for them. They are taught separately and do not interfere in any way with the education of normal boys and girls.

In our night schools we even offer a course in the training of dogs. I would have opposed such a course if it were not for the fact that the people who wanted it were prepared to pay for their lessons.

Nonsense? Perhaps, but, so long as a goodly percentage of our citizens wish to keep dogs, it is better for everyone concerned if their dogs are well-behaved.

No "life-adjustment" courses are taught in Rock Island. We try to develop character and personality in every course we teach. We believe that home, church and school are interdependent institutions, and that all should work together.

One of my saddest recollections is the fate of a student in the high school of which I was once the principal. He refused to study, threw lead slugs in the study hall, and eventually began to steal. I tried to reason with him, but to no avail. Finally I telephoned his father to ask him to come to see me. The father refused.

"He's your responsibility in school," he said, "and my responsibility at home. You do your job, and I'll do mine."

The son is now in the penitentiary.

Critics of the Right believe that character building is the responsibility of home and church, and that our schools should confine themselves to imparting abstract knowledge. Critics of the Left believe that character building, or "life adjustment," is the most important responsibility of our schools, and that the acquisition of abstract knowledge is secondary.

We of the middle way in education reject both points of view. We refuse to believe that knowledge and character are mutually exclusive. We believe that a child's character is molded by what and how he is taught, in school as at home and in church. Some subjects and some teachers may affect his character more than others, but they will all affect it to some degree. It behooves us, therefore, to see that every child is taught every subject in such a way as to make him a better citizen as well as a more learned one. . . .

Learning is of little value unless the child can put it in perspective and relate it to the other things he learns. Reading, writing and arithmetic are important, but nothing is so important as the child's need to use what he learns in harmonious association with others.

What most critics are complaining about is neither Rightism nor Leftism, but simply bad education.

Some progressive-education ideas may be good in themselves, but may be carried out badly. For instance, the idea of bringing cooperation between teachers is good, but it may be worked out in a silly way. In one school, in the South, it was decided to celebrate the importance of cotton. Instead of confining the topic to the social-science class, however, it was celebrated in every class for a week. In the English classes the students were required to write themes about some aspect of the cotton industry; in the physical-education classes, they were required to imitate the movements of cotton pickers; and in the music classes, they were required to sing such songs as "Way Down Upon the Swanee River." It was a "cotton-picking" experiment in every sense of the phrase.

The idea of helping students to see the connection between subjects may be "progressive" but it is good if carried out sensibly. One of our social-science teachers, in an effort to acquaint her students with the customs of the Western states, asked them to prepare and serve a meal consisting solely of Western food products. If she had allowed the preparation of the meal to dominate what she was teaching, she could rightly have been criticized as a Leftist. But she didn't. She simply used the preparation of the meal as a means of interesting her students in the history, geography and economy of the Western states. And, in so doing, she taught them more than she could have taught them in any other way. I know she did, because her students consistently did better in their examinations than the students of any other teacher of social science.

In 1937, when I became the superintendent of schools, there were 170 teachers and 5700 students in Rock Island. Today there are 350 teachers and 9600 students. The average class has been reduced in size from about thirty-four to about twenty-seven.

Rock Island, unfortunately, is an exception. Throughout the United States as a whole, there are more students and fewer teachers than there were twenty years ago. The explanation once again is the great depression. During the 1930's, when most of our teachers were going to school, our national birth rate was declining. Since the Second World War, however, our birth rate has been rising. The inevitable result is a growing shortage of teachers.

This, I think, is the greatest shortcoming of our public schools today. Old school buildings and overcrowded classrooms are serious problems, but even more serious is the lack of competent teachers. No school, however modern and spacious, can be better than its teaching staff, and in the absence of competent teachers the education of our children is bound to suffer.

Critics of the Right and the Left, therefore, are barking up the wrong tree when they complain of the methods rather than the quality of contemporary public education. Everything, in the end, depends upon the teacher, and no good teacher, in my experience, has ever been an extremist. Good teachers never neglect the needs of their students, whether they be bright, average or dull. Although teachers naturally appreciate bright students, and help them to push ahead, they also encourage the average majority and take special pains to aid the dullards.

A good teacher must love children and love learning, but he or she must be paid enough to lead a normal life. If we want good teachers for our children, we must make it possible for them to marry and have children of their own, and to go to the theater now and then without having to sit in the peanut gallery. The problem of public education in the United States today can thus be reduced to the problem of municipal economics. Make the teaching profession attractive enough, and we can find all the teachers that we require; stint on their salaries, as we have too often done in the past, and our children's education will suffer from a lack of competent instructors.

New school buildings are important, but I would prefer, if forced to make the choice, to staff an antiquated school with a sufficient number of good teachers than to acquire a new school without sufficient funds to provide it with an adequate teaching staff. Ideally, of course, I would prefer a new and spacious school building with a plenitude of good teachers. But such an ideal depends upon the demands of the community and its willingness to pay the necessary taxes. Our schools are what we make them. Thomas Jefferson was right when he said, "If a nation expects to be ignorant and free, in a state of civilization, it expects what never was and never will be."

EDUCATION AND THE FUTURE OF AMERICA [11]

Ultimately the source of a nation's greatness is in the individuals who constitute the living substance of the nation. A concern for the realization of individual potentialities is deeply rooted in our moral heritage, our political philosophy, and the texture of our daily customs.

Our devotion to a free society can only be understood in terms of these values. It is the only form of society that puts at the very top of its agenda the opportunity of the individual to develop his potentialities. But in its deepest sense our concern for human excellence is a reflection of our ideal of the overriding importance of human dignity.

Our success or failure in this task is of crucial importance not for ourselves alone. All over the world peoples are striving for a new and fuller meaning of life. No challenge is more important than to give concrete meaning to the idea of human dignity. . . .

The Nature of the Challenge

[The] pattern of future population will present two vital problems. The first concerns the flood of young people who will place an immense pressure on educational institutions in the next twenty years, and on the labor market shortly thereafter. The second problem involves the social and individual problems posed by a rapidly expanding older group.

One of the striking features of contemporary life is the growing range and complexity of the tasks on which our social organization depends. This is dramatically apparent in science but is no less a reality in nearly every field of endeavor.

The demand for highly trained talent is not a sudden development. It has been coming for a long time. The increase in skill and training needed by our labor force can be expected to accelerate in the years ahead. Automation will reduce the number of routine jobs and will replace them by more demanding tasks

[11] From text of summary of the report *The Pursuit of Excellence: Education and the Future of America,* prepared by Panel V of the Special Studies Project of the Rockefeller Brothers Fund, Inc. New York *Times.* p 16. June 23, 1958.

of supervision, maintenance and regulation in addition to the production of the machines themselves.

There is a constant pressure by an ever more complex society against the total creative capacity of its people. Our most critical need a decade hence may be unknown today. Rather we must prepare ourselves for a constant and growing demand for talents of all varieties, and must attempt to meet the specific needs of the future by elevating the quality and quantity of talented individuals of all kinds.

One of our great strengths as a people has been our flexibility and adaptability under the successive waves of change that have marked our history. Never have we needed the trait more than today. It is for this reason that we should educate our young people to meet an unknown need rather than to prepare them for needs already identified. . . .

Excellence in a Democracy

The eighteenth-century philosophers who made equality a central term in our political vocabulary never meant to imply that men are equal in all respects. Nor do Americans today take such a view. It is possible to state in fairly simple terms the views concerning equality which would receive most widespread endorsement in our country today. The fundamental view is that in the final matters of human existence all men are equally worthy of our care and concern. Further, we believe that men should be equal in enjoyment of certain familiar legal, civil and political rights. They should, as the phrase goes, be equal before the law.

But men are unequal in their native capacities and their motivations, and therefore in their attainments. In elaborating our national views of equality, the most widely accepted means of dealing with this problem has been to emphasize equality of opportunity. . . .

With respect to the pursuit of excellence there are several considerations that we must keep firmly in mind. First, our conception of excellence must embrace many kinds of achievements at many levels. Second, we must not assume that native capacity is the sole ingredient in superior performance. Excellence is a product of ability and motivation and character. Finally, we must recognize that judgments of differences in talent are not judgments of differences in human worth.

The Educational System

The formal educational system offers only part of the purposeful education that goes on in a society. Family, church and school share the fundamental responsibility for education. But in a sense every institution in a society is constantly teaching its members, molding their behavior, contributing to their development: in childhood it may be the scout leader, the playground director, the policeman on the corner; in later years the employer, the union, the mass media.

The most effective educational system can be defeated by a social environment that blunts or destroys aspiration. There can be no striving for excellence without models to inspire emulation.

Our schools are overcrowded, understaffed, and ill-equipped. In the fall of 1957, the shortage of public school classrooms stood at 142,000. There were 1,943,000 pupils in excess of "normal" classroom capacity. These pressures will become more severe in the years ahead. Elementary school enrollments will rise from some 22 million today to about 34 million by 1960-1961. By 1968 high schools will be deluged with 50 to 70 per cent more students than they can now accommodate; by 1975, our colleges and universities will face at least a doubling and in some cases a tripling of present enrollments.

If we are to meet these pressures, our schools will need greatly increased public support and attention and much more money. But they also need something besides money: an unsparing re-examination of current practices, patterns of organization and objectives.

From time to time one still hears arguments over quantity versus quality education. Behind such arguments is the assumption that a society can choose to educate a few people exceedingly well or to educate a great number of people somewhat less well, but that it cannot do both. But a modern society such as ours cannot choose to do one or the other. It has no choice but to do both.

The Teaching Profession

The number of new school teachers needed in the next decade is between one third and one half of all the four-year college graduates of every kind in the same period. The danger of a decline in the quality of our corps of teachers is obvious.

The problem of recruitment is inseparable from the preparation required to enter the teaching profession. If the programs for the preparation of teachers are rigid, formalistic and shallow, they will drive away able minds as fast as they are recruited. Unhappily, preparation for pre-college teaching has come all too close to that condition. In some states the requirements for certification are so technical and trivial as to make it unlikely that individuals with a first-class liberal education would even apply—or be eligible if they did apply.

Fortunately, there appears to be a lively movement to correct these difficulties. As for the preparation of college teachers, the problem is one of reforming and expanding graduate education. There has been more emphasis on research and research training than on the preparation of teachers.

But even with aggressive recruitment there appears to be little or no likelihood that we can bring into teaching at any level anything approaching the number of qualified and gifted teachers we need. We can be certain that there will never be enough teachers with the extraordinary human gifts which make for inspired teaching. We must therefore utilize our superior teachers more effectively.

One way to make better use of the ablest teachers is to eliminate many of the petty tasks which occupy a teacher's time. Less highly trained classroom assistants may accomplish much in the lightening of this burden. Another measure is the employment of such devices as television to bring extraordinarily effective teachers into contact with larger numbers of students than they would otherwise face. Films may be similarly useful.

Such innovations as the teacher aide and television should not be thought of as stopgap measures to surmount the immediate teacher shortage, but as the beginnings of a long overdue revolution in teaching techniques.

But the root problem of the teaching profession remains financial. Salaries must be raised immediately and substantially. Almost as important is the fact that promotional policy for most school systems is routine and depends much more on seniority than on merit.

The Curriculum

At the pre-college level, the gravest problem today is to reach some agreement on priorities in subject matter. This problem is particularly critical for those academically talented students who will go on to college. Without presuming to lay down an inflexible set of recommendations, we may suggest what these high-priority items in a solid high school curriculum might be for those of considerable academic ability:

In addition to the general education prescribed for all—four years of English, three to four years of social studies, one year of mathematics and one year of science—the academically talented student should have two to three additional years of science, three additional years of mathematics, and at least three years of a foreign language. For certain students the study of a second foreign language, for at least three years, might replace the fourth year of mathematics and the third year of science.

Particularly with respect to the highest priority subjects, we must modernize and improve the quality of the courses themselves.

Science Education

The crisis in our science education is not an invention of the newspapers, or scientists, or the Pentagon. It is a real crisis.

The U.S.S.R. is not the "cause" of the crisis. The cause of the crisis is our breath-taking movement into a new technological era. The U.S.S.R. has served as a rude stimulus to awaken us to that reality.

The heart of the matter is that we are moving with headlong speed into a new phase in man's long struggle to control his environment, a phase beside which the industrial revolution may appear a modest alteration of human affairs. Nuclear energy, exploration of outer space, revolutionary studies of brain functioning, important new work on the living cell—all point to changes in our lives so startling as to test to the utmost our adaptive capacities, our stability and our wisdom.

We need an ample supply of high caliber scientists, mathematicians and engineers. We need quality and we need it in considerable quantity! We must develop guidance efforts designed to reach all able youngsters, and we must engage in a major expansion of the facilities for science teaching.

There is a danger of training scientists so narrowly in their specialties that they are unprepared to shoulder the moral and civic responsibilities which the modern world thrusts upon them. But just as we must insist that every scientist be broadly educated, so we must see to it that every educated person is literate in science.

The Identification of Talent and the Uses of Diversity

One of the most important goals of any education system is to identify and guide able students and to challenge each student to develop his capacities to the utmost. Tests are most effective in measuring academic aptitude and achievement.

Used with a sound understanding of their strengths and limitations, present testing procedures can contribute significantly to a program of talent identification.

But testing procedures unwisely used can do harm. A few basic considerations must be understood: First, tests are effective on a limited front. Second, no single test should become a basis for important decisions. Third, test scores are one kind of data to be placed alongside other kinds of data.

The identification of talent is no more than the first step. It should be only part of a strong guidance program. As many teachers as possible should be trained to take part in it. As many high schools as possible should have special guidance officers.

The objective of all educational guidance should be to stimulate the individual to make the most of his potentialities. The fact that a substantial fraction of the top quarter of high school graduates fail to go on to college is a startling indictment of our guidance system. . . .

A more special problem is presented by the top 2 per cent of the high school population. For this group particularly the Advanced Placement Program is important. . . . [See "The Advanced Placement Program" in this section, above—Ed.] Another approach is represented by the experimental Program for Early Admission to College, under which about a thousand able students have entered twelve different colleges over the last five dents have entered twelve different colleges over the last five years before completing the last year or two of high school.

Financing

All of the problems of the schools lead us back sooner or later to one basic problem—financing. It is a problem with which we cannot afford to cope half-heartedly. An educational system grudgingly and tardily patched to meet the needs of the moment will be perpetually out of date.

It is likely that ten years hence our schools and colleges will require at least double their present level of financial support.

It is the weakness in the state and local taxing systems more than anything else that gives rise to current proposals for increased Federal support of education. For those who wish to resist or postpone the resort to Federal funds and at the same time not constrict educational services there seems to be only one alternative: a thorough, painful, politically courageous overhaul of state and local tax systems.

Federal programs in education now exist on a large scale. It is certain that they will increase both in scale and in variety. There are educational problems gravely affecting the national interest which may be soluble only through Federal action.

It would be well to bear in mind four principles in appraising proposals for Federal support of education:

1. The Federal Government should address itself to those needs which educational leaders have identified as having a high priority.

2. Federal funds should constitute one source of support among many. State, local and private sources of funds should continue to be the major factor in the support of education.

3. It should preserve local leadership and local control over education.

4. It should be based on a recognition that the Government inevitably exercises a certain leadership function in whatever it does.

Perhaps the most popular form of Federal support for education is the scholarship program. Scholarships involve a minimum hazard of Federal interference. As long as very few institutions charge tuition covering the full cost of education, a scholarship program which enables the student to pay his tuition should provide the college with a supplementary grant to make up the full cost of his education.

To the extent that the Federal Government can assist in building construction, either through loans or outright grants, it will be engaging in one of the most helpful and least hazardous forms of support to education. . . .

The Inadequate Use of Talent

1. The fuller use of underprivileged minorities. Primary among these groups is, of course, the Negro, who has been disadvantaged economically as well as politically and socially in the United States. The end of segregation, with all the difficult adjustments it imposes, is of course a step in the right direction. Legislation such as fair employment practices acts will add a necessary stimulus to private reorientation of attitudes. Until the Negro has been offered equal opportunity with the non-Negro to develop and use his individual talents to the utmost, and until he can be encouraged to make the most of his opportunity, we shall have failed to achieve our moral goal.

2. Better use of the talents of women. One out of every three workers in our regular labor force of nearly 70 million is a woman. To this already large contribution, we can expect a substantial increase over the next decades due to the age composition of our population. There are still relatively few professional fields beyond nursing and teaching in which women

participate extensively. Many firms still hesitate to use women in executive capacities or to include in executive training programs even those women who expect to remain in employment.

3. The rehabilitation of economically depressed areas and segments of the population. The nation is paying a high price for its depressed areas in terms of the wastage of human abilities.

4. Better use of older workers. Only for a portion of older people has retirement with economic security become a treasured period of leisure when one can do "what one always wanted to." For others it is a dreaded break in the texture and tempo of life, leading to personal dissatisfaction on the one hand, and to wasted ability on the other. Remedial action might take the form of a later retirement age. Or it might involve the development of special job opportunities for people over sixty-five. Such opportunities have already been provided in college teaching: the professor retiring from one campus may be hired on special status by some other college.

The Use of Talent in Large Organizations

Every corporation, union, government agency, military service and professional group, should—in its own best interest as well as that of its personnel—conduct a never-ending search for talent within its own staff.

Sometimes a change of jobs is extremely useful in lifting the individual out of his rut and exposing him to new challenges. In this connection it must be noted that nontransferable pension and benefit plans weaken the incentives of men and women to move to positions where better use could be made of their capacities and experience. There seems to be a need for more vesting of pension rights, so that the employees who move to another job need not leave behind years of accumulated benefits.

Improved opportunities for further education within employing organizations and under community auspices can help mature people to test their own unexplored interests and abilities and to develop their potentialities more fully. . . .

Motivation and Values

Some of our more discerning critics are uneasy about the current aspirations and values of Americans. They sense a lack of purpose in Americans; they see evidence that security, conformity, and comfort are idols of the day; and they fear that our young people have lost youth's immemorial fondness for adventure, far horizons and the challenge of the unpredictable.

Fortunately we do not need to decide whether the situation is seriously deplorable or only mildly so. The truth is that never in our history have we been in a better position to commit ourselves wholeheartedly to the pursuit of excellence in every phase of our national life. Intellectual and moral excellence has come to play a uniquely important role. It is essential that we enable young people to see themselves as participants in one of the most exciting eras in history and to have a sense of purpose in relation to it.

Still another challenge is that of providing "models" for young people. The life goals of young people are in considerable measure determined by the fact that they identify themselves with admired figures in the adult world.

If we ask what our society invites in the way of high performance we are led to the conclusion that we may have, to a startling degree, lost the gift for demanding high performance of ourselves. It is a point worth exploring.

What most people, young or old, want is not merely security or comfort or luxury—although they are glad enough to have these. They want meaning in their lives. If their era and their culture and their leaders do not or cannot offer them great meanings, great objectives, great convictions, then they will settle for shallow and trivial meanings. People who live aimlessly, who allow the research for meaning in their lives to be satisfied by shoddy experiences have simply not been stirred by any alternative meanings—religious meanings, ethical values, ideas of social and civic responsibility, high standards of self-realization.

This is a deficiency for which we all bear a responsibility. It is a failure of home, church, school, government—a failure of all of us.

No inspired and inspiring education can go forward without powerful undergirding by the deepest values of our society. The students are there in the first place because generations of Americans have been profoundly committed to a republican form of government and to equality of opportunity. They benefit by a tradition of intellectual freedom because generations of ardent and stubborn men and women nourished that tradition in Western civilization. Their education is based upon the notion of the dignity and worth of the individual because those values are rooted in our religious and philosophical heritage.

We would not wish to impose upon students a rigidly defined set of values. Each student is free to vary the nature of his commitment. But this freedom must be understood in its true light. We believe that the individual should be free and morally responsible: the two are inseparable. The fact that we tolerate differing values must not be confused with moral neutrality. Such tolerance must be built upon a base of moral commitment; otherwise it degenerates into a flaccid indifference, purged of all belief and devotion.

In short, we wish to allow wide latitude in the choice of values but we must assume that education is a process that should be infused with meaning and purpose; that everyone will have deeply held beliefs; that every young American will wish to serve the values which have nurtured him and made possible his education and his freedom as an individual.

BIBLIOGRAPHY

An asterisk (*) preceding a reference indicates that the article or a part of it has been reprinted in this book.

Bibliographies

British Information Services. 23p. Select list of books and documents on education in Britain. The Services. 45 Rockefeller Plaza. New York 20. '58.

Education in the U.S.S.R. and in the U.S.A. (Bibliography no28) 6p. University of Florida Education Library. Gainesville, Fla. '58.

National Education Association. Educational Research Service. Education in lay magazines. The Association. 1201 16th St. Washington 6, D.C. '57-'58.

Books, Pamphlets, and Documents

Adler, Irving. What we want of our schools. 256p. John Day. New York. '57.

Adler, M. J. and Mayer, Milton. Revolution in education. 255p. University of Chicago Press. Chicago. '58.

Aly, Bower, ed. American education (National University Extension Association. Committee on Discussion and Debate Materials and Interstate Cooperation. Discussion and Debate Manual 32. 1958-59) 2v. Lucas Brothers. Columbia, Mo. '58.

Aly, Bower, ed. Youth education. (National University Extension Association. Committee on Discussion and Debate Materials and Interstate Cooperation. Discussion and Debate Manual 29. 1955-56) 2v. Lucas Brothers. Columbia, Mo. '55.

American Association of School Administrators. High school in a changing world; 36th yearbook. 383p. The Association. 1201 16th St., N.W. Washington 6, D.C. '58.

Benson, G. C. S. and Payne, J. M. National aid to higher education. 38p. American Enterprise Association. 1012 14th St. Washington 5, D.C. '58.

Benton, William. This is the challenge. 254p. Associated College Presses. New York. '58.

Bestor, Arthur. Restoration of learning. 459p. Dryden Press. New York. '55.

Blaustein, A. P. and Ferguson, C. C. Desegregation and the law. 333p. Rutgers University Press. New Brunswick, N.J. '56.

*British Information Services. Fact sheets on Britain. Education in Britain. 2p. The Services. 45 Rockefeller Plaza. New York 20. Ap. '58.

*British Information Services. Fact sheets on Britain. Universities in Britain. 2p. The Services. 45 Rockefeller Plaza. New York 20. Jl. '56.

Brubacher, J. S. and Rudy, Willis. Higher education in transition. 494p. Harper and Bros. New York. '58.

Carnegie Foundation for the Advancement of Teaching. Federal programs in higher education. 19p. The Foundation. 589 Fifth Ave. New York 17. '57.

Center for the Study of Liberal Education for Adults. Liberal education. (Notes and Essays on Education for Adults no 18) 29p. The Center. 940 E. 58th St. Chicago. '57.

Childs, J. L. American pragmatism and education; an interpretation and criticism. 373p. Henry Holt and Co. New York. '56.

Collier's Encyclopedia. Library and Education Division. Collier's Encyclopedia reports on the White House Conference on Education. 24p. P. F. Collier and Son. New York. '56.

Eddy, E. D. Colleges for our land and time. 328p. Harper and Bros. New York. '56.

Edman, Irwin. John Dewey: his contribution to the American tradition. 322p. Bobbs-Merrill. Indianapolis, Ind. '55.

Ehlers, Henry, ed. Crucial issues in education. 227p. Henry Holt and Co. New York. '55.

Fleming, H. C. and Constable, John. What's happening in school integration? (Public Affairs Pamphlet no244) 20p. Public Affairs Committee. New York. '56.

Fletcher, C. S. Battle of the curriculum; address delivered January 7, 1958. 18p. Fund for Adult Education. 200 Bloomingdale Road White Plains, N.Y. '58.

Foreign Policy Association. Science and foreign policy. (Headline Series no 130) 62p. The Association. New York. '58.
"Science and education: U.S. and U.S.S.R." R. E. Marshak.

Freeman, R. A. School needs in the decade ahead. 301p. Institute for Social Science Research. Washington, D.C. '58.

Fund for Adult Education. Continuing liberal education, report for 1955-1957. 95p. The Fund. 200 Bloomingdale Road. White Plains, N.Y. '58.

Ginsberg, Eli. Human resources: the wealth of the nation. 183p. Simon and Schuster. New York. '58.

Good, H. G. History of American education. 570p. Macmillan Co. New York. '56.

Gould, S. B. Address delivered at Antioch College June 28, 1958. 27p. Antioch Press. Yellow Springs, Ohio. '58.

Hogarth, C. P. Crisis in higher education. 60p. Public Affairs Press. Washington, D.C. '57.

Houle, C. O. and Nelson, C. A. University, the citizen and world affairs. 179p. American Council on Education. Washington, D.C. '56.

Hutchins, R. M. Some observations on American education. 112p. Cambridge University Press. London. '56.

Kandel, I. L. American education in the twentieth century. 247p. Harvard University Press. Cambridge, Mass. '57.

Keats, John. Schools without scholars. 202p. Houghton Mifflin. Boston. '58.

*Killian, J. R., Jr. Text of address delivered March 23, 1958. mimeo. press release. The White House. Washington 25, D.C. '57.

Kline, G. L., ed. Soviet education. 192p. Columbia University Press. New York. '57.

Korol, Alexander. Soviet education for science and technology. 513p. John Wiley. New York. '57.

Latimer, J. F. What's happened to our high schools? 196p. Public Affairs Press. Washington, D.C. '58.

Mallinson, Vernon. Introduction to the study of comparative education. 249p. Macmillan Co. New York. '57.

Meyer, A. E. Education for a new morality. 91p. Macmillan Co. New York. '57.

Mills, C. W. Mass society and liberal education. (Notes and Essays on Education for Adults no9). 17p. Center for the Study of Liberal Education for Adults. 940 E. 58th St. Chicago 37. '54.

National Association of Manufacturers. Does public education need Federal aid? (Economic Series no72) 24p. The Association. 2 E. 48th St. New York 17. '56.

National Education Association. Ten criticisms of public education. (Research Bulletin v35, no4) 45p. The Association. 1201 16th St. Washington 6, D.C. '57.

National Education Association. Today and tomorrow in elementary and secondary education. 19p. The Association. 1201 16th St. Washington 6, D.C. '58.

National Education Association. Educational Policies Commission. Higher education in a decade of decision. 152p. The Association. 1201 16th St. Washington 6, D.C. '57.

National Education Association. Educational Policies Commission. Public education and the future of America. 98p. The Association. 1201 16th St. Washington 6, D.C. '55.

Ratner, Joseph, ed. Intelligence in the modern world: John Dewey's philosophy. 1077p. Modern Library. New York. '39.
Chapters 10-12.

*Rickover, H. G. Education in the nuclear age; address delivered December 6, 1957. 14p. mimeo. press release. United States Atomic Energy Commission. Washington 25, D.C. '57.

*Rockefeller Brothers Fund, Inc. Pursuit of excellence: education and the future of America; panel report V of the special studies project of the Fund. (Doubleday News Book) 49p. Doubleday and Co. Garden City, N.Y. '58.

Reprinted in this book: Text of the summary of the report. New York Times. p 16. Je. 23, '58.

Shoemaker, Don. With all deliberate speed. 239p. Harper and Bros. New York. '57.

Smith, G. K., ed. Current issues in higher education. 249p. National Education Association. Association for Higher Education. 1201 16th St. Washington 6, D.C. '57.

Smith, Mortimer. Public school in crisis. 164p. Henry Regnery Co. Chicago. '56.

Stanley, W. O. Social foundations of education. 638p. Dryden Press. New York. '56.

Stiles, L. J., ed. Teacher's role in American society. 298p. Harper and Bros. New York. '57.

Traxler, A. E., ed. Vital issues in education. 176p. American Council on Education. 1785 Massachusetts Ave. Washington 6, D.C. '57.

*UNESCO. European educators discuss secondary school revolution. 3p. UNESCO press release. United Nations. New York. Ap. 23, '58.

*United States. Committee for the White House Conference on Education. Report to the President. 126p. Supt. of Docs. Washington 25, D.C. '56.

United States. Department of Health, Education and Welfare. Education in the U.S.S.R. (Bulletin no 14) 226p. Supt. of Docs. Washington 25, D.C. '57.

United States. Department of Health, Education and Welfare. Germany revisited; education in the Federal Republic. A. M. Lindegren. (Bulletin no 12) 107p. Supt. of Docs. Washington 25, D.C. '57.

*United States. President's Committee on Education Beyond the High School. Second report to the President. 108p. Supt. of Docs. Washington 25, D.C. '57.

*United States. Senate. Science and education for national defense; hearings before the Committee on Labor and Public Welfare. 1602p. 85th Congress, 2d session. Supt. of Docs. Washington 25, D.C. '58.

*United States. Supreme Court. Reports. Brown v. Board of Education of Topeka [decision in desegregation case], May 17, 1954, by Chief Justice Earl Warren, speaking for a unanimous court. v347, p483-96. Supt. of Docs. Washington 25, D.C. '54.

United States Steel Foundation. Release on grants to education. 4p. The Foundation. New York. My. 1, '58.

Woodring, Paul. Fourth of a nation. 255p. McGraw-Hill Book Co. New York. '57.

Woodring, Paul. New directions in teacher education. 142p. Fund for the Advancement of Education. 477 Madison Ave. New York 22. '57.

PERIODICALS

America. 98:365. D. 21, '57. Federal aid to improve the schools.
America. 98:569. F. 15, '58. Panic among the educators. W. T. Costello.
Annals of the American Academy of Political and Social Sciences. 301:1-210. S. '55. Higher education under stress. F. J. Brown; Thorsten Sellin, eds.
Annals of the American Academy of Political and Social Sciences. 302:100-5. N. '55. Education and other public services in France. T. G. Munson, tr.
*Atlantic Monthly. 199:47-50. Ap. '57. Pay and the professor. Beardsley Ruml.
*Atlantic Monthly. 200:73-7. N. '57. Education in the Western world. J. B. Conant.
Atlantic Monthly. 200:110-13. D. '57. Textbooks that don't teach. Oscar Handlin.
Atlantic Monthly. 201:45-9. Ja. '58. Scientist in the U.S.S.R. John Turkevich.
Atlantic Monthly. 201:29-34. Ja.; 26-9. Ap. '58. Race and the schools: a crisis North and South. A. E. Meyer.
Atlantic Monthly. 201:55-8. Ap. '58. Russia's new schooling. A. C. Eurich.
Atlantic Monthly. 201:59-63. Ap. '58. What strangles American teaching: the certification racket. Lydia Stout.
Atlantic Monthly. 202:34-9. Jl. '58. Certification racket; discussion. Daniel Tanner and others.
British Affairs (British Information Services). 2:85-8. Je. '58. Technical education.
*Bulletin of the Atomic Scientists. 12:333-7. N. '56. Plight of science education. H. A. Meyerhoff.
*Bulletin of the Atomic Scientists. 14:83-6. F. '58. Nature of the Soviet scientific challenge. R. E. Marshak.
Bulletin of the Atomic Scientists. 14:154-6. Ap. '58. Contrasts in education. W. C. Davidson.
Business Week. p 132-4+. D. 14, '57. Red formula produces technical supermen.
Business Week. p73. Ja. 4, '58. Administration's school plan.
*Business Week. p 155-61. Ap. 19, '58. Education—special report.
*Business Week. p74-102. Ap. 26, '58. Education—special report, part II: What's being planned for tomorrow's schools.
*Carnegie Corporation of New York Quarterly. 6:1-4. Ap. '58. Can our high schools do the job?

Commentary. 23:336-43. Ap. '57. Education in democratic society; the U.S. and Britain compared. David Daiches.

Congressional Digest. 36:257-88. N. '57. Controversy of the month: federal aid for school construction?

Congressional Digest. Ag.-S. '58.
Entire issue on education.

Coronet. 43:90-4. Ap. '58. Push-button pedagogy. N. V. Carlisle.

Cosmopolitan. 144:36-9. Ap. '58. How progressive education failed us. Bernard David.

Current History. 32:257-302. My. '57. Integration: the South's historic problem; symposium.
Entire issue.

Current History. 35:1-64+. Jl. '58. Soviet Union: education at mid-century.
Entire issue.

Current History. 35:65-128. Ag. '58. France: education at mid-century.
Entire issue.

Current History. 35:1-64. Jl. '58. Soviet Union: education at mid-century.
Entire issue.

*Educational Record. 39:89-96. Ap. '58. Is European education better? B. S. Hollinshead.
Also separate. 8p. American Council on Education. 1785 Massachusetts Ave. Washington 6, D.C. '58.

Foreign Affairs. 35:564-80. Jl. '57. Education and the national interest. H. M. Wriston.

Foreign Affairs. 36:209-20. Ja. '58. Inward look. J. R. Oppenheimer.

Freedom and Union. 13:16-18. My. '58. Education and class systems swell British emigration. G. W. Oakes.

Harper's Magazine. 215:58-62. O. '57. British and American Schools. D. K. Colville.

*Homiletic and Pastoral Review. 58:27-33. O. '57. "Freedom of choice" in schools. V. C. Blum.

Ladies' Home Journal. 75:11+. F. '58. Do American educators know what they are up to? Dorothy Thompson.

Life. 44:26-35. Mr. 24; 93:101. Mr. 31; 89-97. Ap. 7; 117-25. Ap. 14; 103-11. Ap. 21, '58; Crisis in education.
Discussion. 44:10. Ap. 14, '58.

Life. 44:36-7. Mr. 24, '58. It's time to close our carnival. Sloan Wilson.
Same abridged. Reader's Digest. 72:31-5. Je. '58.

*Life. 44:32. Mr. 31, '58. Deeper problem in education.
Discussion. 44:16. Ap. 21, '58.

Life. 44:120-1. Ap. 14, '58. Famous educator's plan for a school that will advance students according to ability.

Life. 44:34. Ap. 21, '58. Painful crisis, the long hard cure.

Look. 21:33+. Je. 11, '57. What is a school and the big school controversy: adjustment vs. knowledge. G. B. Leonard, Jr.

Look. 22:79-88. Je. 10, '58. Who runs our schools? G. B. Leonard, Jr.

Nation. 185:262-4. O. 19, '57. Revolution in Soviet education. Joshua Kunitz.

*Nation. 186:309-12. Ap. 12, '58. Free minds and open universities. L. M. Hacker.

*Nation. 186:407-09. My. 10, '58. Teacher shortage: cause and cure. Irving Adler.

*Nation. 186:411. My. 10, '58. A Britisher's view. W. K. Richmond.

National Education Association Journal. 46:189-90. Mr. '57. Higher education in the national spotlight. H. E. Wilson.

National Education Association Journal. 47:79-90. F. '58. Science, mathematics and the humanities; let's balance the program.

National Educational Association Journal. 47:111-12. F. '58. High price of poor education. J. E. Russell.

National Education Association Journal. 47:153. Mr. '58. Search for talent. J. W. Gardner.

*National Education Association Journal. 47:188+. Mr. '58. Contemporary challenge to American education: official statement by the Educational Policies Commission of the Association.

Also separate. 31p. The Association. 1201 16th St. Washington 6, D.C. '58.

National Education Association Journal. 47:218-19. Ap. '58. Academically talented pupil. J. B. Conant.

National Education Association Journal. 47:221-33+. Ap. '58. Special section on testing and evaluation. J. W. Wrightstone and others.

National Educational Association Journal. 47:245-6. Ap. '58. Education course controversy. C. H. Wilson.

National Parent-Teacher. 52:2-3. My. '58. American education: an evaluation. E. G. Brown.

National Parent-Teacher. 52:22-3. My. '58. Are foreign schools so much better than ours?

Nation's Business. 45:44-6. S. '57. Adverse effects of Federal aid to education.

New Republic. 136:12-16. Mr. 4, '57. Educating the gifted child. Arthur Bestor.

New York Herald Tribune. p2-3. Jl. 14, '57. Some facts on education in Russia. F. M. Hechinger.

New York Herald Tribune. Sec. 2. p3. F. 16, '58. Discipline called chief lack in U.S. Schools. W. D. Gombar.

New York Times. p 14. N. 14, '57. Text of President's talk in Oklahoma City citing need for rise in funds for science.

New York Times. p 10. Ja. 24, '58. Excerpts from speech by Senator J. W. Fulbright.

*New York Times. p 18. Ja. 28, '58. President's message to Congress, January 27, 1958.

Same. School Life. 40:5+. Mr. '58.

New York Times. pE9. Mr. 2, '58. Education in review (reappraisal of graduate programs). Benjamin Fine.

New York Times. pE9. Ap. 6, '58. Education in review (on higher regard for intellectual work). Gene Currivan.
*New York Times. p 1+. Ap. 20, '58. Costs of college soaring; likely to double by 1970. Milton Bracker.
New York Times. pE9. Ap. 27, '58. Education in review (on current educational debate). Gene Currivan.
New York Times. pE9. My. 4, '58. Education in review (on academic freedom). Gene Currivan.
New York Times. pE9. My. 18, '58. Education in review (case against Federal aid to colleges). Gene Currivan.
*New York Times. p6. My. 19, '58. Moscow outlines school reforms.
New York Times. p22. My. 23, '58. In the nation (on Army program for public schools). Arthur Krock.
New York Times. p4. Je. 14, '58. Text of address by Dr. L. G. Derthick to the National Press Club, June 13, 1958, on Soviet education.
New York Times. p 18. Je. 21, '58. What are we doing? editorial.
New York Times. p37. Je. 22, '58. Long-range plan for science eyed.
New York Times. pE9. Je. 22, '58. Education in review (status of education bills before Congress). Gene Currivan.
New York Times. p 16. Je. 27, '58. Educator scores teacher training. Leonard Buder.
New York Times. p5. Jl. 14, '58. Text of preliminary report on higher education in the Soviet. E. H. Litchfield.
New York Times Magazine. p 13+. Ja. 9, '55. Education for all is education for none. Douglas Bush.
New York Times Magazine. p 15+. Ap. 1, '56. Now the cold war of the classroom. William Benton.
New York Times Magazine. p 13+. Je. 2, '57. Case for TV in education. C. A. Siepmann.
New York Times Magazine. p9+. Je. 30, '57. Bringing up your children; French way, our way. L. W. Wylie.
*New York Times Magazine. p25+. S. 8, '57. Progressive education: a debate; The case for it, William H. Kilpatrick; the case against it, Arthur Bestor.
New York Times Magazine. p 19+. S. 29, '57. Integration: the pattern emerges. Wayne Phillips.
New York Times Magazine. p 19+. N. 10, '57. If we are to catch up in science. J. R. Dunning.
*New York Times Magazine. p7+. Ja. 26, '58. We do not teach them how to think. Marc Raeff.
Discussion. p 19-20. F. 9; 6+. F. 16, '58.
New York Times Magazine. p 15+. Ap. 6, '58. Dual education problem: school and home. A. E. Stevenson.
Discussion. p66. Ap. 20, '58.
New York Times Magazine. p 13+. Je. 15, '58. Rejoinder to critics of John Dewey. Oscar Handlin.
New York Times Magazine. p5+. Je. 22, '58. Report on Russia's big red schoolhouse. Marc Raeff.

Newsweek. 50:106. D. 16, '57. Stressing the sciences, Britain.
Newsweek. 51:64-5. Ja. 20, '58. Challenge (Russian education).
*Newsweek. 51:82-4. Mr. 3, '58. New avalanche of college-age Americans. H. R. Allen.
Parents' Magazine. 32:35+. N. '57. Coming college crisis. F. M. Hechinger.
Parents' Magazine. 33:35+. F. '58. Has Sputnik taught us a lesson? F. M. Hechinger.
Reader's Digest. 72:176-9. Mr. '58. Russia rings the school bell; excerpt from Inside Russia today. John Gunther.
Reporter. 18:8-9. F. 20, '58. Our cut-rate education. Max Ascoli.
Discussion. 18:6. Mr. 20; 3. Ap. 3, '58.
*Reporter. 18:10-14. F. 20, '58. Are Soviet schools better than ours? A. R. MacAndrew.
Saturday Evening Post. 229:23-5+. Je. 15; 32-3+. Je. 22; 20-1+. Je. 29; 230:30+. Jl. 6; 32-3+. Jl. 13, '57. Deep south says never. J. B. Martin.
Saturday Evening Post. 230:39+. S. 21, '57. Are the public schools doing their job? H. L. Brown, Jr.
*Saturday Evening Post. 230:33+. F. 22, '58. Middle way is the best way; ed. by L. White. E. H. Hanson.
Saturday Review. 40:15-27+. S. 14, '57. New year, new problems; Saturday Review's annual educational survey.
Saturday Review. 41:10-12. F. 1, '58. Money is not enough. C. M. Fuess.
Discussion. 41:26. F. 22; 23 Mr. 1, '58.
Saturday Review. 41:11-18. F. 15, '58. New world in education.
Saturday Review. 41:12-14+. My. 3, '58. Victims of success. H. S. Commager.
School and Society. 82:68-70. S. 3, '55. Progressive and traditional education: a synthesis. F. A. Shaw.
School and Society. 85:84-6. Mr. 16, '57. Higher education in transition. D. D. Henry.
School and Society. 85:99-103. Mr. 30, '57. British views of higher education. Ifor Evans.
School and Society. 85:112. Mr. 30, '57. U.S.A. compared with U.S.S.R. P. R. Anderson.
School and Society. 86:18-19. Ja. 4, '58. Superiority of American higher education.
School and Society. 86:103-4. Mr. 1, '58. Challenge to American education; address, December 15, 1957. R. M. Nixon.
School and Society. 86:104-5. Mr. 1, '58. Basic criteria of good education. E. D. Smith.
School and Society. 86:146+. Mr. 29, '58. Educational criticism in Britain. W. W. Brickman.
School Life. 39:5-6+. Mr. '57. Status of American education; message to Congress, January 28, 1957. D. D. Eisenhower.

Scientific American. 198:44-6. Ja. '58. Education in the U.S.S.R.
Senior Scholastic. 72:1T. Mr. 7, '58. Conant high school report.
Senior Scholastic. 72:27+. Ap. 4, '58. German education.
Senior Scholastic. 72:47. Ap. 18, '58. U.S. vs. Europe. B. S. Hollinshead.
*Teachers College Record. 59:69-75. N. '57. Great challenges for education. H. L. Caswell.
Teachers College Record. 59:101-9. N. '57. Reflections on the White House Conference. J. E. Russell.
Teachers College Record. 59:330-7. Mr. '58. Education within industry. H. F. Clark; H. S. Sloan.
Teachers College Record. 59:344-9. Mr. '58. Television and education: a critical analysis. Daniel Tanner.
*Teachers College Record. 59:450-9. My. '58. Spirit of American education. G. S. Counts.
Time. 70:56+. D. 16, '57. Dark side of the moon (on Russian education).
U.S. News & World Report. 43:106-7. N. 8, '57. Is the north really mixing its schools?
U.S. News & World Report. 43:134-5. N. 8, '57. Protestant view against plan for government aid to parents of pupils. G. L. Archer.
U.S. News & World Report. 43:65. N. 15, '57. We have suffered a very serious defeat; excerpts from address. Edward Teller.
U.S. News & World Report. 43:137-41. N. 15, '57. Three R's in Russia are really tough.
U.S. News & World Report. 43:86-91. D. 6, '57. Size-up of what's wrong with American schools; excerpts from address, Nov. 22, 1957. H. G. Rickover.
U.S. News & World Report. 44:85-7. Ja. 10, '58. Who will get the billion in school aid?
*U.S. News & World Report. 44:68-77. Ja. 24, '58. What went wrong with U.S. Schools; interview. Arthur Bestor.
U.S. News & World Report. 44:83-4. Ja. 24, '58. White House missile expert takes a look at U.S. schools; excerpts from address, January 7, 1958. J. R. Killian, Jr.
U.S. News & World Report. 44:75. F. 7, '58. We've been asked about Ike's plan for scholarships.
U.S. News & World Report. 44:66-75. F. 21, '58. How to get better schooling; interview. M. S. Eisenhower.
*U.S. News & World Report. 44:77-80. My. 2, '58. Junior colleges: low-cost answer to crowded campuses?
*U.S. News & World Report. 44:99-101. My. 16, '58. Debate over quality of U.S. schools; symposium. H. G. Spalding; S. M. Lambert.
U.S. News & World Report. 44:73-9. Je. 13, '58. Three R's—and more—are coming back.

U.S. News & World Report. 45:68-71. Jl. 4, '58. Is U.S. really too stingy with its schools?

United States Department of State Bulletin. 37:25-9. Jl. 1, '57. Education, Communist style, American style; address, June 3, 1957. E. L. Dulles.

Same. Vital Speeches of the Day. 25:590-3. Jl. 15, '57.

Vital Speeches of the Day. 21:1453-8. S. 1, '55. Adjustment versus education. M. B. Smith.

Vital Speeches of the Day. 23:418-20. My. 1, '57. Wider education of our people; address, April 4, 1957. D. D. Eisenhower.

Same with title: Education, the most important subject. National Education Association Journal. 46:300-2. My. '57.

Vital Speeches of the Day. 23:719-22. S. 15, '57. Education for survival; address, May 18, 1957. Grayson Kirk.

Vital Speeches of the Day. 24:298-300. Mr. 1, '58. Too much programmed education. C. V. Newsom.

*Vital Speeches of the Day. 24:496-9. Je. 1, '58. Communications and education; address, April 19, 1958. J. L. Burns.

Also separate. 14p. Radio Corporation of America. 30 Rockefeller Plaza. New York 20. '58.

Yale Review. 47:161-74. D. '57. End of illusion? D. W. Brogan.

McClellan, Grant S ed.
America's educational needs. New York, H. W. Wilson Co., 1958.

269 p. 20 cm. (The Reference shelf, v. 30, no. 5)

"Prepared to provide material on the 'problem area' designated by the National University Extension Association for high school debate and discussion in the academic year 1958-1959."
Bibliography: p. [259]-269.

1. Education—U. S.—1945- I. Title. (Series)

LB7.M2 370.973 58-12646

Library of Congress

370.973 McClellan, Grant Samuel, ed.
America's educational needs. Wilson, H.W. 1958
269p (Reference shelf v30, no. 5)

Contains 41 articles dealing with such phases of American education as the problem of an educational philosophy; specific problems of classroom and teacher shortages; of rising costs of education; lessons to be learned from foreign educational experience, and possible improvements at home
Bibliography: p259-69

1 Education—U.S. I Title II Series 370.973

58W2724 (W) The H. W. Wilson Company